PC SOFTWARE APPLICATION SKILLS

CS-612

For

Bachelor of Computer Applications

[B.C.A.]

Useful For

IGNOU, Vinayaka Mission University, IP University, Delhi University, CCS University, JMI University, B. M. V. Open University (KOTA), M. P. Bhoj Open University(M.P.), Tamilnadu Open University, YCM Open University (Maharashtra), Mahatma Gandhi University (Kottyam), M. D. University, and all other Indian Universities.

AF529955

GULLYBABA PUBLISHING HOUSE (P) Ltd.

AN ISO 9001:2008 CERTIFIED CO.

GullyBaba Publishing House (P) Ltd.
2525 / 193, Ist Floor, Onkar Nagar-A,
Tri Nagar, Delhi-110035
Ph: 9350849407, 9312235086, 011-27387998

E-mail: info@gullybaba.com
info@degreewala.com
WebSite: www.gullybaba.com
www.ignouonline.com

Edition : 2011

Author : Dinesh Verma, Vimal Kumar Sharma
Price : 280/-

Preface

This book is mainly targeted for BCA exam of PC Software Application Skills. It has been introduced in market after seeing the huge demand of ready to grasp material for exams with high level of quality, and its un-availability in market. We the GullyBaba Publishing House took a step ahead to publish the quality material focusing on exams at the same time giving you indepth knowledge about the subject.

GPH Book is the pioneer effort that provides a unique methodology so as to perform better in exams. If your goal is to attain higher grade use this powerful study tool independently or along with your text.

*On the Web : **www.gullybaba.com** is the vital resource for your exams acting as catalyst to boost up your preparation. Now you can access us on the net through **www.doctorignou.com, www.doeacconline.com, www.gphindia.com, and www.gullybabapublishinghouse.com.***

Feedback about the book can be sent at **cs612writers@gullybaba.com.**

Acknowledgments :

We appreciate the staff and facility support provided by GullyBaba Publishing House. In particular, we appreciate the encouragement and professional advises received from Mr. Ajay Saini, Mr. Tarun Sharma, H. Faheem Ahmed and many more.

Also we would like to thank typesetting and designing team Mrs. Bhawna Verma, Mr. Shravan Vats, Mr. Mukesh.

We gratefully acknowledges the significant contributions of Mr. Mahesh Chand, Mrs. Bimla Devi, Mrs. Bhawna Verma and our experts in bringing out this publication.

New Delhi

Feedback is the breakfast of Champions.

Ken Blanchard

You can Help other students.
"Inform any error or mistake in this book."

We and Universe
will reward you for Your Kind act.

Email at : feedback@gullybaba.com
or
WhatsApp on 9350849407

Table of Contents

STUDY NOTES

SOLVED PAPERS

Chapter-1

Classical Problems and Puzzles

Q1. What is graph ? Explain the concept of Crossing the Konigsberg Bridges. Also define Eulerian Circuit.
#. Discuss the Koingsberg Bridges Problem using the graph method.
[JUN03]

Graph is a discrete mathematical structure of points and connecting lines, which can be used to model a variety of situations.

Koingsberg Bridges Problem : Konigsberg was a city in Parssia (now a part of Russia) situated on the Pregel River, which served as the residence of the dukes of Prussia in the 16th century. The river Pregel flowed through the town, creating as island, as in the following picture. Seven bridges spanned the various branches of river, as show

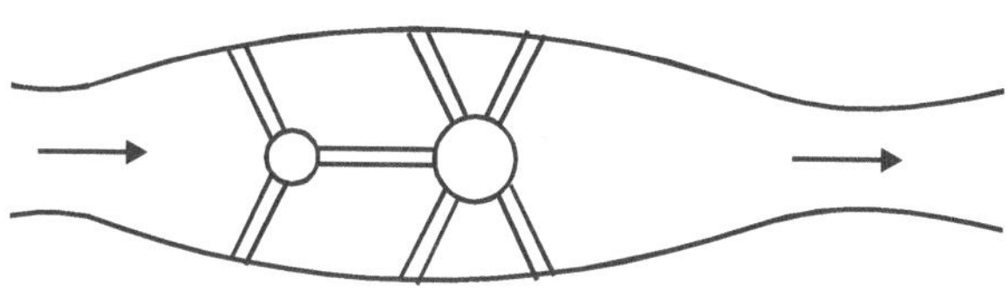

The Bridges of Konigsberg

Is it possible, Euler was asked, for person to return to the starting point after having crossed the seven bridges once, and only once?

Eulerian circuit : Euler converted the problem to a graphic representation, in which each land mass becomes a vertex, and each bridge and edge between two vertices. In graph-theoretic terms, the problem reduces to the question: Can one trace the figure starting at one of the vertex? Try this without lifting your pencil from the paper. And termed this closed trail as Eulerian Circuit.

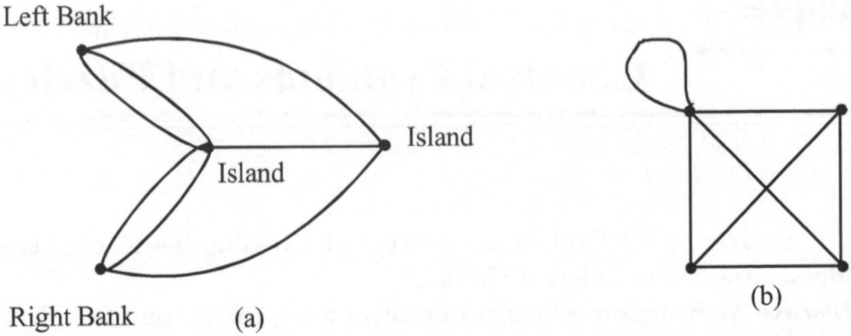

And Eulerian circuit in his honour-does not exist for the graph of Fig. (a). He proved in fact: a graph G (which we may define as a composition of two sets: vertices and edges) contains a circuit if every vertex of G is of even degree. The degree of a vertex is the number of edges, which meet at it. Note that in Fig.(a) the degree of each vertex is written alongside it. For each vertex in the circuit there must be an edge by which the vertex is reached, and another by which it is exited. A loop (Fig. (b)) contributes two, and not one, to the degree of a vertex. Let's see why an Eulercian circuit in a graph forces all its vertices to have even degree. Start at some vertex on the circuit, and follow the circuit from vertex to vertex, erasing which edge as you go along it. In passing through a vertex, you erase one edge entering and one edge exiting, or else you erase a loop. In each case you reduce the degree of the vertex by two. Eventually every edge gets erased, and all vertices are reduced to zero degree, so all vertices must have had even degree to begin with. The graph of the Konigsberg brides has vertices of odd degree, and cannot include an Eulerian circuit.

Q2. Explain the theory of Cannibals and Missionaries.

#: There is three edible missionaries, who are all initially on the left bank of river, and wish to cross it. The only boat available is one capable of carrying two persons; and the condition of safe crossing is that at no time can the cannibals outnumber the missionaries. How do they cross the river, with no one getting eaten?

It is convenient to label the "states" which represents the number of missionaries and cannibals on a given side of river as the vertices of a graph. A state in which there are c cannibals and m missionaries is represented by the symbol (c,m). Clearly, some states are impossible: (3, 2) on the left bank, or (1, 2) on the right bank. Following table the set of sixteen possible states:

	1	2	3	4	5	6	7	8	9	10	11	12	13	14	15	16
Left Bank (c,m)	3,3	3,2	3,1	3.0	2,3	2,2	2,1	2,0	1,3	1,2	1,1	1,0	0,3	0.2	0,1	0,0
Right Bank (c,m)	0,0	0,1	0,1	1,0	1,0	1,1	1,2	1,3	2,0	2,1	2,2	2,3	3,0	3,1	3,2	3,3

The letter 1 or r used to specify the position of the boat in any state; thus (1,1) is the start, state in which three cannibals and three missionaries are standing on the left bank, where the boat is also only three of which are however acceptable: (r,5), (r,6) and (r,9).

The final way to cross the river with no one getting eaten is-

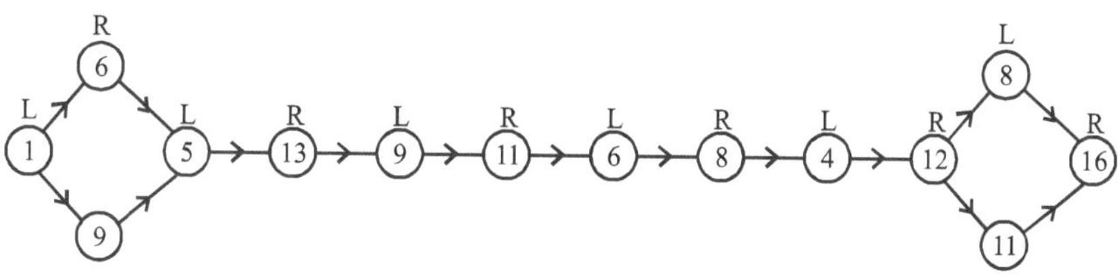

where, L = Left bank and R = Right bank

In the above figure number under circle denotes the situation and L shows that boat is on the left bank and R shows that the boat is on the right bank of the river.

Q3. Explain about the Decanting problems and mention different solving techniques with an example. [DEC99]

#: Decanting problems are most directly solved using trilinear coordinates. Support this statement and discuss the above problem by giving an example. [JUN00,Q1(b)]

Decanting problems are most directly solved using coordinates, in which three sets of parallel lines divide the plane into a tessellation of equilaterals. In this systems the coordinates (x,y,z) of a point P are defines as the distances of the point from the sides of an equilateral Triangle ABC, with side a and altitude h. In figure x,y and z are the distances of P from BC, CA and AB repressively. The coordinates are regarded as positive when the point is within the triangle. The coordinates (x, y, z) of P are its distances from BC, CA and AB respectively. Since the area of any triangle is half the base times altitude, we see that:

Area(ABC) = Area(PBC) + Area(PBC) + Area (PAB)

$\therefore$ 1/2ah = 1/2(ax) + 1/2(az)

$\therefore$ h = x + y + z

Thus trilinear coordinates can be useful when three variable quantities have a constant sum, and the application to pouring in immediate.

Consider a example, in which we are given a vessel filled with eight liters of wine, and two empty vessels of capacities five and three liters respectively, the aim being to divide the wine into two equal parts. The initial state is represented by the vertex A(8,0,0) of the triangle and the domain of the solution is bounded by the vertices P(3,5,0), Q(0,5,3), and R(5,0,3) which lie on a parallelogram bounded by the lines y = 0, y =5, z = 3. The figure show how the desired point (4, 4, 0) can be reached. Suppose the first move is to fill the five-litre jug, so the new state becomes (3, 5, 0). The solution path runs along a direction parallel to one side of the triangle of reference, and bends whenever it reaches a vertex or side of the parallelogram. Solution Path :

First A(8, 0, 0) is initial state. Then from A jug we pour wine in C to get R (5, 0, 3). Then from C we pour into B to get I (5, 3, 0). Again from A into C to get J (2, 3, 3), then from C to B to get K (2, 5, 1). Pouring from b to A get L (7, 0, 1), then from C to b to get M (7, 1, 0), then from C to B to get M (7, 1, 0). Next we pour from A to C to get N (4, 1, 3) and finally from C into B to get O (4, 0, 0).

: A (8, 0, 0) → R (5, 0, 3) → J (2, 3, 3) → K (2, 5, 1)→ L (7, 0, 1) → M (7, 1, 0) → N (4, 1, 3) → O (4, 0, 0)

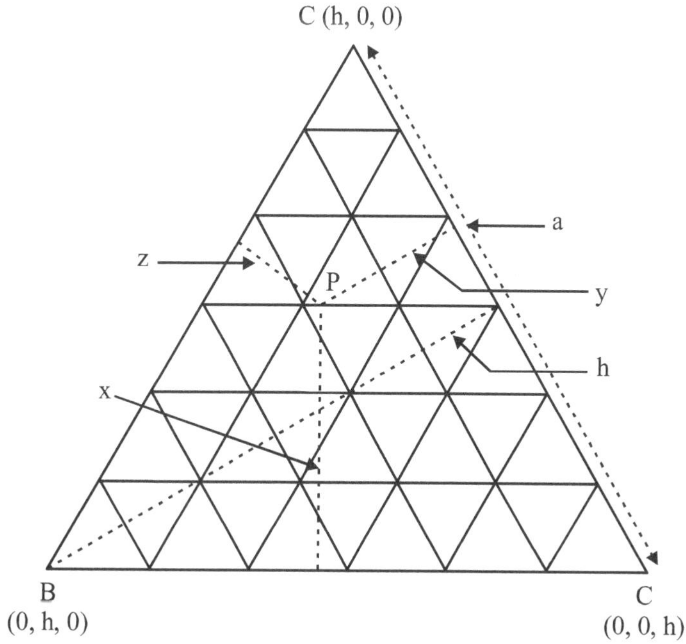

Q4. Given a 12-litre vessel filled with milk and two empty vessels with capacities of 9 liters and 5 liters. How can you divide the milk into 2 equal portions? Explain and write the sequence of steps to solve.

[DEC01][JAN01]

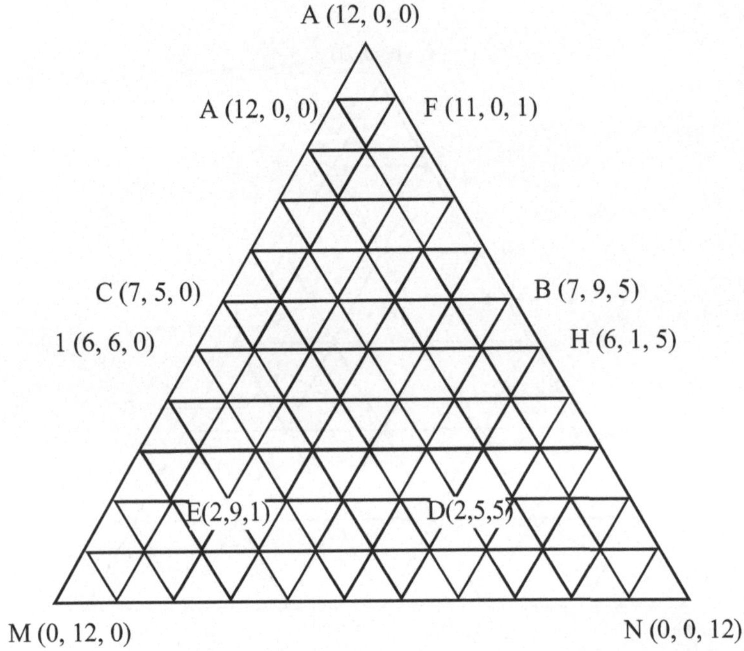

A (12, 0, 0) → B (7, 0, 5) → C (7, 5, 0) → D (2, 5, 5) → E (2, 9, 1) → F (11, 0, 1) → G (11, 1, 0) → H (6, i, 5) → I (6, 6, 0)

Q5. You are given two uncalibrated jugs, one of capacity five liters and the other of capacity, three liters and an unlimited supply of water. Show a sequence of filling and emptying of the jugs and of pouring back and forth between two jugs, so that exactly four liters of water is obtained in the first jug. [JUN01]

Solution Path ABCDEFGZ

A (0, 0) → B (5, 0) → C (2, 3) → D (2, 0) → E (0, 2) → F (5, 2) → G (4, 3) → Z (4, 0)

Another Solution Path ABCDEFGZ

A (0, 0) → B (0, 3) → C (3, 0) → D (3, 3) → E (5, 1) → F (0, 1) → G (1, 3) → Z (4, 0)

Q6. Suppose that you have eight coins and are told that one is counterfeit and has a different weight (heavier or lighter) than the other seven. Determine which coin is different in no more than three weighings (Hint: To start with, weigh three coins in the left pan against three in the right.

#: You are given eight coins, out of which seven are of same weight, however eighth coin is slightly heavier than the others, Find the heavier coin in no more than three weighings. Explain the process. [JUN01]

Such type of question is solve by Decisions tree.

Let 1, 2, 3, 4, 5, 6, 7 and 8 are given coins.

Steps of making Decision Tree

(1) Make two groups of coins and put both groups in different pan. Every group have 4- 4 coins.

(2) Weigh both group.

(3) It is clear that heavier group have heavier coin.

(4) Choose heavier group and divide them two subgroup. Now both subgroups have 2-2 coins.

(5) Again weight both subgroup and choose heavier group. Now selected group have only two coins.

(6) Weigh both coins and detect heavier coins.

Graphical representation of Decision Tree:

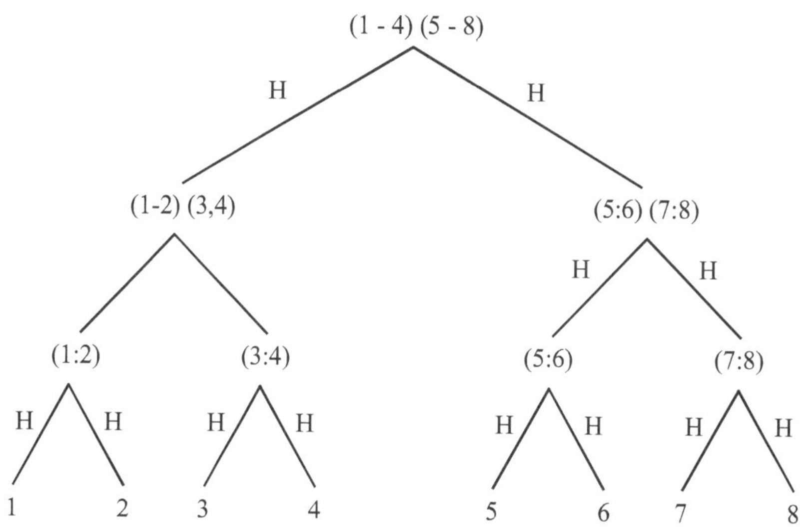

Q7. If you are given the information that the counterfeit coin is heavier than the others, how will you pick it in only two weighings? [DEC01]

Consider the number of coins is 8. We name the coins through their number 1 to 8.

Now, we make two groups of 3-3 coins and put 2 rest coins separate.

Group 11, 2, 3
Group 24, 5, 6

CASE I

First weighing : Weigh both group of coins putting one group in left pan and another in right rest two coins.

Second weighing : Now weigh rest two coins, one putting one left pan and other putting on right pan of balance.

CASE II

First weighing : After first weighing, if we find one group is heavier, then it will be clear that heavier coin will must reside in heavier group.

Second weighing : Now, choose two coins from heavier group and weigh them according to aforsaid method. Counterfeit coin is detected through getting heavier coin. If both coins are equal then third must be heavier coin.

Decision Tree for the given problem :

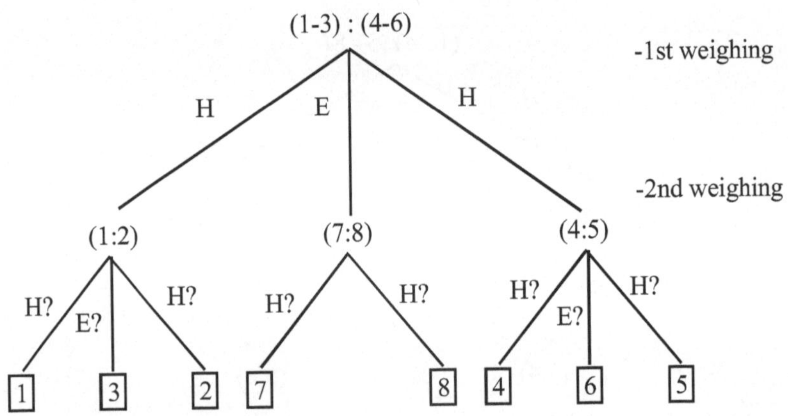

Here, H = Heavier
E= Equal to

Q8. Given 13 coins, one of them heavier than the rest, how can you determine it in no more than 3 weighings using decision tree.

[DEC02][JUN02]

Let 13 coins are named by their number 1 to 13.

You make two group of 6-6 coins and keep one extra coin separate. Now, both group, putting one group in left pan and other in right pan of balance. If both group are equal, it is clear that extra (13th) coin will heavier. So, heavier coin will be detected in one weighing.

If both groups are not equal, it is clear that heavier coin will be resided in heavier group of coins. So, you select heavier group coins which have 6 coins and again divide them in two groups 3-3 coins. Weight both group, putting one group in left pan and another in right pan. It will be second weighing. Choose heavier group. Now you will get three coins left. Choose two coins of them and weight it will be third weight. If both coins are equal then third will be heavier otherwise one of them is heavier. In this way, we can determine heavier coin in three or less than three weighing.

DECISION TREE

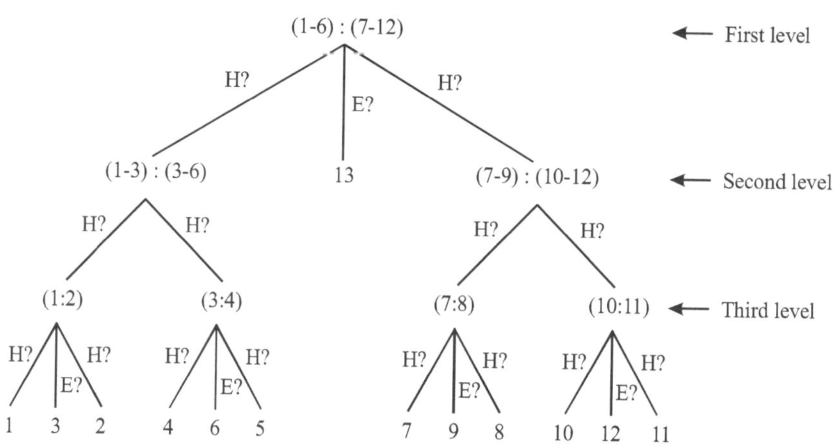

Q9. A certain street contains 1000 buildings. A signmaker is contacted to number the houses from 1 to 1000. How many zeros will he need?

[JUN01][JAN01]

1. All zeroes at the end of a number upto 990

= 10, 20 ..... 100 .... 160, 170 990

= 10 × 10

= 100 zeroes.

2. All zeroes as middle digit *i.e*....

100, 101, 101 .... 200, 201, ... 900 , 901

$= 10 \times 9$

= 90 zeros.

Three zeros of 1,000

3. Total $100 + 90 + 3 = 193$ zeroes.

Q10. Explain the paradox in the following sentence: [JUN01]
I declare 'I am lying'

The Speaker can speaks either truth or false.

Case I : He speaks truth, since the statement says that the speaker declares that he speaks lie. One assumption that the speaker speaks truth is violated or it is clear that he is liar.

Case II : He speaks false : In this case the statement says that he declares that he speaks lies actually must be speaking the truth which again contradicts our assumption that the speaker speaks lies.

Q11. At what time after 4 P.M. is the minutes hand of a clock exactly aligned with the hour hand? [JAN01]

At 4 P.M. the angle between minutes hand and hour hand is 120°. Now time taken for minutes hand to rotate 360° is 60 minutes and time taken for hour to rotate 30° is 60 minutes.

∴ Angular velocity of minutes had = 360 / 60 = 6° /min

∴ Similarly angular velocity of hour hand = 30 / 60 = (0.5)°/min

∴ Relative angular velocity of minutes hand with respect to hour = (6 – 0.5)°/min = (5.5)°/min

∴ Required time to overcome (5.5)° = 1 minutes

∴ Required time to overcome (120)°

= 120 / 5.5 minutes = 21°49'

∴ At time 4 : 21 : 49PM the minutes hand of a clock exactly aligned with the hour hand.

Q12. A carpenter cuts a board of wood twelve feet long into one foot pieces without stacking. How many cuts must he make ? [JAN01]

From the 12 feet long log the woodcutter wants to 12 one - foot pieces.

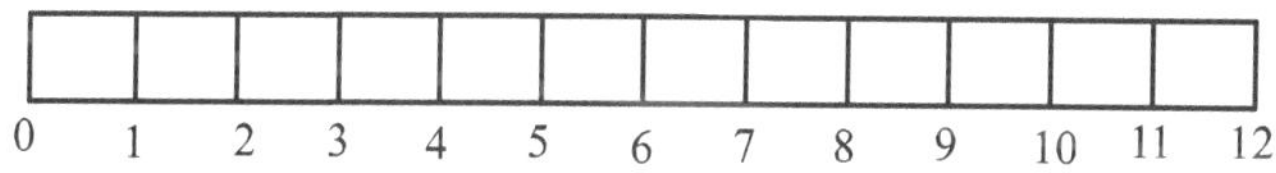

Wood cutter will begin cutting board from spot 1 and go next to spot 11 to make 12 pieces of 1 foot. Hence it is specify that 11 cuts he build.

Q13. My friend collects antique stamps. She purchased two, but found that she needed to raise money urgently. So she sold them for Rs. 8000 each. On one she made 20%, and on the other she lost 20%. How much did she gain or lose in the entire transaction?

Let purchase price of first stamp be Rs. x and that of second shop be Rs. y.

∴ 1.2 x = 8000 i.e. x = Rs. 6666.66
0.8 y = 8000 y = Rs. 10000
Total purchase price Rs. 16666.66
Total sales price Rs. 16000
So she lost Rs. 666.66

Q14. There are four seats in a row at a cinema. Sudhir will sit next to Shrin, but not text to Ganesh. If Ganesh will not sit next to Geeta, who is sitting next to Geeta?

A truth table is made

Seats / Names	1	2	3	4
Sudhir	×	✓	×	×
Ganesh	×	×	×	✓
Shirin	×	×	✓	×
Geeta	✓	×	×	×

Now, Sudhir seats next to Shirin so he is at least not sitting in seat No.1. The question is who sits next to Geeta is not in at least seat No.4. Ganesh is also not sitting next to Geeta so he is not at least in seat No. 1. So either Shirin or Geeta is in seat No.1.

But if Shirin is seat No. 1 then Sudhir is No.2, Geeta in No.3 and Ganesh in No.4, but Ganesh does not sit next to Geeta (give condition). Hence Geeta must be in seat No.1
Sudhir in No.2
Shirin in No.3
and Ganesh in No.4

Q15. Put the appropriate plus or minus signs between the number below, in the correct places, so that the value of the expression on the left will equal the value on the right:

0 1 2 3 4 5 6 7 8 9 = 1

0 + 1 + 2 + 3 + 4 - 5 - 6 + 7 - 8 + 9 = 1

Q16. A man just finished having his house built, and needs something more. At the hardware store the shopkeeper shows him what he wants says, "Each is Rs. 10," "OK", says the man, "I'll take 1243, so here's Rs. 40." What had he bought?

House number plates.

Q17. How many odd-numbered pages are there in a book 749 pages long?

A book can't have odd number of pages. However, upto 749 pages it will have 374 odd numbered pages.

Q18. Cubical dice have the following numbers written upon them :
5 17 19 37 41 46 50 66

The dice are tossed, and the winner is the person who first reaches 100 with the fewest dice possible, and with no repeats. What numbers does the winner need?

To reach exact 100, three dice tossing with numbers 17, 37 and 46 are needed.

Q19. Next week I am going to collect rent from my tenant, visit the new museum, go to the UTI office, and have my teeth checked at the dentist's. My tenant is not home on Wednesday or Friday the UTI office is closed on weekends, and the museum is closed Mondays. My dentist can give me an appointment on Tuesday, Thursday or Saturday. What day can I do everything I've planned?

A possible truth table is prepared-

Day	Rent Collect	Museum	UT? Office	Dentist
MON	✓	×		×
TUE	✓	✓	✓	✓
WED	×			×
THR	✓	✓	✓	✓
FRI	×			×
SAT			×	
SUN			×	×

	M	T	W	T	F	Sa	Su
Days	×	✓	×	✓	×	×	×

Either Tuesday or Thursday can be chosen.

Q20. How many minutes is it before six o'clock, if fifty ago it was four times as many minutes past three o'clock?

Let the present time be x minutes after 3.00 am and let there be y minutes to 6.00 am.

(i.e. 180 minutes).

Let 3.00 am be our reference point i.e. we treat it as 0 minutes.

From given conditions

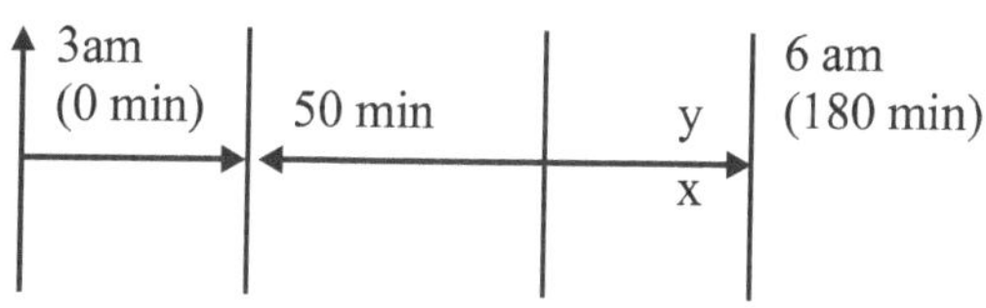

180-y=x

4y + 50 = x

Solving

y = 26 minutes

x = 154 minutes

=> it is 26 minutes before 6 am

=> Now the time is 5:34 am

Q21. Multiply by 7 the number of 8's followed by 3, but not by 8, in the number below:

381654783298514285838385737983256941837408326

The given number is :

3 8 1 6 5 4 7 8 3 2 9 8 5 1 42 8 5 8 3 8 3 8 5 7 3 7 9 8 3 2 5 6 4 1 8 3 7 4 0 8

3 2 6

From the left to right

Number of 8's followed by 3, but not followed by 8 = 3

Multiplied by 7, we get result 7 x 3 = 21

From right to left

Number of 8's followed by 3, but not followed by 8 = 6

Multiplied by 7, we get result = 7 x 6 = 42

Q22. When Alexander the Great attacked the forces of Porus, an Indian soldier was captured by the Greeks. He had displayed such bravery in battle, however, that the enemy offered to let him choose how he wanted to be killed. They told him, " If you tell a lie, You will be put to the sword, and if you tell the truth you will be hanged." The soldier could make only one statement. He made the statement, and went free. What did he say?

The soldier made the statement "I will be put to sword".

(a) Now if this is true he must be hanged, but then it will be false.

(b) If it is a lie he will be put to sword, but then it becomes true. So they could neither hang him nor could put to sword and he was set free.

Q23. Visiting a new town, you discover that there are only two barber shops, with only one hair dresser in either. In need of hair cut, you explore further and find that one barber is messy and disorganised and had a terrible haircut, while the other is neat and tidy and has a beautiful haircut. Which one do you choose to cut your hair?

The Messy and disorganised barber whose own haircut is terrible. Because he must be busy in doing good business and so must be a good barber who has not time for his own haircut.

Q24. Jack had some beans that grew into trees very quickly. The trees double in height every hour. At 10 a.m. the trees were four thousand feet high. When were they two thousand feet high? What is their height at 5.00 am.?

The tree double in height every hour.

So, if they are four thousand feet high at 10.00 am., they will be 2000 feet high one hour earlier i.e. at 9.00 am.

Height at 5.00 am can be worked out like this :

Height at 9.00 am 2000 feet

Height at 8.00 am 1000 feet

Height at 7.00 am 500 feet

Height at 6.00 am 250 feet

Height at 5.00 am 125 feet
therefore height at 5.00 am was 125 feet

Q25. My doctor gave me eight pills, and told me to take one every half-hour. How long does it take me to use up all of the pills?
Three and half hours (not 4 hours).

Q26. On another occasion, both Professors made the following statements :
First Prof: (1) " I lie on Saturdays."
(2) "I lie on Sundays."
Second Prof : "I will be tomorrow."
What day of the week as it?
From the first professor's second statement i.e. "I lie on Sundays" it is obvious that he is lying because on Sundays both speak truth. So his first statement "I lie on Saturdays" is false and he speaks truth on Saturdays i.e. he must be Prof. Ahmed. Now Prof. Ahmed lies only on Monday. Tuesdays and Wednesdays, so the day has to be one of these days.
The second is Prof. Chaturvedi. He speaks truth on Mondays, Tuesday and Wednesdays. So if his statement "I will lie tomorrow" is true he can make it only on (a) Wednesday, because he lies on Thursday.
So, the only day possible today is Wednesday.

Q27. Five rooms are interconnected with themselves and an outside verandah by doors on every wall, as shown in following figure. Is it possible to start in one room, or the outisde, walk through every doorway exactly once, and return to the starting point?

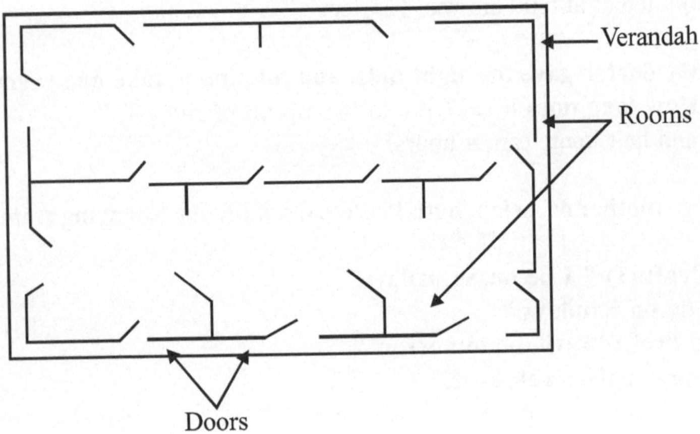

The graph of given figure is as follows :

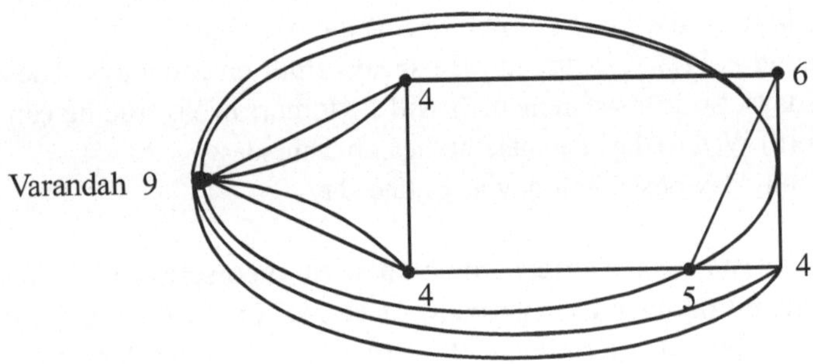

The vertices represent rooms and varandah. The edges represent doors. The numbers at each vertex each of number of degree of that vertex. Since at some vertices the degree is odd, the graph is not an Eulerain circuit and it is not possible to start in one room, or the outside, walk through every doorway exactly once and return to starting point.

Q28. Professors Ahmad and Chaturvedi are extremely strange persons. Prof. Ahmed lies on Mondays, Tuesdays and Wednesdays, but tells the truth on the other day of the week. Prof. Chaturvedi lies on Thursdays, Fridays and Saturdays, but tells the truth on other days of the week. They made the following statements:
Prof. Ahmad :"Yesterday was one of my lying days."
Prof. Chaturvedi: "Yesterday was one of my lying days too."
What day of the week was it?

Both are not telling truth. One is lying.

1. Suppose Prof. Ahmed is speaking truth. Then he is speaking on Thursday. Now Prof. Chaturvedi is lying. So it has to be Thursday and he is talking about Wednesday the day on which he speaks truth.

2. Suppose Prof. Ahmed is lying. It means 'Yesterday was his day of telling truth' He must be speaking on Monday.

But in case of Prof. Chaturvedi if he is also lying the day has to be Thursday and if he is speaking truth it cannot be at least Monday. Thus, we conclude that Prof. Ahmed is telling truth, Prof. Chaturvedi is lying and the day is Thursday.

Q29. Which word becomes smaller when you append more letters to it?

The word SMALL becomes SMALLER and SMALLEST when more letters are appended to it.

Chapter-2

The Higher Arithmetic-I

Q1. Prove that there is atleast one prime number between K^2 and $(K+1)^2$ for all integers K satisfying $1 \leq K \leq 20$. **[DEC01,Q4(a)][JUN00]**

Given the value of K is $1 \leq K \leq 20$

Following is the table based on the given value of K :-

K	K^2	$(K+1)^2$	Prime Number
1	1	4	2,3
2	4	9	5,7
3	9	16	11,13
4	16	25	17,19,23
5	25	36	29,31
6	36	49	37,41,43
:	:	:	:
10	100	121	103,113
:	:	:	:
19	361	400	367
20	400	441	403

It is observed that atleast one prime number occurs between K^2 and $(K + 1)^2$ for K between 1 and 20.

Q2. Verify that there is at least one prime between k and 2k for all integral k satisfying 1 < k <=100.

We prepare following table to verify the given claims:-

K	2K	Exist Prime
2	4	3
3	6	5
4	8	7
5	10	7
6	12	7,11
7	14	11,13
-	-	-
-	-	-
-	-	-
-	-	-
-	-	-
100	200	-

So, is the above table we see that there is atleast one prime number between K and 2K.

Q3. List 10 primes of the form $k^2 + 1$, where k is an even integer. Can $k^2 + 1$ be prime for odd integers k? Can $k^2 - 1$ be prime for any integers k?

K^2	$K^2 + 1$	Remarks
2	5	Prime number
4	17	"
6	37	"
10	101	"
14	197	"
16	257	"
20	401	"
24	577	"
26	677	"
30	901	Prime number

In the above table we have 10 prime numbers $K^2 + 1$, where K is an even integer.

K^2	K^2+1	Remarks	K^2	K^2-1	Remarks
1	2	Prime no.	1	0	
3	10	Not Prime	2	3	
5	26	"	3	8	
7	50	"	4	15	
9	82	"	5	24	
11	122	"	6	35	
-	-	-	7	48	
-	-	-			

From the above table, we see that $K^2 + 1$ can not be prime for odd integer.

Q4. Verify that every even integer k such that 6 <= k <= 100 can be partitioned as the sum of two odd primes.

(Christian Goldbach later to Euler (1742) conjectured that every even number greater that 4 can be decomposed into two odd primes, thus:

16 = 5 + 11;

32 = 13 + 19;2 computers have been applied to the inquiry)

Q5. Find the smallest number such that if its leftmost digit is placed at its right end, the new number so formed is precisely 50% larger than the original number. Prove it. **[DEC02][JUN00]**

Let the n+1 digits comprising the number-beginning from the left-d_0, d_1, d_2..., d_n, where d_0 is different from 0, and d_1, d_2..., d_n are in [0-9]. Then the condition of the problem implies :

$$d_1d_2d_3.....d_nd_0 = (3/2) \times d_0\ d_1d_2....d_n$$

By explicitly stating the "weight" of each digit as determined by its position, we rewrite the above condition :

$$2 \times (d_1 \times 10^n + d_2 \times 10^{n-1} + d_3 \times 10^{n-2} + ... + d_0 =$$
$$3 \times (d_0 \times 10^n + d_1 \times 10^{n-1} + d_2 \times 10^{n-2} + ... + d_n)$$

Transposing the terms involving to the right hand side of the equation, and the other terms to its left hand side, we find:

$$17 \times (d_1 \times 10^{n-1} + d_2 \times 10^{n-2} + ... + d_n) = 3 \times 10^{n-2} x d_0$$

From the Fundamental Theorem of Arithmetic it is clear that 17 must be a factor of the right and side of the above equation. But what is d_0? Well, the problem specifies that we must find the smallest number with the required property. Since d_0 is the first digit of the number, and since the smallest number will have the least value of d_0, it is reasonable to set d_0 equal to 1. We must now find the least such that $2 \times 10^{n-2}$ is divisible by 17. Trying with n at 1, 2, 3, 4 etc. we look for the first number of the sequence 28, 298, 2998, 29998,.... that leaves no remainder on division by 17. That number is 2999999999999998. The quotient obtained on dividing this number by 17 is 176470588235294. Therefore d_1 is 1, d_2 is 7, d_3 is 6, ...d_{15} is 4, and the number we seek (with d_0=1 written at the appropriate place) is of 16 digits :1.

Q6. Prove the lemma: It two integers a and b are each of the form 4k + 1, their product is also of the same form. [JUN00]

Let $a = 4i + 1, b = 4j + 1;$

then $ab = (4i + 1) \times (4j + 1)$

$= ij + 4i + 4j + 1$

$= 4 (4ij + i + j) + 1$

$= 4k + 1$, where $k = 4ij + i + j$

Hence proved.

Q7. What is the remainder left after dividing 1! + 2! + 3! + ... + 100! by 7 ? [DEC01][DEC99][JUN01][JAN01]

From 7! onwards, every term gives as the remainder as every term contains 7 as a factor Therefore, we need to find the remainder when

$1! + 2! + ... + 6!$ is divided by 7

$1! + 2! + ... + 6! = 1 + 2 + 6 + 24 + 120 + 720$

$= 873$

Now

$873 = 5 \pmod{7}$

Hence, the remainder is 5.

Q8. For any prime p > = 5, prove that $p^2 + 2$ is composite. [DEC02][JUNE02][JUN99]

Here, $p \geq 5$ and as p is a prime, therefore, p must not be divisible by 3.

=> $p = 3k + 1$ or $3k + 2$ for some integer k

=> Either $(p - 1)$ or $(p + 1)$ is divisible by 3.

Now, $p^2 + 2 = (p^2 - 1) + 3 = (p - 1)(p + 1) + 3$

$= 3k' + 3 = 3(k' + 1)$

=> $(p^2 + 2)$ is divisible by 3 and hence, $(p^2 + 2)$ is composite.

Q9. Find a prime divisor of the form 4K+3 for the integer 4(3×7×11×19) - 1. [DEC01][JUN99]

$4(3 \times 7 \times 11 \times 19) - 1$
$= 17556 - 1$
$= 17555$
$= 5 \times 3511$

Now,

$4k + 3 = 3511$

or, $4k = 3511 - 3$

$\therefore \quad k = \dfrac{3508}{4} = 877$

Hence,

$(4(877) + 3)$ is prime divisor of the form $4k + 3$.

Q10. Prove from lemma 1, for any positive X < 1, the series:

$1 + x + x^2 + x^3 + ... x^n$ converges to $\dfrac{1}{(1 - x)}$ as n tends to infinity.

[DEC04,Q2(b)][DEC01][JUN99]

Let $S = 1 + x + x^2 + ... + x^n$ .... (i) multiplying (i) by x on both sides we get

$xS = x + x^2 + x^3 + ... x^{n+1}$ Now subtract (i) by new equation

$S(1 - x) = 1 - x^{n+1}$

$S = 1/(1 - x) - x/(1 - x)$

therefore, $S = \dfrac{1}{(1 - x)} - \dfrac{x^{n+1}}{1-x}$

where clearly the second term tends to be zero with n., for x <1. In particular, for any prime p. Since, 1/p<1

$$\left(1+\frac{1}{p1}+\frac{1}{(p1)^2}+........\frac{1}{(pn)^2}+.........\right)\left(1+\frac{1}{p2}+\left(\frac{1}{p2}\right)^2+.........\left(\frac{1}{p2}\right)^{1/n}+.........\right)$$

$$\left(1+\frac{1}{pN}+\frac{1}{(pN)^2}+.........\right)$$

$1 + 1/P + 1/P^2 + 1/P^3 + ... = 1/(1 - 1/p)$

so as $n \to \infty$ $\boxed{S = \dfrac{1}{1 - x}}$ proved

Q11. Prove from lemma 2, the sum $1 + \dfrac{1}{2} + \dfrac{1}{3} + \dfrac{1}{4} + ... + \dfrac{1}{n}$ tends to infinity with n. **[DEC03,Q6(a)][JUN99]**

The sum: $1 + 1/2 + 1/3 + 1/3 + ...1/n$

tends to infinity with n. (This series of terms is called the Harmonic series).

Proof :

With four terms we find:

$$1 + 1/2 + 1/3 + 1/4 > 1 + 1/2 + 1/4 + 1/4 = 2$$

while with eight terms:

$$1 + 1/2 + 1/3 + 1/4 + 1/5 + 1/6 + 1/7 + 1/8 + 1/8 + 1/8 + 1/8 + 1/8 = 5/2.$$

With sixteen terms:

$$1 + 1/2 + 1/3 + ...+ 1/16 > 5/2 + 1/16 + ...1/16 = 5/2 + 1/2 = 3.$$

Thus, with a sufficiently large number of terms, the series can be made to exceed any preassigned number, however larger. In other words, the sum of the series approaches infinity, as the number of terms in it becomes infinite.

Euler's Proof :

Suppose that the number of primes is finite, say N. Let these primes be p_1, p_2, p_3....p_n. Then the product:

$$1/(1 - 1/p_1) \times 1/(1 - 1/p_2).....1/(1 - 1/p_n)$$

must also be finite.

By Lemma 1, this product is written as

$$\left(1+\frac{1}{p1}+\frac{1}{(p1)^2}+\cdots\cdots\frac{1}{(pn)^2}+\cdots\cdots\right)\left(1+\frac{1}{p2}+\left(\frac{1}{p2}\right)^2+\cdots\cdots\left(\frac{1}{p2}\right)^{1/n}+\cdots\cdots\right)$$

$$\left(1+\frac{1}{pN}+\frac{1}{(pN)^2}+\cdots\cdots\right)$$

By Lemma 2 the harmonic series has an infinite sum. Therefore the number of primes cannot be finite.

Q12. Prove that the number (single number) 412,078,521,834 is not a perfect square. **[JUN01]**

Given number is : 412,078,521,834.

On solving it :

	641932
6	412,078,521,834
	36
124	520
	496
1281	2478
	1281
12829	1197752
	115461
128383	429118
	385149
1283862	3396934
	2567724
	829210

Remainder is 829210
So, we can say that given number is not a perfect square.

Q13. Prove that 12, 078, 521, 834 is not a square, while 1, 354, 896 is a square. [JAN01]

2	12,078,521,834
	6,039,260,917

The number after the fraction is 6,039,260,917. So we can say that it is not a perfect square. Another number is 1354896.

Chapter-3

The Higher Arithmetic -II

Q1. Prove that the expressions 3x + 7y and 9x + 4y are divisible by 17 for the same set of integral values of x and y. [DEC02][JUN00]

To prove that if 3 x + 7y is divisible by 17 for some integer, values of x and y, then, for the same values of x & y, 9x + 4y is divisible by 17 and this also holds vice-versa.

First, let us suppose that for some set of integer values of x & y, 3x + 7y is divisible by 17 i.e.

Let $3x + 7y = 17k$

$\Rightarrow 3x = 17k - 7y$

$\Rightarrow 9x = (51k - 21y)$

$\Rightarrow 9x + 4y = 51k - 21y + 4y = 51k - 17y$

$\Rightarrow 17(3k - y)$ (multiple of 17)

9x + 4y is also divisible by 17 for the same set of integer values of x & y. Now, vice-versa, let

$9x + 4y = 17k$

$$\Rightarrow 3x = \left(\frac{17k - 4y}{3}\right)$$

$$\therefore 3x + 7y = \left(\frac{17k - 4y}{3}\right) + 7y$$

$$\Rightarrow 3x + 7y = \left(\frac{17k - 4y + 21y}{3}\right)$$

$$= \left(\frac{17k - 17y}{3}\right) = 17\left(\frac{k - y}{3}\right) (\textit{multiple of } 17)$$

$\Rightarrow$ 17 divides (3x + 7y)

($\because$ 17 does not divide by 3 and 17 is a prime number)

Hence, 3x + 7y is divisible by 17 for the same for integer values of x & y for which 9x + 4y is divisible by 17.

Q2. Determine all positive integers for which 2^n+1 is divisible by 3. [JUN03][JUN02][JUN00]

The given expression is $2^n + 1$. We wish to determine all positive integers for which 2^n+1 is divisible by 3.

i.e. $n \geq 1, 2, 3, \ldots n$

Now for	$n = 1$	$2^n + 1 = 3$
	$n = 2$	$2^n + 1 = 15$
	$n = 3$	$2^n + 1 = 9$
	$n = 4$	$2^n + 1 = 17$
	$n = 5$	$2^n + 1 = 33$
	$n = 6$	$2^n + 1 = 65$
	$n = 7$	$2^n + 1 = 129$

It is observed that whenever n is a odd positive integer i.e. 1, 3, 5, 7,.....2^n + 1 is divisible by 3. And for odd n, we can rewrite the given expression as

$2^n - (-1)^n$

This expression for the form $a^n - b^n$ is always factorable. Therefore, for all positive odd n integers, the expression $2^n + 1$ is always divisible by 3.

Q3. Let $a_1, a_2, a_3, \ldots a_N$ be an arbitrary arrangement of the number 1, 2, 3, … n. Prove that, if n is odd the product $(a_1, - 1)$ $(a_2 - 2)$ $(a_3 - 3)$ … $(a_n - n)$ is even number. [JUN02][DEC99]

The number of factors in the following product

$(a_1 - 1) X (a_2 - 2) X (a_3 - 3) \ldots\ldots\ldots (a_n - n)$ is odd.

Since given n is odd.

By inspection, the sum of all factors is 0. This is impossible if each of the factors was odd, because and odd numbers cannot sum to an even, the product.

$(a_1 -1) X (a_2 - 2) X (a_3 - 3) \ldots\ldots\ldots (a_n - n)$ is an even number.

Q4. Prove that for every integer (n > 2), $(n!)^2 > n^{n.}$

[DEC02][JUNE02][JUN99]

We are given that n>2, where n is an integer. We have to prove that

$(n!^2) > n$

Now, the expansion for (n!) can be written as the product

$1 \times n \times 2 \times (n -1) \times 3 \times (n -1) \times \ldots\ldots\ldots \times (n - 1) \times 2 \times n \times 1$

In this set of products, each of the terms, $1 \times n$, $2 \times (n -1)$, $3 \times (n - 2)$, etc. is greater than or equal to n.

The fist and the last terms are $(1 \times n)$. These are smaller than others. Each of the other terms is of the form $(K + 1) \times (n - K)$ and exceeds, because

$(K + 1) \times (n - K) = K (n + K) + (n - K)$

$= K + (n - k)$

$= n$

And there are n such products. Therefore,
$(n!)^2 > n \times n \times n \times \ldots\ldots\times n$ (n terms) = n
=> $(n!)^2 > n^n$

Q5. An arithmetic progression is a sequence of equally spaced terms:
a, a + d, a + 2d, a + 3d, . . .
where a is the first term of the progression, and d is the common difference. Prove that in an infinite arithmetic progression of natural numbers in which the common difference is not zero, not all the terms can be primes.

If nth term of the progression be denoted as Tn, term,
it is clear that $T_n = a + (n - 1)\,d$
Thus, the ath term after a must be $a + (a - 1)d$, and the following term must be,

$$a + (a - 1)d + d, \text{ i.e. } a(1 + d)$$

Which is a composite number.

Q6. Prove that the product of four consecutive natural numbers cannot be the square of an integer. [DEC04,Q1(d)][DEC99][JUN99]

Examine the product of the consecutive numbers.

$1 \times 2 \times 3 \times 4 = 24$
$2 \times 3 \times 4 \times 5 = 120$
$3 \times 4 \times 5 \times 6 = 360$ and so on.

In each case we find that the product is one less than a perfect square. Thus 24 is
5^2-1, 120 is 11^2-1, 360 and so on.
Now consider the product of four consecutive integers.

$$n(n + 1)(n + 2)(n + 3)$$

where n is arbitrary. We will prove the result after rewriting this product in the form f(n)
1. Where f(n) is a perfect square expression on n, we first note that the term n (n + 2) in the product looks "almost" like a perfect square.

$n(n + 2) = n^2 + 2n$
$= n^2 + 2n + 1 - 1$
$(n + 1)^2 - 1$
$(n + 1)(n + 3) = n^2 + 4n + 3$
$= n^2 + 4n + 4 - 1$
$= (n + 2)^2 - 1$

$\therefore$ $n(n + 1)(n + 2)(n + 3) = [(n + 1)^2 - 1]$, **which is an expression not like that kind we are looking for 1**. Lets therefore experiment with a different order of expansion:

$[n(n + 3)] [(n + 1) (n + 2)] = (n^2 + 3n + 2)$
$= (n^2 + 3n)^2 + 2 (n^2 + 3n)$
$[n(n + 3)] [(n + 1) (n + 2)] = (n^2 + 3n) + (n^2 + 3n) + 1 - 1$
$= (n^2 + 3n + 1)^2 - 1$

Q7. For any integer n greater than 2, prove that the nth power of the length of the hypotenuse of a right triangle is greater than the sum of the nth powers of the lengths of the smaller sides.

Let the hypotenuse be c, and the smallest sides be a and b. Then
$c^n = c^2c^{(n-2)} = (a^2+b^2)\ c^{(n-2)} = a^2c^{(n-2)} + b^2c^{(n-2)}$
But $c^{(n-2)} > a^{(n-2)}$, and $c^{(n-2)} > b^{(n-2)}$
Therefore:
$c^n > a^2a^{(n-2)} + b^2b^{(n-2)} = a^n + b^n$

Q8. For any three consecutive integers, the cube of the largest cannot be the sum of the cubes of the other two. **[JUL04][JUN02]**

Suppose that three consecutive integers are , n, n+1, n+2
Now, according to question we have to prove that,
$(n+2)^3 \neq n^3 + (n+1)^3$ where n+2 may be as n+(n+1)
$\Rightarrow n^3 + 6n^2 + 8n + 8 = n^3 + n^3 + 2n^2 + 2n + 1$
$\Rightarrow n^3 - 4n^2 - 6n - 7$
$\Rightarrow n(n^2-4n-6) - 7$
Equation is not true for any integer. Hence, the given condition holds.

Q9. Prove that the fraction (21n + 4) / (14n + 3) cannot be reduced for any n. **[JAN01][JUN01]**

Let n = 1,
$21n + 4 = 21 \times 1 + 4 = 25$
and $14n + 3 = 14 \times 1 + 3 = 17$
There is no any common factor between both equation.
Again, if we put n = 2
$21n + 4 = 21 \times 2 + 4 = 46$
and $14n + 3 = 14 \times 2 + 3 = 31$
No any common factor between them.
Now, given n = 3,
$21n + 4 = 21 \times 3 + 4 = 67$
and $14n + 3 = 14 \times 3 + 3 = 45$
There is no any number factor.
Thus, we can say that both expression have no factors in common for any value of n.

Q10. Determine all 3 digit numbers N such that N is divisible by 11, and N/11 equals the sum of the squares of the digits of N. [JUN03][DEC01]

A three digit number is represented by

$N = 100a + 10b + c$ ....(I)

Some 3 – digit numbers which is divisible by 11:-

110, 121, 132, 143, 154, 165 etc.

According to question:-

$N/11 = a^2 + b^2 + c^2$ ....(II)

After observation equation (I) and (II), we obtained

$N = 803$

which is divisible 11.

Q11. For any integer n > 2, prove that the nth power of the length of the hypotenuse of a right triangle is greater than sum of the nth powers of lengths of the smaller sides.

To prove :- $a^n > b^n + c^n$ for $n > 2$

In the right-angled Δ ABC shown in the figure, we have,

$a^2 = b^2 + c^2$

$a^3 = a^2.a = (b^2 + c^2).a = b^2 a + c^2.a > b^2.b + c^2.c$

(a>b and a>c)

$\Rightarrow a^3 > b^3 + c^3$

Similarly,

$a^4 = a^3.a = (b^3 + c^3).a = b^3.a + c^3.a > b^3.b + c^3.3$

$\Rightarrow a^4 > b^4 + c^4$

Carrying out this operations for n-2 times, we finally get,

$a^n > b^n + c^n$ for $n > 2$.

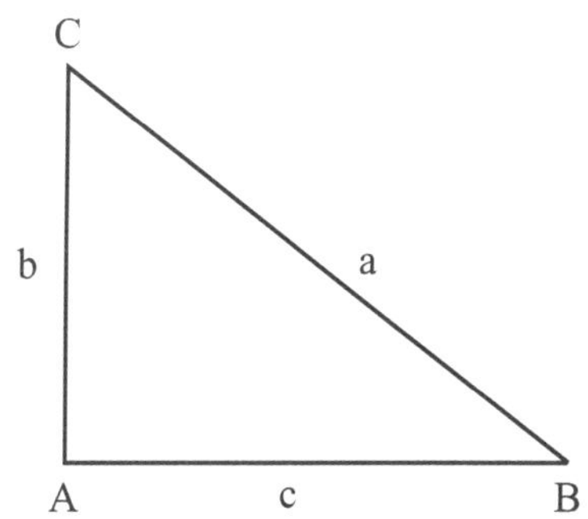

Q12. Find R_1 the maximum number of regions into which a plane can be divided by a infinite straight lines, no two of which are parallel, and no three of which pass through the same point. [JUN01]

We start considering the numbers of regions formed by zero, one, two, three line etc.

According to above consideration, when there are no line, the plane consist of one region.

Mathematically : $R_0 = 1$

One line divides the plane in two regions :

$R_1 = 2$ as 4(½)

Two lines divides the plane into four regions and three lines into seven as :

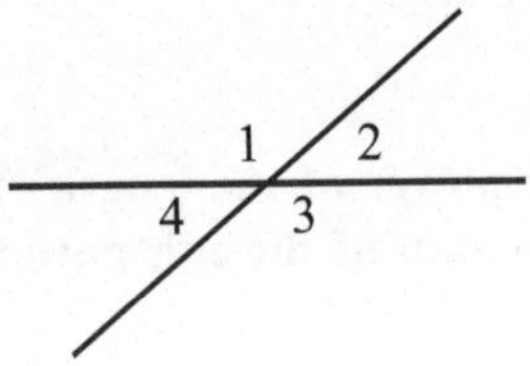

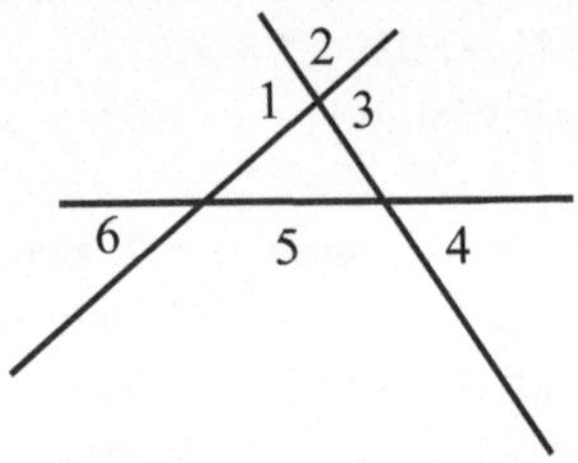

Further, 4 lines divides the plane into 11 regions.

Therefore, we can assume a formula :

$$R_n = R_{n-1} + n \text{ for small value of } n$$

The nth line increases the number of region by n, because it outs the previous n-1 lines in n-L places.

Since R_0 is 1 (It is thought of as boundary condition)

By backwards from R_n to these general formula in terms of n alone.

$$\begin{aligned}
R_{nj} &= R_{n-1} + n \\
&= R_{n-1} + n \\
&= R_{n-2} + (n-1) + n \\
&= R_{n-3} + (n-2) + (n-1) + n \\
&= R_0 + 1 + 2 + 3 + \ldots\ldots.. + (n-2) + (n-1) + n. \\
&= 1 + S_n
\end{aligned}$$

Whereas S_n is the sum of the first n positive integers.

Using Gauss's trick we can write :

$$S_n = 1 + 2 + 3 + \ldots\ldots.. + (n-2) + (n-1) + n$$

$$S_n = \frac{n(n+1)}{2}$$

$$2S_n = n(n+1)$$

$$R_n = 1 + n(n+1)/2$$

Q13. Write short notes on Minimum Spanning Circles.[DEC03][JUN03]
#: Explain the concept of Minimum Spanning Circles and Jung's Theorem.

Consider a finite set of n points in the plane; then the set of distances between any two points is also a finite set, which has a largest member, say d, called the span of the set of points. Clearly, if a set of points has span d, then it is possible to draw a circle of radius d that encloses all the points.

But it is possible to draw a smaller circle that still enclose the entire set : first locate a pair of points, P and Q, whose distance from each other is d. (If there are several such pairs, we may choose any one). Construct two circles of radius d with centers at P and Q.

The circle entered at P passes through Q, while the circle at Q passes through P. These circles intersect at R and S. The entire set of n points lies within each circle. Therefore it must lie within their intersection. But the intersection itself is enclosed within die circle which has RS for its diameter. Since PS is maximally d, the radius of this spanning circle, by Pythagoras Theorem is $d\sqrt{3}/2$, (why?) a bound lower than the one we had started with. This bound lean be further improved, and this is Jung's Theorem : Every finite set of points of span d has a spanning circle no greater than $d\sqrt{3}/3$, a still better bound. Though smaller spanning circles are possible for certain finite sets of points, there are some which require the spanning circle to be atleast this large.

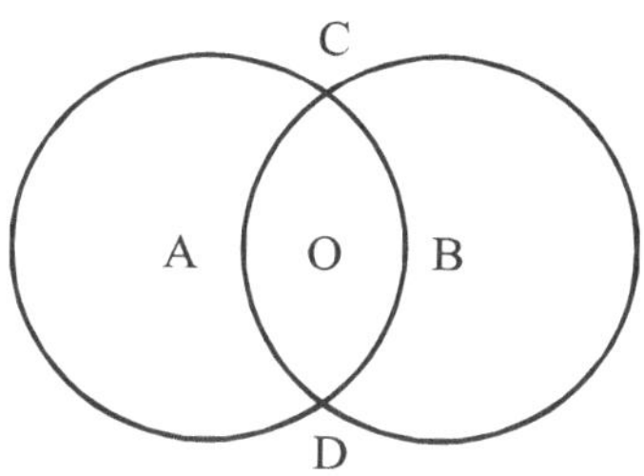

PQ=d, OP=d/2, PS=d, maximally

Q14. Given a set A consisting of 10 numbers between 1 and 100: prove that there exist two distinct subsets of A whose elements sum to the same number. [JUL04]

Given that a set consisting of 10 number between 1 to 100.

Let subset of A is a_1 which contains the number

{0, 1, 2, 3, 4, 5, 6, 7, 8, 9} and other subset of A i.e. a_2 is

{0, 1, 2, 3, 4, 5, 6, 7, 8, 9} and

then sum is i.e. A

A = {0, 2, 4, 6, 8, 10, 12, 14, 16, 18}

Q15. A cylindrical hole of length three inches is drilled through a sphere. Find the volume of material removed? [JAN01]

Length or height of the hole $h = 3$ inches.

Let, radius of spherical hole is r inches.

We, know that,

Volume of spherical hole = volume of material removed by hole

So,

Volume of hole $= \pi r^2 h$

$= \pi r^2 3$

$= 3\pi r^2$ cube inches

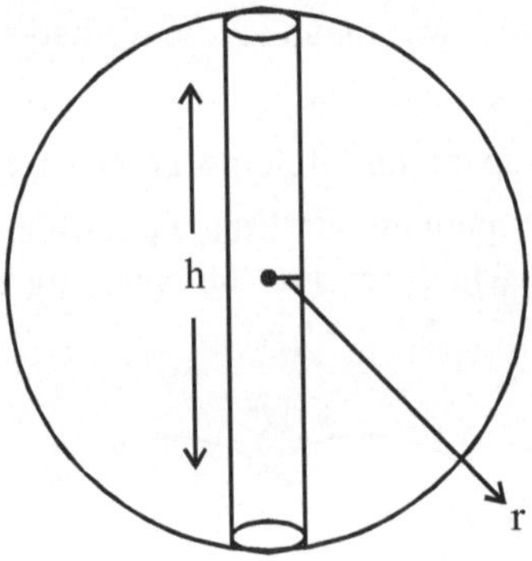

Chapter-4

General Methods

Q1. Find the sum of the first n cubes, $S_n = 1^3 + 2^3 + 3^3 + 4^3 + ...n^3$

In the equation if n = 1, then S_1=1; if n = 2, S_2 = 9; if n=3, S_3=36; if n =4, S_4=100.

The sum of the first n cubes is a perfect square. Testing for a few more values, the results are :

$S_1 = 1 = 1^2$

$S_2 = 9 = 3^2$ $\quad$ $S_5 = 225 = 15^2$

$S_3 = 36 = 6^2$ $\quad$ $S_6 = 441 = 21^2$

$S_4 = 100 = 10^2$ $\quad$ $S_7 = 784 = 28^2$

There is a pattern in the squares. When n increases from 1 to 2 the changes from S_1 to S_2 is from 1^2 to 3^2. When n changes from 2 to 3 the change from S_2 to S_3, is that the number

$\because 2^2 = 4 > 2^? - 1 = 3$

$\because 4 > 3$.

Let P_k be true for some fixed k.

i.e. $2 > k^2 - 1$ & assuming P_k is if we prove that P_{k-1} is true then we have that the square of number is larger by 3 from the preceding; in going from S_3 to S_4, it's larger by 4, and in going from S_4 to S_5, it's larger by 5. Then s_8 is $(28+8)^2$ or 36^2. And S_9 is 45^2. There is a pattern here, S_n can thus be expressed as a formula which is a perfect square expression in terms of n.

$$S_n = \left[\frac{1}{2}n(n+1)\right] \textbf{ power 2}$$

Q2. Prove by the method of induction that the sum of first n cubes is S_n $(1/2n\,(n+1)^2)$. **[DEC04, Q1(c)]**

The sum S_n of the first n cubes obeys the formula :

$$S_n = \left[\frac{1}{2}n(n+1)\right] \textbf{ power 2}$$

We prove this formula by the method of induction as follows. The formula is certainly true for n=1 called the base case, since

$$1^3 = \left[\frac{1}{2}(1+1)\right]^2$$

We now establish the inductive case, namely that if the formula is true for n=k, then it is true also for n = k+1;

Assume that for some fixed k,

$S_k = (1/2k\ (k+1)^2$

$S_{k+1} = [1/2(k+1)(k+1+1)2]^2 = 1/2k(k+1)^2+(k+1)^3$

$= (k+1)^2\ (k+1+(1/2k))^2$

$= (k+1)^2(1/2(k+2))^2$

$= (1/2(k+1)(k+2))^2$

Thus, if the formula is true for some k then it is true for k+1. In particular, if the formula is true for k=1, it is necessarily true for k=2. But we know by direct testing that the formula does hold for k=2. Therefore it holds for k=3. Therefore for k=4. And similarly for any k. This is the method of induction.

Q3. For all n, prove that $2^n \geq 2n$. **[DEC03]**

We will prove it by mathematical induction:

$2^n \geq 2n$

$n = 1$

$2^1 \geq 2.1$

2 = 2 which is true.

Let it is true for n = r, then

$2^r \geq 2r$

Multiplying both sides by 2

$2^{r+1} \geq 2r.2$

$= 4r$

Q4. For all n, prove that $2^n \geq 3n - 2$. **[DEC99]**

$2^n \geq 3n - 2$

for $n = 1$

$2 \geq 3 - 2$

$2 \geq 1$ which is true.

Let it is true for n = r, then

$2 \geq 3r - 2$

Multiplying both sides by 2

$2^{r+1} \geq 3 \times 2^r - 2 \times 2$

$= 3r + 3r + 3 - 7$

$= (3r - 7) + 3(r + 1)$

$= 3(r + 1) - 2 + 3r - 5$

As for r = 1, it is true

So, for $r \geq 2$, $3r - 5 > 0$

$= 2^{r+1} \geq 3^{r+1} - 2$

= for (r + 1) it is true.

So the given statement is true for n = 1 and if true for n = r then it is true for n = r + 1

So, it is true for any value of n.

Q5. Prove that for all n, $2^n \geq n^2 - 1$ **[DEC00]**

Let P_n, $2^n > n^2 - 1$ which is a statement for $n \in N$.

Let n = 1

$\therefore$ We prove that P_1 is true

L.H.S = $2^1 = 2$

R.H.S = $1^2 - 1 = 0$

$\therefore$ L.H.S $\geq$ R.H.S

$\therefore$ P_1 is true.

Also P_2 is true.

$\because 2^2 = 4 > 2^2 - 1 = 3$

$\because 4 > 3$.

Let P_k be true for some fixed k.

i.e. $2^k > k^2 - 1$ & assuming P_k is if we prove that P_{k+1} is true then we have proved the result for all $n \in N$.

Now,

L.H.S = $2^{k+1} \quad = 2^k.2$

$\geq 2k^2 - 2$

$= k^2+2k+1+k^2-2k-1-2$

$= (k+1)^2-1$ = R.H.S

($\because k^2-2k-2>0$ for $k > 2$, k Î N)

P_k is true

=> P_{k+1} is true

$\therefore$ By induction $2n >= n^2 - 1$ for all $n \in N$.

Q6. Prove that for all $n \geq 4$, $2^n \geq n^2$. **[JUNE03]**

Given that n > 4

First we take, n = 5

$2^5 = 2 \times 2 \times 2 \times 2 \times = 32$

and $5^2 = 5 \times 5 = 25$

we know that 32 > 25

so, $2^5 > 5^2$ ....(I)

and $6^2 = 6 \times 6 \times = 36$

we know that 64 > 36

so, $2^6 > 6^2$ ....(II)

Again, we take, n = 7

$2^7 = 2 \times 2 \times 2 \times 2 \times 2 \times 2 = 128$

and $7^2 = 7 \times 7 = 49$

we know that 49 > 138

so, $2^7 > 7^2$ ....(III)

After observing condition (I), (II) and (III), we can say that $2^n > n^2$ for n>4.

Also solved that

Let, formula is correct for n = k

$\therefore \quad 2^{k7} \geq k^2$

or, $2^k.2 \geq 2k^2$

or, $2^{k+1} \geq k^2 + k^2$

or, $2^{k+1} \geq k^2 + 2k \quad \left[\because k^2 > 2k \text{ for } n > 6\right]$

or, $2^{k+1} \geq (k + 1)^2$

So, formula is correct for n = k + 1

Hence, by mathematical induction we have proved that, for all $n \geq 4$ $\boxed{2^n \geq n^2}$.

Q7. Prove that for all $n \geq 10$, $2^n \geq 100n$. **[DEC03,Q4(b)]**

Given that n>10

First we take, n = 11

$2^{11} = 2 \times 2 \times 2 \times 2 \times 2 \times 2 \times 2 \times 2 \times 2 \times 2 \times 2 = 2048$

and $100.11 = 1100$

we know that 2048 > 1100

so, $2^{11} > 100.11$ ....(I)

now, we take, n = 12

$2^{12} = 2 \times 2 \times 2 \times 2 \times 2 \times 2 \times 2 \times 2 \times 2 \times 2 \times 2 \times 2 = 4096$

and $100.12 = 1200$

we know that 4096 > 1200

so, $2^{12} > 100.12$ ....(II)

Again, we take, n = 13

$2^{13} = 2 \times 2 \times 2 \times 2 \times 2 \times 2 \times 2 \times 2 \times 2 \times 2 \times 2 \times 2 \times 2 = 8192$

and $100.13 = 1300$

we know that 8192 > 1300

so, $2^{13} > 100.13$ ....(III)

after observing condition (I), (II) and (III), we can say that 2^n>100n for n>10.

Also solved that

Let, formula is correct for n = k

$\therefore \quad 2^k \geq 100k$

or, $2^k.2 \geq 200k$
or, $2^{k+1} \geq 100k + 100k$
or, $2^{k+1} \geq 100k + 100$
or, $2^{k+1} \geq 100(k + 1)$
so, formula is correct for n = k + 1

Hence, by the mathematical induction, we have proved that. $\boxed{2^n \geq 100n}$ for n ≥ 10.

Q8. Prove that the sum of the squares of the first n integers is 1/24 (2n)(2n + 1)(2n+2). **[DEC05, Q5(c)]**

We have to prove that sum of the squares of the first n integer n is

$$= \frac{2n\,(2n+1)\,(2n+2)}{24}$$

Mathematically which may be written as;

$$1^2+2^2+3^2+4^2+\dots\dots\dots+n^2 = \frac{2n\,(2n+1)\,(2n+2)}{24}$$

i.e. P(n) : $1^2+2^2+3^2+4^2+\dots\dots\dots+n^2 = \frac{2n\,(2n+1)\,(2n+2)}{24}$ ....(1)

Let n = 1, $1^2 = \frac{2\times 1(2\times 1+1)(2\times 1+2)}{24}$

$1 = \frac{2(3)(4)}{24}$

$1 = \frac{24}{24}$

$1 = 1$

L.H.S. = R.H.S

$\Rightarrow P(1)$ is true.

Let us suppose that P(K) is true

putting n=k in (1) we have

$1^2+2^2+\dots\dots\dots+K^2 = \frac{2K\,(2K+1)\,(2K+2)}{24}$ ....(2)

i.e. P(K) is true

Now we want to check equation (1) is also true for k+1, so, we replace K by K+1 to last term of L.H.S. i.e. in K^2 which become $(K+1)^2$
adding $(K+1)^2$ to both side of equation (2) we have

$$1^2+2^2+3^2+\dots\dots\dots\dots\dots+K^2+(K+1)^2 = \frac{2K\,(2K+1)(2K+2)}{24}+(K+1)^2$$

$$= \frac{2K(2K+1)(2K+2)+24(K+1)^2}{24}$$

$$= \frac{4K(K+1)\{K(2K+1)+6(K+1)\}}{24}$$

$$= \frac{(K+1)}{6}\{2K^2+K+6K+6\}$$

$$= \frac{(K+1)}{6}\{2K^2+7K+6\}$$

$$= \frac{(K+1)}{6}\{(2K+3)(K+2)\}$$

$$= \frac{(K+1)\times 2\times 2}{6\times 2\times 2}\{(2K+3)(K+2)\}$$

$$= \frac{(K+1)2}{24}\{(2K+3)(2K+4)\}$$

$$= \frac{2(K+1)(2K+3)(2K+4)}{24}$$

$\therefore$ P(n) is true for n = (K+1)

i.e. P(K+1) is true

$\therefore$ By principle of mathematical induction P(n) is true for all natural number n.

Hence $1^2+2^2+\ldots\ldots\ldots\ldots+n^2 = \frac{2n(2n+1)(2n+2)}{24}$ proved.

Q9. Prove that the sum of the fourth powers of the first n integers is 1/30 n(n + 1)(2n + 1)(3n² + 3n - 1) [DEC03]

Let S^n denote the sum of the fourth of the first n integers.

Let n = 1

$$\therefore S_1 = \frac{1}{30}(1)(1+1)(2(1)+1)(3(1)^2+3x1-1) = \mathbf{\frac{1}{30}\ (1)(6)(3+3-1)}$$

$$= \frac{1}{30}(30)$$

$$= \frac{1}{30}k(k+1)(2k+1)(3k^2+3k-1)+(k+1)^4$$

$$= (k+1)\left[\frac{1}{30}(k)(2k+1)(3k^2+3k-1)+k+3k+3k+1\right]$$

$$= \frac{1}{30}(k+1)(6k^4 + 9k^3 + k^2 - k + 30k^3 + 90k^2 + 90k + 30)$$

$$= \frac{1}{30}(k+1)(6k^4 + 39k^3 + 91k^2 + 89k + 30)$$

$$= \frac{1}{30}(k+1)(6k^4 + 12k^3 + 27k^3 + 54k^2 + 37k^2 + 74k + 15k + 30)$$

$$= \frac{1}{30}(k+1)\ (k+2)(6k^3 + 27k^2 + 37k + 15)$$

$$= \frac{1}{30}(k+1)\ (k+2)(6k^3 + 9k^2 + 18k^2 + 27k + 10 + 15)$$

$$= \frac{1}{30}(k+1)\ (k+2)(2k+3)(3k^2 + 9k + 5)$$

$$= \frac{1}{30}(k+1)\ (k+2)(2(k+1)+1)(3k^2 + 6k + 3 + 3k + 3 - 1)$$

$$= \frac{1}{30}(k+1)\ (k+2)(2(k+1)+1)(3k+1)^2 + 3(k+1) - 1)$$

$$= S_{k+1}$$

Hence by method of induction $= S_n = \frac{1}{30} n(n+1)(2n+1)(3n^2 + 3n - 1)$ is true for all for all $n \in N$.

Q10. What is the power of 10 that divides 100! (factorial of 100)?

[JAN01]

100 ! = 1 × 2 × 3 × 4 × 5 × 6 × .... × 100

In this product we get factors:

10, 20, 30, 40, ..., 90, 1000

Each of these numbers is a product of 10 and 100 is 10^2. Thus, the 100 ! is divisible by atleast 10 raised power 11 i.e. 10^{11}.

Now, 100 ! has

2 × 5
12 × 25
22 × 25
32 × 35
....

....

92×95

Each of the products above is divisible by 10. Thus, 100 ! is further divisible by 1010. So, 100! is divisible by $10^{11}, 10^{10}$.

$= 10^{21}$

Q11. Prove that for every integer $n > 2$, $(n!)^2 > n^n$. **[JUN03]**

We want to prove that

$(n!)^2 > n^n$ for $n > 2$

The term $(n!)^2$ can be expanded in the following form:

$1 \times n \times 2 \times (n - 1) \times 3 \times (n - 2) \times .... \times (n - 1) \times 2 \times n \times 1$

In the set of products : $1 \times n$, $2 \times (n - 1)$, $3 \times (n - 2)$, etc each term is greater than or equal to n. The first (and the last) product $(1 \times n)$ is smaller than others while each of the other, being of the form $(k + 1) \times (n - x)$ exceeds n, because

$$(k + 1) \times (n - k) = k (n - k) + 1 (n - k)$$
$$= (k + 1) (n - k)$$
$$> k + (n + k)$$
$$= n$$

There are n such products

Therefore $(n!)^2 > n^n$

Chapter-5

Introduction To Excel

Q1. What is MS-Excel

MS-Excel is a Windows based application package that can be used to automate tasks such as calculation and analysis of data. MS-Excel works the way you want i.e. it can be customised.

Q2. List the various features available in MS-Excel.

Following are the various features available in MS-Excel :

✓ **Tip Wizard** - Guides you to work more effectively while you work by displaying various helpful tips and techniques based on what you are doing.

✓ **Drag and Drop Feature** - It helps you to reposition the data and text by simply dragging the data with the help of mouse.

✓ **Autofill** - It helps you to fill rows or columns with the series of data.

✓ **Autosum** - You can add a large range of data by simply selecting a tool button.

✓ **Windows Interface** - As Excel is Windows based package therefore the user interface is consistent.

✓ **Shortcut Menus** - Commands appropriate to the task that you are doing appear by clicking the right mouse button.

✓ **Built-in Spell Check** - You can maintain a dictionary of the words usually used in your work and spell-check your spreadsheet.

And many other features are being incorporated in newer versions.

Q3. Give the shortcuts to select the following using keyboard in MS-EXCEL: **[DEC01,Q2(a)]**

(i) Current cell

(ii) Entire column

(iii) Entire Row

(iv) Entire worksheet

(v) Open a new worksheet

(vi) Open an existing worksheet

(vii) Extend selection to End of Data Block.

(i) Enter

(ii) Ctrl + Spacebar

(iii) Shift + Spacebar
(iv) Ctrl+A **or** Ctrl + Shift + Spacebar
(v) Ctrl + N
(vi) Ctrl + O
(vii) Shift, End + Arrow key

Q4. Explain the different types of data that can be entered in worksheet cells. [DEC01,Q2(b)][JAN01][JUN00]

The various kinds of entries that can be made in a cell are :

i) Text:- First select the cell in which the data has to be entered and type- in the text.

Press ENTER key to finish your entry. The data will be displayed in the active cell as well as in the formula bar. To enter digits as text (calculations cannot be done using these kind of entries) use an apostrophe(') as the first character.

ii) Number:- Numbers include digits from 0 to 9 and one special characters like:

$ % + - / ( ) , . E e

iii) Date and Time:- Date and Time entries are interpreted in a special way in Excel. They are represented as numbers for Excel given to each day from 01:01:1990 (serial number 1) to 31:12:2078(serial number 65380). Although when you type a date in the cell like 01/01/97, it will be displayed as it is.
Example Type TODAY( ) in a blank cell and press ENTER key. (This function will display the system date and time).

iv) *Data in Series* - You can fill a range of cells either with the same value or with the series of values. This can be done using Autofill handle (small square on the bottom-right corner of the active cell).
Drag this handle till the last cell to create a range of cells which are to be filled-in with the values.

Example

1. Enter MONDAY in cell E20.
2. Drag the Autofill handle till the cell K20.

(The whole range will be filled with days from MONDAY to SUNDAY)

Q5. How many ways of referencing the cells are there ? [JAN01]
#: Explain the 3 ways of referencing the cells in MS-EXCEL worksheet. [DEC01]

#: Explain the three ways of referencing the cells.

There are 16384 rows and 256 columns in one worksheet. The first cell is labelled as A1 (column as A and row number as 1) or R1C1.

Example

R3 C3 refers to row 3 column 3 and is equivalent to C3. Thus the last cell is labelled as IV 16384. This is called the cell address and they reused to identify the cell.

Following are the ways of referencing the cells :

(i) Relative → This refers to the cell relative to the given position.

Example

Enter the following values:

In cell A3 enter the value 34
In cell A4 enter the value 23
In cell A5 enter the value 89
In cell A6 enter the formula = A3 + A4 + A5
Copy this formula to the cell A7, and see the result.

Observe the formula entered in cell A7. It is A4 + A5 + A6. The formula entered in cell A6 means the sum of the values given in the three cells given above the current cell. Therefore, when we move down, the relation specified in the formula was copied (i.e. the three values given above the current cell which is A7 now).

(ii) Absolute → This refers to the specific cell irrespective of the position of the formula. The '$' sign is used to denote an absolute reference.

Example

In the cell B3 copy the formula $A$3 + $A$4 + $A$5

Copy this formula to the cell B4.
We find that the result and the formula remains the same.

(iii) Mixed → It is a combination of both relative and mixed references. It has one absolute co-ordinate and one relative co-ordinate. $D1 and D$1 are both examples of mixed references.

Q6. Differentiate between Workbook and Worksheet.[JAN01][DEC05]

Following are the differences between a work book and a work sheet :

(i) A workbook is the MS Excel file in which you enter and store related data. A worksheet (also known as a spreadsheet) is a collection of cells on a single "sheet" where you actually keep and manipulate the data.

(ii) Each workbook can contain many worksheets. But reverse is not possible. (It's a lot like a book. One book contains an entire story. Each page of the book contains part of the story.)

(iii) Often one workbook has a single theme, such as a personal budget. Each worksheet would then have a part of the theme, such as the budget broken down by month.

Q7. How the access of the Workbook can be restricted from other users?

In MS-Excel, it may be necessary to protect the data from being seen or used by unauthorised people. For this facility of password is available.

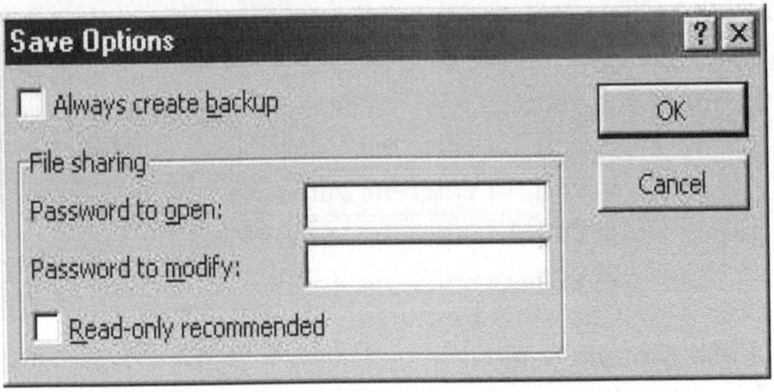

From the File→Save As dialogue box click on options....button.

The access to a workbook to other users can be restricted in 3 different ways:

1) Protection Password

(a) Type the password, which will be required to open the workbook. The password can be upto 15 characters long, can include alphabets (uppercase or lowercase), numbers and special characters. It is case sensitive also.

(b) Excel will ask to re-enter the same password. Enter the password again.

(c) Click on OK.

2) Write Reservation Password

This password will be required when changes in the existing workbook are made and then workbook is saved. This prevents the unauthorised users to make any modification in the workbook. The rules to give the password are same as Protection Password.

3) Read-only Recommended

If this option is checked, the following dialogue box will be displayed every time you try to open the workbook.

This option is checked if one wants to discourage the other users from making any changes by mistake or want to prevent the changes to be made by more than one users simultaneously.

Q8. What is Fill-handle and how is it useful?

In Excel, the active cell has a heavy bordered box surrounding it. The box has a small square in the bottom corner. This square is known as the fill handle. The fill handle is used to copy information from one cell to the next by clicking on the square and dragging. The Fill Handle in Excel is possibly one of Excels most under utilized features. In it's simplest form it will increment any series of numbers. For example, if you type the number **1** in any cell and then the number **2** in a cell that adjoins it, you can use the Fill Handle to increment up to any number desired. To do this you simply select you two cells (starting from the one with the number **1**) and then hover your mouse pointer over the Fill Handle (until it changes to a small black cross), left click and drag in the direction you want the incremented numbers to show. You can also do the same by entering any starting number in any cell, selecting the cell, holding down the Ctrl key and then dragging down with the Fill Handle. If you do not hold down the Ctrl key Excel will simply copy the same number.

The best bit about this feature is that we can alter the amount we increment by simply typing any two numbers we want eg **5** and **10** would result in **5, 10, 15, 20, 25** etc. If you wanted a blank cell between each number simply use the method below:

Type **5** in cell **A1**

Leave **A2** blank

Type **10** in cell **A3**

Leave **A4** blank

Select cells **A1:A4**

Drag down using the Fill Handle

The exact same principle applies to **dates**, after all dates in Excel are only numbers (**Serial Values**).

The other thing that you can do with the Fill Handle is drag it up or to the left to clear the contents of selected cell(s). You can even insert or delete rows or columns by holding down the **SHIFT** key while dragging the fill handle.

Chapter-6

Formatting And Printing Worksheet

Q1. Explain
(i) Steps required to Apply 'Autoformat' to a Range of cells **[JUN03][JUN01][JUN99]**
(ii) Autofit **[JUN03][JUN99]**
(iii) Format Painter **[DEC05,Q2(c)][JUN03][JUN99]**
(iv) Autoformat **[DEC05,Q4(a)(i)]**
(v) Font
(vi) WYSIWYG
(vii) Page Setup

(i) Steps required to Apply 'Autoformat' to a Range of cells :
To apply Autoformat to a range of cells follow the given steps:
1. Select the range of cells.
2. Select **Autoformat** option from the **Format** menu.
3. Choose the appropriate format from the list of **Table Format**.
4. Click on OK.

(ii) Autofit : Autofit selection is available in deciding the width of a column in MS Excel. It adjusts the width of the column according to the widest entry in that column.

(iii) Format Painter : This feature of Excel provides the facility to copy the format of cell(s) to the selected cells easily and quickly by clicking on the Format Painter tool button(picture given below) on the Standard Toolbar.

Applying Format Painter :

1. Select the formatted cells whose format you want to copy.
2. Press the left mouse button on the Format Painter tool button.

3. Drag the mouse pointed through the cell(s) where you want to apply the formatting.

This formatting technique can be repeated without going through the steps given above. If you double-click the Format Painter tool button, the cursor remains active until you click on the button again.

(iv) Autoformat : This is a built-in table format that can be applied to the range of cells. This feature includes the formatting of numbers, border alignment, font, colour, row height and column width.

(v) Font : Fonts are the typefaces (e.g. TIMES NEW ROMAN, ARIAL etc.) which have Size (in points) colour special effects (like strike through, superscript, and subscript). Fonts can be in bold, italics, or regular. They could also be underlined. Fonts can be changed either through Formatting Toolbar **Or,** through the menu command.

Through Formatting Toolbar :

(a) Select the cells or characters to be formatted.

(b) Click on the appropriate options on the Toolbar.

Through the menu command :

(a) Select the cells or characters to be formatted.

(b) Choose **Format→Cells.**

Select the **Font** tab.

(vi) WYSIWYG : (pronounced "wiz-ee-wig") Page set up means page layout or the final version of how the data should look on printing. It involved choosing paper size, orientation of data, scaling of the area, margins, header/footer etc.

WYSIWYG is the short version of 'What you see is what you get.' This is feature Excel also provides like other Windows programmes. It simply means what one sees on the screen, one will get printed too.

(vii) Page Setup : With the 'What you see is what you get' feature of Excel it is always better to start with page layout which one also wants as printed copy.

The steps are as follow:

1. Open the File menu by clicking on the file.

2. Click on the page set up.

The following dialogue box is displayed.

The Page option allows the user to set the paper size, orientation of the data, scaling of the area etc. Excel inserts automatic page-breaks also.
The Margins tab, when clicked, displays the dialogue box. One can set the top, bottom, left and right margins of the page. These are the distances in inches from edge of the page. This also allows the user to see the preview of the data before it is printed.

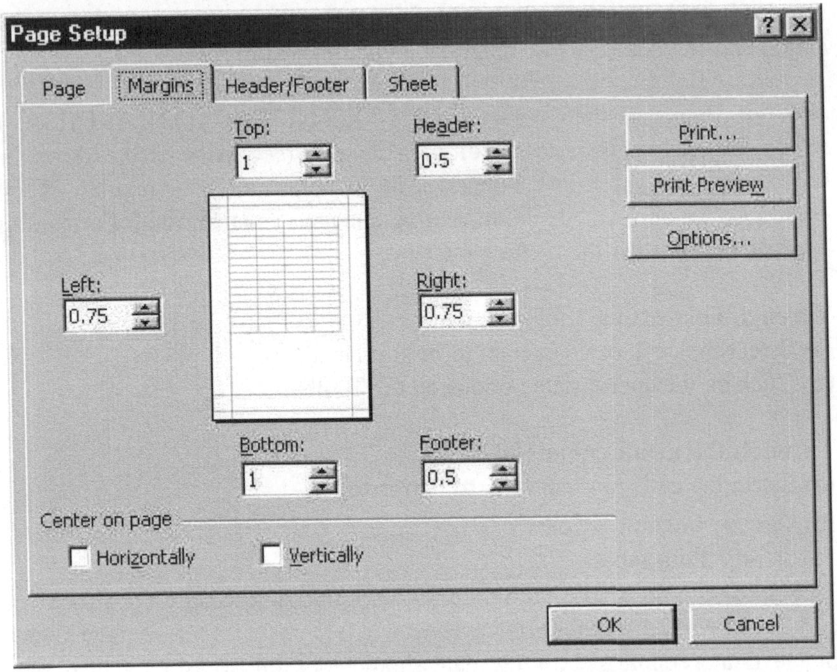

Header/Footer tab gives the option to set the header (which will be displayed on top of every page) and the footer (which will be displayed at the bottom of every page). The header may include the name of the organisation or date or any other thing one may wish to write. The footer may include the page number or a line or something one may wish to write. To add more data as header or footer, click on Custom Header or Custom Footer.
The Sheet tab has the option to select the area to be printed (i.e. the range of cells), set the row or column titles (these will be printed on every page), or select the page order from the multiple worksheets etc.

Q2. What is Alignment ? What are its different options that are available? [JAN01][JUN99]

 # : What is "Alignment"? Explain the four alignment options which can be used for document alignment. [DEC,05Q1(d)]

Alignment is the positioning of text/matter in a cell. In general, by default in Excel the text is left aligned and the numbers are right aligned. Alignment is done in two ways which are Vertical and Horizontal alignment. Vertical alignment determines whether text is positioned at the top, bottom or center of the page.

The various **Horizontal Alignment** options are :

General - the text is left aligned and the numbers are right aligned. This is the default status.

Left - aligns the contents to the left of the cell.

Center - aligns the cell contents to the center of the cell.

Right - aligns the contents to the right of the cell.

Fill - fills the selected cells with the single character.

Justify - this option is selected with multiple lines of text as it wraps the contents from left to right.

Center Across Selection - centers the text across multiple columns.

The various **Vertical Alignment** options are :

Top - aligns the text at the top of the cell.

Center - places the text in the center of the cell.

Bottom - aligns the text on the bottom of the cell.

Justify - wraps the text from top to bottom.

Chapter-7

•••••••••

Customizing Workplace

Q1. Define workplace.

Workplace is the area of the worksheet which is visible and where we work.

Q2. What are the different workplace displays.

Toolbars, Menu bar, Formula bar or Status bar are some of the displays on your workplace. All these displays are not required always. Like, once you have created the workbook, you do not require the toolbars, status bar, formula bar. These can be hidden.

To hide toolbars

1. Select **View → Toolbars.**

2. Uncheck all those toolbars which you want to hide by clicking on the toolbars name.

To hide formula and status bars

✓ Select **View → Formula Bar** to toggle hide or displays of the bar.

or

✓ Select **View → Status Bar** to toggle hide or display of status bar.

Q3. What is the use of creating more than one window at a time?

In Excel, one workbook can be displayed in more than one window. The additional window can be created by going to Windows ® New window command.

Similarly, one can create more than one window to arrange the workspace. This is done to quickly access the information needed. It saves time and helps in organising work efficiently.

Q4. There are different ways for arranging the windows on screen. What are these?

There are different ways to arrange the windows. Create 3 or 4 windows of your workbook and follow the given method:

Choose **Window → Arrange** command

The following dialog box is displayed.

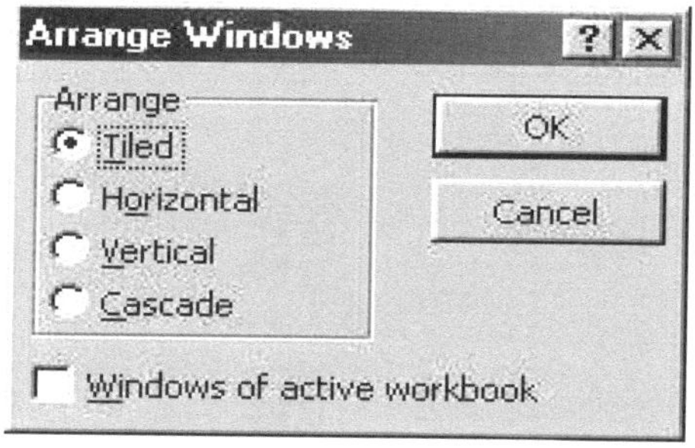

The various options available are :

Tiled - Each window is completely visible in the total workspace which is divided evenly to all the windows.

Horizontal - The windows are arranged horizontally and are fully visible.

Vertical - Again all the windows are completely visible but are arranged vertically.

Cascade - The windows are overlapped on each other and only the title are visible of each window.

Q5. What are custom controls? Explain their use on the worksheet. Write the sequence of steps for creating controls on the worksheet. [DEC01][JUN00]

#: How Controls are created on the Worksheet? Give the steps in sequence.

#: Explain the meaning and purpose of custom control. [DEC05,Q4(a)(iii)]

A software routine that adds some enhancement or feature to an application. Custom controls are written to provide as little as a few graphical interface improvements to as much as providing full imaging, spreadsheet and text editing extensions to the application. Depending on the development system, custom controls are either linked into the application when it is written or maintained as independent executable files that are called at runtime. DLLs, VBXs and OCXs are examples.

Example : instead of typing-in the response, you can select the appropriate option from the drop-down list. The tool buttons that are used to draw control objects are found on the **Forms Toolbar**. To display this toolbar -

Choose **View → Toolbars**.

Some of the custom controls are: lable(text), edit box, group box, check box, option box, list box, drop down list box, list box link to edit control, combination of edit control and drop-down, scroll bar control and spinner control. Following is the picture of all the tool buttons and the short description.

	label (text)		edit box
	group box		button
	check box		option box
	list box		drop-down list box
	list box link to edit control		combination of edit control & drop-down
	scrollbar control		spinner control

The edit control, list box linked to edit control, and combination of edit control & drop-down tool buttons cannot be linked to worksheet cell. These controls can be used inside dialog box only. One control can be linked to only one cell. But one cell can have many controls linked to it.

Following are the steps to place the control on the worksheet :

1. Display the Forms Toolbar on the worksheet.

2. Click the control object tool which is to be placed on the worksheet.

3. As the shape of the mouse pointer changes (crosshair), the object is drawn on the worksheet as other objects are drawn.

4. Choose **Format → Object** command.

5. Click on the Control tab from the dialog box which is displayed.

6. Enter the cell reference or cell name in the Cell Link box.

Chapter-8

Calculation In Worksheet

Q1. What is the significance of formula in calculations? Give the basic properties of formula. Give the sequence of steps to enter a formula and to edit it also. [JUN99]

#: In Excel, what is the significance of formulae in calculations ? Give the basic properties of formulae. Write a step-by-step procedure to enter a formula and perform calculations, with the help of an example. [DEC04,Q1(e)]

#: What is the significance of formulas in calculations?

#: What is the significance of formulae in calculations? Give three basic properties of formulae. [JUN04,Q2(a)]

Significance of formula : Formulae are the building blocks for simple to advanced computing. They are widely used to perform simple mathematical operations like addition, subtraction, multiplication or division and also complex computations. They provide the power to analyse data in depth and extensively.

Following are the basic properties of formula :

(1) A formula may consist of operators, cell references, range names, values and functions.

(2) A formula always start with an equal to (=) sign.

(3) When a formula is entered in the cell, after the Enter key is pressed, only the calculated result is displayed in the cell and not the formula.

(4) If we make a cell, containing formula, as an active cell, through it still shows the value, but in the formula bar, the formula is displayed.

Following are the sequence of steps to enter a formula and to edit it also :

The formula is entered as shown below.

1. In the cell D5, enter the formula as: =(40%)*C5

2. Copy this formula in cells D6 to D9.

3. In the cell E5, enter the formula as: =(20%)*C5

4. Copy this formula in cells E6 to E9.

5. In the cell F5, enter the formula as :=C5 + D5 + E5

6. Copy this formula in cells F6 to F9.

Formulas can be entered by referring to the values of other worksheets of the workbook, or by referring to the values stored in other workbook.

Example

	A	B	C	D	E	F
1						
2			MADE EASY WEB SOLUTIONS			
3						
4	NAME	AGE	BASIC	HRA	DA	GROSS
5	ANITA	23	1500			
6	VIJAY	24	1450			
7	SANJAY	25	1700			
8	RAJESH	23	1400			
9	PARVEEN	22	2000			

By referring to other worksheet cell =Sheet2! B3 + A2

(Sheet 2! B3 refers to the value stored in the cell B3 of Sheet 2 while user is working in Sheet1.)

By referring to the cell of other workbook = 100([Employee.xls] Sheet1!$D$2)

(In the formula given above, [Employee.xls] Sheeta!$D$2 refers to the cell D2 of Sheet1 of workbook Employee.xls.)

This also creates a link between worksheets and workbooks. Therefore, while making changes in these linked worksheets and workbooks one has to be careful as the change will affect the dependent and linked cells also.

Editing Formula :

The formulas can be edited in the similar way as you have been editing text or number entries.

- You can edit the formula by pressing F2 key, and make changes directly in the cell.
- Type the changes in the formula bar.
- Double-click on the cell containing the cell and make changes as the formula is displayed in the cell.

Q2. What is a function? Give two examples of arithmetic and logical category of functions. Also explain what is the function Wizard in Excel. [DEC04,Q2(a)]

#: Enumerate various types of functions in MS-Excel and explain one type of these functions with examples. [JUN01]

#: What are functions? Explain each category of functions with two examples. [JAN01]

#: Explain the use of the following functions : [JUN03]

(i) SUMIF(num1, num2, ...) (ii) FACT(num) (iii) RAND() (iv) EXACT()

#: What does 'function' mean in MS-EXCEL? How are functions used in solving problems? Briefly explain the use of any six functions available in MS-EXCEL. [JUL04]

#: Give the syntax for the following built-in functions with the help of an example of each:

(i) ROUND

(ii) FIND [DEC04,Q6(c)]

Function : The built-in formulas are called functions. The users have to provide the cell references or addresses only. Theses are called arguments of the function that are given between a pair of parenthesis like ( ). The functions perform the operation on the given values and return the result that is displayed in the same cell where the function was entered. The use of functions also shortens the formula. **Example :** Suppose you want to add the values of cells C10 through C20. You can enter the formula as := C10 + C11 + C12 + C13 + C14 + C15 + C16 + C17 + C18 + C19 + C20. You can get the same result if you use the function instead, like = SUM(C10:C20). Complex formulas can be created using functions. Some of the tasks can be accomplished through functions only.

There are four categories of functions available in EXCEL to perform various tasks :

(i) Arithmetic Functions : These functions are used for simple mathematical calculations of number data. See below :

a) Sum (num 1, num 2....) : This returns the sum of all the numbers in the list of arguments.

Example

= SUM(B4, H4)
= SUM(A6:G6)

b) SUMIF(range, criteria, SUM range) : This adds the cells specified by a given criteria where,

Range- is the range of cells under evaluation.

Criteria- is the criteria in the form of a number, expression, or text that defines which cells will be added.

Example

SUMIF(C2:C10,">50", D2:D10)
SUMIF - (D5:D15"<75",F5:F15)

c) EXP(number) : Returns e raised to the power of number specified as argument. The constant e equals 2.71828182845094, the base of the natural algorithm.

Number - is the exponent applied to the base e.

Example

= EXP(3)

d) INT(number) : Rounds a number down to the nearest integer.

Number - is the real number one wants to round down to an integer.

Example

= INT(6.2)

= INT(6.2)

e) FACT(number) : Returns the factorial of a number.

Number - is the non-negative number one wants the factorial of. If number is not an integer, it is truncated.

Example

= FACT(5)

f) MOD(number, divisor) : Returns the remainder after number is divided by divisor. The result has the same sign as divisor.

Number- is the number for which one wants to find the remainder.

Divisor- is the number by which one wants to divide number.

Example

= MOD(15, 2)

= MOD(15,-2)

g) PRODUCT(number1, number2,....) : Multiplies all the numbers given as arguments and returns the product.

Number1, Number2,......-are 1 to 30 numbers that one wants to multiply.

Example

= PRODUCT (B5:F5)

h) ROUND (number, num_digits) : Rounds a number to a specified number of digits.

Number - is the number one wants to round.

Num_digits - specifies the number of digits to which one wants to round number.

Example

= ROUND(96.54,0)

i)SQRT(number) : Returns a positive square root.
Number - is the number for which one wants the square root. If number is negative, SQRT returns the # NUM! error value.
Example

SQRT(100)

j) CEILING(number, significance) : Returns number rounded up to the nearest multiple of significance.
Number - is the value one wants to round.
Significance - is the multiple to which one wants to round.
Example

Ceiling (97.8,1)

k) RAND( ) : Returns an evenly distributed random number greater than or equal to 0 and less than 1. A new random number is returned every time the worksheet is calculated. If one wants to use RAND to generate a random number but don't want the numbers to change every time the cell is calculated, one can enter = RAND ( ) in the formula bar and press F9 to change the formula to a random number.
Example To generate a random number greater than or equal to 0 but less than 100 : = RAND ( )* 100.

l) LOG (number, base) : Returns the logarithm of a number to the base specified.
Number **-** is the positive real number for which one wants the logarithm.
Base - is the base of the logarithm. If base is omitted, it is as summed to be 10.
Example

LOG (16, 2)

(ii) Text Functions : These functions are used to manipulate textual data.
(a) Concatenate (text 1, text 2, . .) : Joins several text items into one text item. The "&" operator can be used instead of CONCATENATE to join text terms.
Text1, text2, . . are 1 to 30 text items to be joined into a single text item. The text items can be text strings, numbers, or single cell references.
Example

= CONCATENATE ("Soft", "ware")

b) EXACT (text1, text2) : Compares two text strings and returns TRUE if they are exactly the same, otherwise FALSE. It is case-sensitive but ignores

formatting differences.
Text1 - is the first text string.
Text2 - is the second text string.
Example
= EXACT("poor", "pour")

c) FIND (find_text, within_text, start_num) : Finds one string of text within another string of text and returns the number of the character at which find_ text first occurs. Find_text-is the text one wants to find.
Within_text - is the text one wants to find.
Start_num - specifies the character at which to start the search. If not specified the start_num, it is taken as 1 - the first character of within_text.
Example
= FIND("&", "Harry & Harren")

d) LEFT(text, num_chars) : Returns the first (or leftmost) character in a text string.
Text - is the text string containing the characters in a text string.
Num_chars - specifies how many characters one wants LEFT to return. Num_chars must be greater than or equal to zero.
Example
= LEFT("Batssman", 5)

e) RIGHT(text, num_chars) : Returns the last (or rightmost) characters in a text string.
Text - is the text string containing the characters one wants to extract.
Num_chars - specifies how many characters one wants to extract.
Example
= RIGHT("Education", 3)

f) LEN (text) : Returns the number of characters in a text string.
Text - is the text whose length one wants to find. Spaces count as characters.
Example
= LEN("Gullybaba dot com")

g) LOWER (text) : Converts all uppercase letters in a text string to lowercase.
Text - is the text one wants to convert to lowercase. LOWER does not change characters in text that are not letters.
Example
= LOWER("Limit")

h) UPPER(text) : Converts text to uppercase.
Text - is the text one wants to be converted to uppercase. Text can be a reference or text string.
Example
=UPPER("dinesh")

i) MID(text, strat_num, num_chars) : Returns a specific number of characters from a text string, starting at the position specified.
Text- is the text string containing the characters one wants to extract.
Start_num- is the position of the first character one wants to extract in text. The first character in text has start_num1, and so on.
Num_chars- specifies how many characters to return from text.
Example
= MID("Microchip", 3, 4)

j) PROPER(text) : Capitalizes the first letter in text and any other letters in text that follows any character other than a letter. It converts all other letters to lowercase.
Text - is text enclosed in quotation marks, a formula that returns text, or a reference to a cell containing the text one wants to partially capitalise.
Example
= PROPER("the best QUALITY")

k) REPLACE(old_text, start_num, num_chars, new_text)- Replaces part of a text string with a different text string.
Old _text- is text in which one wants to replace some characters.
Start_num- is the position of the character in old_text that one wants to replace with new_text.
Num_chars- is the number of characters in old_text that one wants to replace with new_text.
New_text- is the text that will replace characters in old_text.

l) SEARCH(find_text, within_text, start_num) : Returns the number of the character at which a specific character or text string is first found, reading from left to right. It is not case-sensitive.
Find_text- the text one wants to find.
Within_text- is the text in which one wants to search for find_text.
Start_num- is the character number in within_text, counting from the left, at which ones wants to start searching.
Example
= SEARCH("L", "Quantity")

m) TRIM(text) : Removes all spaces from test except for single spaces between words.

Text- is the text or the reference to a cell containing text for which one wants to substitute characters.

Old_text - is the text one wants to replace.

New_text- is the text one wants to replace to old_text with.

Instance_num- specifies which occurrence of old_text one wants to replace with new_text.

Example

= SUBSTITUTE("Purchase Price", "Purchase", "Cost")

(iii) Time Functions : Excel stores Date and Times as serial numbers. Though the values are displayed in the appropriate format which is recognised by the user. The functions to manipulate date and time are:

a) DATE(year, month, day)- Returns the serial number of a particular date.

Year- is a number from 1900 to 2078 in Microsoft Excel for Windows.

Month- is a number representing the month of the year.

Day- is a number representing the day of the month.

Example = DATE(99, 2 ,12)

b) DATE VALUE(date_text) : Returns the serial number of the date represented by date_text.

Date_text -is text that returns a date in a Microsoft Excel date format.

Example =DATE VALUE("22-AUG-99")

c) DAY(serial_number) : Returns the day of the month corresponding to serial_number. The day is given as an integer ranging from 1 to 31.

Serial_number- is the date_time code used by Microsoft Excel for date and time calculations.

Example =DAY("16-MAY")

d) MONTH(serial_number) : Returns the month corresponding to serial_number. The month is given as an integer, ranging from 1 (January) to 12 (December).

Serial_number- is the date-time code used by Microsoft Excel for date and time calculations.

Example MONTH("6-JAN")

e) YEAR(serial_number) : Returns the year corresponding to serial_number. The year is given as an integer in the range 1900-2078.

Serial_number- is the date-time code used by Microsoft Excel for date and time calculations.

Example =YEAR("7/5/99")

f) WEEKDAY(serial_number, return_type) : Returns the day of the week corresponding to serial_number. The day is given as an integer, ranging from1 (Sunday) to 7 (Saturday)

Serial_number- is the date-time code used by Microsoft Excel for date and time calculations.

Return_type- is a number that determines the type of return value.

Example =WEEKDAY("2/12/99")

g) HOUR (serial_number) : returns the hour corresponding to serial_number. The hour is given as an integer, ranging from 0 (12:00 A.M.) to 23 (11:00 P.M.).

h) MINUTE (serial_ number) : Returns the minute corresponding to serial_number. The minute is given as an integer, ranging from 0 to 59.

Serial-number - is the date-time code used by Microsoft Excel for date and time calculations.

Example = Minute ("3 : 55 PM")

i) TODAY ( ) : Returns the serial number of the current date.

Example TODAY ( )

j) NOW ( ) : Returns the serial number of the current date and time.

Example NOW( )

(IV) Loopup and References : These functions are used to search for the values in the table.

a) HLOOKUP (lookup_value, lookupref, columnno, nearest) : Searches the top row of an array for a particular value, and returns the value in the indicated cell. Use this function when comparison values are located in a row across the top of a table of data and one wants to look down a specified number of rows.

Lookup_value - is the value to be found in the first row of the table.

Lookupref - is a table of information in which data is looked up.

Columnno - is the row number in table_array from which the matching value should be returned.

Nearest - is a logical value that specifies whether you want HLOOKUP to find an exact match or an approximate match. If FALSE, HLOOKUP will find an exact match.

Example HLOOKUP (“BASIC”, C4 : E9, 6, FALSE)

b) VLOOKUP (lookup_value, lookupref, columnno, nearest) : Searches the leftmost column of an array for a particular value, and return the value in the cell indicated. This function is used when the comparison values are located in a column to the left or right of the data one wants to find.

Lookup_value - is the value to be found in the first column of the table.

lookupref - is the table of information in which data is looked up.

Columnno - is the column number in table from which the matching value should be returned.

Nearest - is a logical value that specifies whether one wants LOOKUP to find an exact match or an approximate match.

Example = VLOOKUP (“DIM”, A4 : B9, 2, FALSE)

(v) Logical : These functions are used to test the conditions. They return the logical value as TRUE or FALSE.

a) AND (logical 1, logical 2.....) : Returns TRUE if all its arguments are TRUE; returns FALSE if one or more arguments are FALSE. LOGICAL1, LOGICAL2.....-are 1 to 30 conditions one wants to test that can be either TRUE or FALSE.

Example = AND(11>2, 4=4)

b) OR(logical, logical2,...) : Returns TRUE if any argument is TRUE; returns FALSE if all arguments are FALSE.

Example OR(2<7, 5>3, 6=2)

c) NOT(logical) : Reverse the value of its argument. NOT is used when one wants to make sure a value is not equal to one particular value.

Logical- is a value or expression that can be evaluated to TRUE or FALSE. If logical is FALSE, NOT returns TRUE; if logical is TRUE, NOT returns FALSE.

Example NOT(5>3)

d) IF(logical_test, value_if_true, value_if_false) : Returns one value if logical_test evaluates to TRUE and another value if it evaluates to FALSE. Upto seven IF functions can be nested.

Logical_test - is any value or expression that can be evaluated to TRUE or FALSE.

Value_if_true - is the value that is returned if logical_test is TRUE.

Value_if_false - is the value that is returned if logical_test is FALSE.

Example IF (35>19, 35,0)

e) FALSE( ) : Returns the logical value FALSE.
Example = FALSE( )

f) TRUE( ) : Returns the logical value TRUE.
Example = TRUE( )

Function Wizard : Refer next question.

Q3. Write short notes on:
(i) Function wizard **[DEC02][JUN02][DEC99]**
(ii) Recalculation features of MS-Excel **[JUN01]**
#: Explain the recalculation feature of MS-EXCEL. Give the basic properties of formulas. **[JAN01]**

(i) Function wizard : Excel provides the facility of built-in functions through the functions wizard. The Function Wizard guides the user through all the steps of writing a function and its arguments. The results and example are displayed as the user works on.

There are two ways to get the function wizard. If you look at the **Standard Toolbar**, the function wizard icon looks like the icon on the right.

The other way to get to the function wizard is to go to the Menu **INSERT** — down to **FUNCTION**.

Either way you get there, at this point Excel will list all of the functions available. Upon choosing the function, Excel will prompt you for the information it needs to complete the function. Mini descriptions are available for each of the cells. It is often necessary for you to understand the functions in order to be able to figure out these descriptions.

(ii) Recalculation features of MS-Excel : MS Excel is a spreadsheet programme. It offers the facility of auto-recalculation. Every time a change is made in the cells recalculation is automatically done in all other dependent cells. This is called ripple effect. There are basically two kinds of recalculations.

1. Automatic: This is the default mode in which a change in the value of any cell causes recalculation of the whole worksheet automatically.

2. Manual: When this option is chosen, the recalculation of the entire worksheet is done only on pressing the F9 key.

This option can be chosen by going to Tools → Option and then clicking on calculation tab.

Following are the basic properties of formula :

(1) A formula may consist of operators, cell references, range names, values and functions.

(2) A formula always start with an equal to (=) sign.

(3) When a formula is entered in the cell, after the Enter key is pressed, only the calculated result is displayed in the cell and not the formula.

(4) If we make a cell, containing formula, as an active cell, through it still shows the value, but in the formula bar, the formula is displayed.

Q4. Explain the various access restriction mechanisms related to the worksheet in MS-EXCEL. [DEC02][DEC99]

#: Explain how the access of worksheet in EXCEL can be restricted from other users. [DEC01,Q1(c)]

#: How can the access of the worksheet be restricted from the users using different password techniques? [JUN00]

#: Discuss about the Save and Protect Workbook in MS-EXCEL. [JUN03]

In MS-Excel, it may be necessary to protect the data from being seen or used by unauthorized people. For this facility of password is available.

From the File ® Save As dialogue box click on options … button.

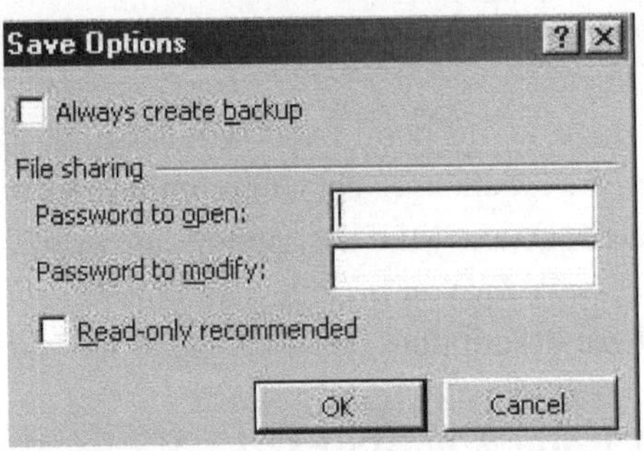

The access to a workbook to other users can be restricted in 3 different ways:

(i) Protection Password

a) Type the password, which will be required to open the workbook. The password can be upto 15 character long, can include alphabets (upper case or lower case), number and special characters. It is case sensitive also.

b) Excel will ask to re-enter the same password. Enter password again.

c) Click on OK.

(ii) Write Reservation Password

This password will be required when changes in the existing workbook are made and then workbook is used. This prevents the unauthorized users to make any modifications in the workbook the rules to give the password are same as Protection Password.

(iii) Read-only Recommended

If this option is checked, the following dialogue box will be displayed every time you try to open the workbook.

This option is checked if one wants to discourage the other users from making any changes by mistake or want to prevent the changes to be made by more than one users simultaneously.

Chapter-9

Charts

Q1. What are charts in MS-Excel.

Charts are the graphic component of Excel. The data which is entered as tables can be viewed in the graphical form as charts which makes the figures of data effective, interesting, easy to understand, and easy to analyse and compare data.

Chart can be of two types :

Embedded Charts : These charts are included in the worksheet and can be moved , copied, and resized as any other graphical object.

Chart Sheet : Separate Chart Sheet are inserted when a chart is created. It contains only one chart. To create chart sheets, choose **Insert → Chart → As New Sheet.**

Excel helps you to create chart as either 2-dimensional or 3- dimensional.

Q2. Explain different chart components. Using chart wizard. Explain the sequence of steps to create a chart. **[DEC02]**

 # : Explain Chart Wizard. **[JUN02][DEC99]**

Chart Components.

Chart Title : A title give to the whole chart.

X-axis Title : a title give to the X-axis range.

X axis Category : This is the categories of the idea which have been plotted.

These are taken from the leftmost column or the top most row.

Y-axis Title : A title given to the y-axis range.

Y-axis value : This is the data-range marked to plot the data series.

Data Labels : These are used to distinguish one data series from another.

Legend : It specifies the color, symbol or pattern used to mark the data series.

Tick Mark : These marks are used to show the scaling of X-axis and Y-axis.

Wall : This is the background of the plotted area.

Floor : This is the base upon which the data series is plotted.

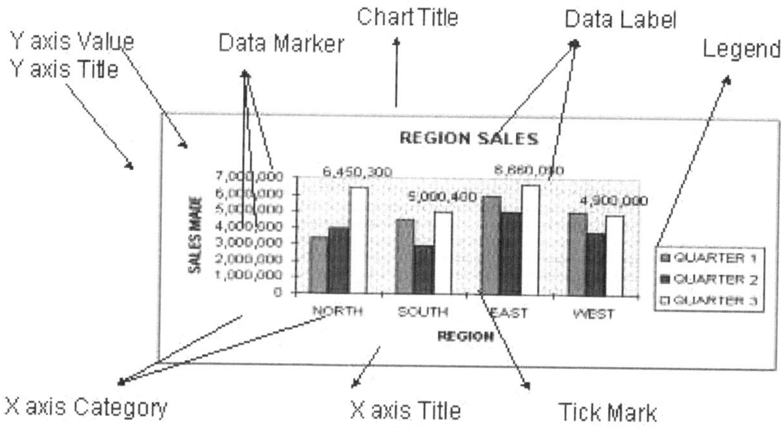

Chart Wizard : The Chart Wizard is a series of dialog boxes that guides the user through the steps required to create a new embedded chart or modify settings for an existing embedded chart. It displays either five steps or two steps, depending on what is selected. If worksheet data is selected, all five steps are displayed because one is creating a new chart. If an existing chart is selected to modify it, only two steps are displayed. When the Finish button is clicked in any of the steps, the Chart Wizard finishes the chart.

Steps to create the chart through Chart Wizard :

Step 1 – To create a new chart, enter the data.

Step 2 – Click on Chart Wizard tool button from standard Toolbar. The pointer changes to crosshair shape.

Step 3 – Mark the area on the worksheet to place the chart.

Step 4 – Enter the range of data from the worksheet in the Range box and click on Next.

Step 5 – Select the chart type from the charts displayed and click on Next.

Step 6 – Select the format for selected chart and click on Next.

Q3. Describe various types of charts offered by Excel.

#: Write a short note on Various types of Charts in MS-Excel [JUN01]

MS-Excel offers 15 different major chart types, each of which has at least one subtype, or variation. You can change the chart type to present your data more clearly and effectively. The various chart types are:

AREA CHART, BAR CHART, LINE CHART, DOUGHNUT CHART, RADAR CHART, XY (Scatter) CHART,

1) AREA CHART

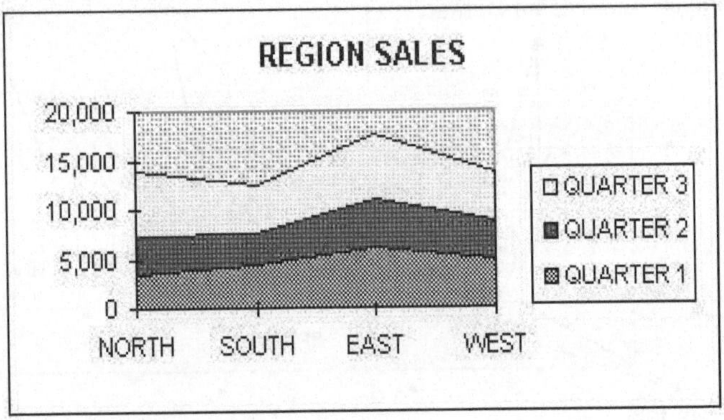

This shows the magnitude of change over time. It is a stacked line chart, with the area between the lines filled with colour and shading. The data series are plotted one on top of the other.

2) BAR CHART

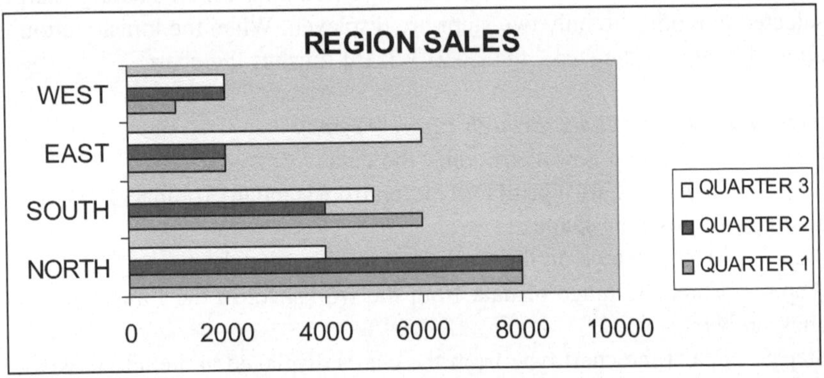

It consists of the series of horizontal bars that allow comparison of the relative size of two or more items.

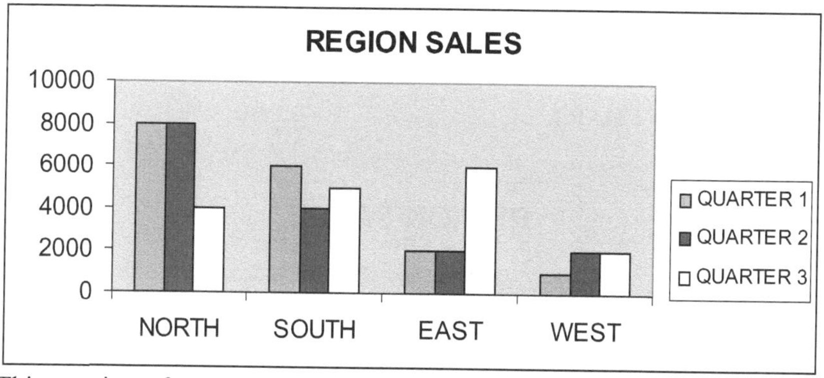

This consists of a series of vertical columns that allows comparison of the relative size of two or more items.

3) LINE CHART

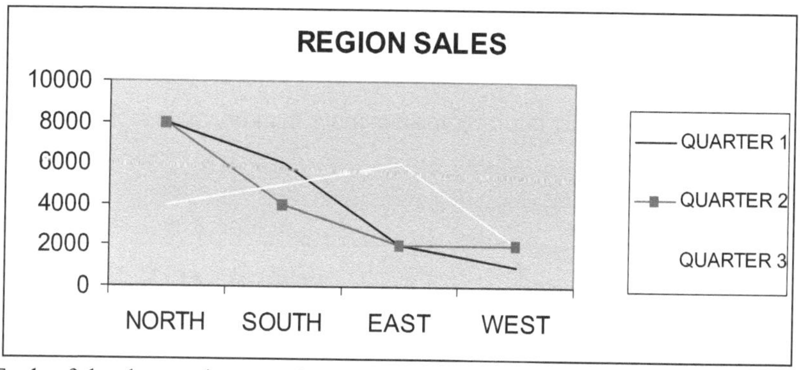

Each of the data series are plotted as line of different colour and shading.

4) PIE CHART

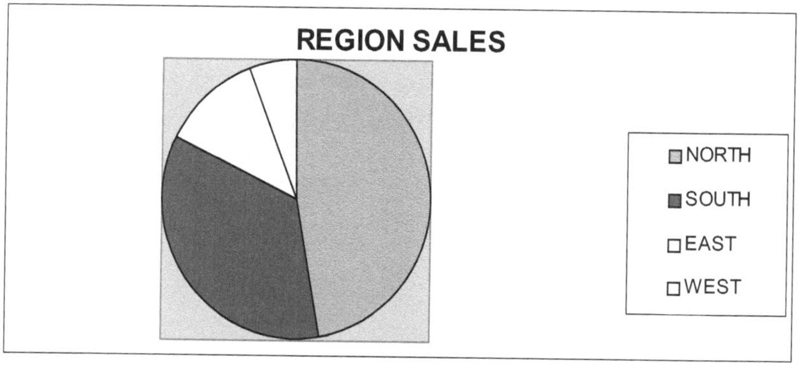

These are the best charts to compare the percentage of the sum the data series. It represents only one data series.

5) DOUGHNUT CHART

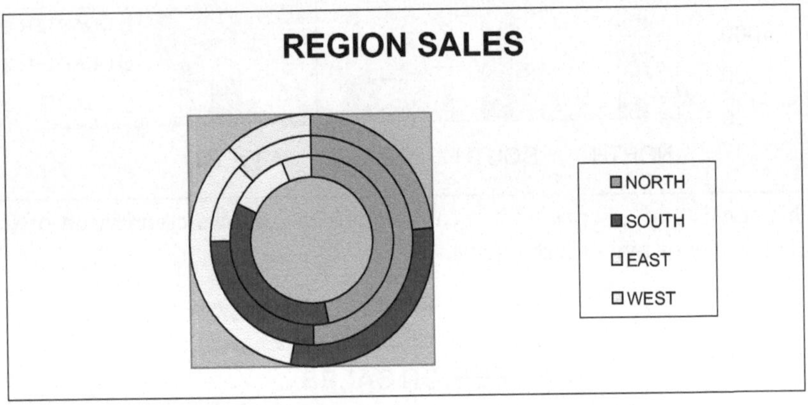

It is similar to Pie Chart but it represents more than one data series.

6) RADAR CHART

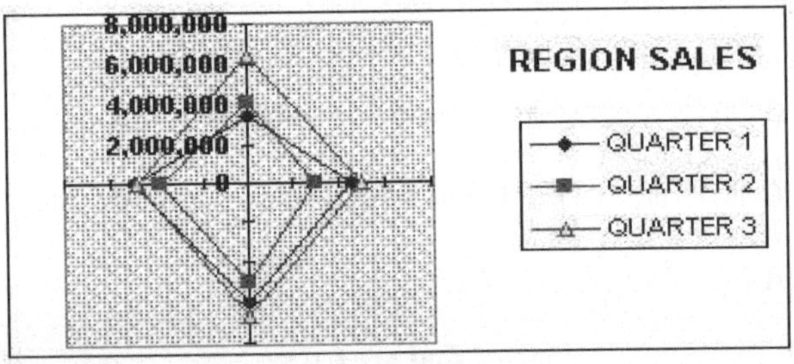

This shows the data values in relation to the centre point and to each-other. Data of the same data series are connected by lines.

7) XY(Scatter) CHART

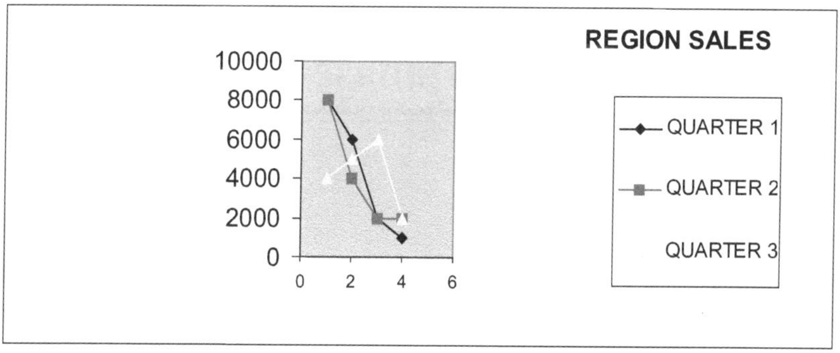

The value of the data series is plotted as the intersection point of the X-axis and Y-axis. The sub-chart types of these charts are also available with different orientations.

Chapter-10

Database Power In Excel

Q1. What do you mean by database.

There are various kinds of data in any company e.g. all the details of the employees, sales details, client data, products data. The purpose of storing and maintaining data is to retrieve it later for day-to-day transactions and management planning.

The data, which is collected from the sources is the raw data. Various operations can be carried out on the data, like sorting, searching and totalling. This is processed and manipulated now and termed as Information. The system which helps us to perform all these activities on the data is termed as DBMS. Database is an organized collection of information. It is also referred to as a list or a table.

There are two kinds of databases :

Internal Database - Databases created in the worksheet.

External Database - Database which is created through other DBMS or RDBMS packages like MS-ACCESS, FOXPRO, dBASE, SQL Server, ORACLE.

Q2. What is a data-table? What purpose does it serve ? State its types and explain how various data table are created.

DATA TABLES - Once formulas have been entered on worksheet, one can perform a "what-if analysis" to see how changing certain values in formulas affects the results of the formula. Data tables provide a shortcut for calculating all the variations in one operation. A data table is a range of cells that shows the results of substituting different values in one or more formulas.

There are two types of data tables :

a) One-input table - With a one-input data table, you type different values for one variable and the effect on one or more formulas is seen. The steps to create one input table are:

1. Enter the data as shown below:

	F	G	H
8			
9	Rate of Interest :		10%
10	Initial Amount :		8,000
11	Monthly Intrest :		800
12			

2. In a single column, enter a list of values to substitute in the input cell.
3. In the row above the first value and one cell to the right of the column of values, enter the formula +H9*H10 that refers to the input cell.

G	H
12%	=+H9*H10
11%	
9%	
11.50%	

4. Choose **Data → Table...**
5. In the column input cell box, enter the cell reference H9.
6. Click on OK button.
MS-Excel substitutes each value in the input cell and displays the result of the right of each input value.

b) Two-input table - With a two-input data table, you enter different values for two variables and see the effect on one formula. Follow the steps as given below to enter the two-input table:
1. Refers to the same data as in the above example.
2. In an empty cell, enter the formula +H9*H10.
3. Starting in the cell below the formula, enter the values that you want to substitute in the same column as the formula.
4. Starting in the cell to the right of the formula enter the values that you want to substitute in the other input cell in the same row as the formula as given below.

G	H	I	J	K
=+H9*H10	10000	7500	9000	8500
12%				
11%				
9%				
11.50%				

5. Choose **Data→Table...**
6. In the column input cell box, enter the cell reference H9.
7. In the row input cell box, enter the reference H10.
8. Click on OK button.

Q3. Write short notes on:
(i) Pivot table [DEC02][JUN02][JAN01][DEC99][DEC05,Q4(a)(ii)]
(ii) Auto filter [JUN02]
(iii) Internal database and External database [JAN01]
(iv) Database
(v) Record
(vi) Field

(i) Pivot table : A pivot table is an interactive worksheet table you use to summarise and analyse data from an existing list or table. You can update a pivot table whenever changes occur in the original source data. The original data remains intact, and the pivot table stays on the worksheet you created it on.

You create a pivot table by using the Pivot Table Wizard, a series of interactive dialog boxes that guide you through the steps of locating and retrieving the data you want to analyse. The Pivot Table Wizard also lets you define how you want to arrange the pivot table using row and column labels, and how you want to present data in the fields. You can create a pivot table from source data that resides in:

1) A Microsoft Excel list or database.
2) An external database, such as a table or file created in an application or database management system external to Microsoft Excel.
3) Multiple Microsoft Excel consolidation ranges.
4) Another pivot table in the same workbook.

Once you create a pivot table, you can rearrange, organizes and analyse the data by dragging and dropping the fields in the pivot table. You can also include subtotals, change the summary function for a field, or select a custom calculation for your pivot table.

(ii) Auto filter : Viewing records that meet certain criteria is called filtering the database. For example, you have stored the data of all the employee of your organisation. The query can be made on the database to view the details of all those employees who have been working with the orgainsation for more than 10 years. This would be your search criteria and finding all those records which have the Date-of-join of 10 years back would meet this criteria.
There are two ways to filter the database - AutoFilters and Advanced Filters. AutoFilter meets most needs. However, when you need to use complex criteria to filter a list, use Advanced Filter. Your list should have column labels for better results.

(iii) Internal database and External database : Every orgainsation works towards maintaining data of various kinds, e.g,. all the details of the employees, sales details, client data, products data. The purpose of storing and maintaining data is to retrieve it later for day-to-day transactions and management planning. The data, which is collected from the source is the raw data. Various operations can be carried out with the data, like, sorting, searching and totalling. This is processed and manipulated to be transformed as Information.
The most important database feature of MS-EXCEL is a powerful and simplified tool to store, manage and analyse data.

There are two kinds of databases:
Internal Database - Database created in the worksheet.
External Database - Database which is created through other DBMS or RDBMS packages like MS-ACCESS, FOXPRO, dBASE, SQL Server, ORACLE.

(iv) Database : Database is an organized collection of information. It is also referred to as a list or a table.
(v) Record : Each row of the list is called as a record.
(vi) Field : Each column is called as a field.

Q4. Explain the concept of Filtering a Database in MS-EXCEL using Autofilters and using Advanced filters. [DEC02,Q2(b)]

#: What do you understand by the term " filtering the database" ? Explain how it is done in MS-Excel.

Filtering the database using AutoFilters : This is an easier and quick method to filter the database. To filter the database follows the given steps:

1. Select any cell of the database range and choose **Data → Filter → AutoFilter** command. MS-Excel inserts drop down arrows next to each column label in the list.

2. Click the arrow in the column that contains the data you want to display.

3. Select the item you want to display.

The various other options other than column items that are available are :

1. All - Shows all records.

2. (Custom...) - To specify two criteria for a column.

3. (Blanks....) - Shows all those records that have no entry in the particular column.

4. (Non Blanks...) - Shows all those record that have some entry in the column.

To remove AutoFilters, again choose **Data → Filter → AutoFilter.**

Using Advanced Filters :

These filters are used to filter the data on the basis of more that one field. Using the same database suppose you want to view only those records where the sale was more than 400 in the third quarter and more than 300 in the fourth quarter. To get the results, follow the given steps:

1. Enter the data as given below.

2. Choose **Data → Filter → Advanced Filter** command.

3. A message dialog box is displayed that asks you to assume the top row of the data range as the header row. Click on OK.

4. A dialog box is displayed with two kinds of action:

a) Filter the list, in-place - displays only those record that match the criteria.

b) Copy to another Location - to copy the records that match the criteria to another location in the worksheet, leaving the database range as it is. Select the first action, i.e, **Filter the list, in-place.**

5. Specify the list range as A3:E9, and the criteria range as H4:15.

6. Click on OK.

Q5. Explain the two ways to create database in MS-EXCEL. [JUN02]

#: What is a database ? What a step-by-step procedure to create a database in MS-EXCEL using Data Form Command. [DEC04,Q4(c)]

There are various kinds of data in any company e.g. all the details of the employees, sales details, client data, products data. The purpose of storing and maintaining data is to retrieve it later for day-to-day transactions and management planning.

The data, which is collected from the sources is the raw data. Various operations can be carried out on the data, like sorting, searching and totalling. This is processed and manipulated now and termed as Information. The system which helps us to perform all these activities on the data is termed as DBMS. Database is an organized collection of information. It is also referred to as a list or a table.

There are two kinds of databases:

Internal Database - Databases created in the worksheet.

External Database - Database which is created through other DBMS or RDBMS packages like MS-ACCESS, FOXPRO, dBASE, SQL Server, ORACLE.

In MS-Excel, database can be created in two simple ways:

1. Enter the data in the form of table in the worksheet.

2. Use **Data Form** command.

To create database using Data Form command, the steps are :

1. Enter the given details:

In Cell	***Enter***
A1	AGE
B1	NAME
C1	SEX
D1	DEPARTMENT

2. Choose **Data, Form** command while keeping one of the field name active.

3. The dialog box is displayed, warning you for taking the row of the selected cell as the header row of the database. Click on OK.

4. Another dialog box is displayed, which shows one record at a time. Fill-in the appropriate details in the box against each field name.

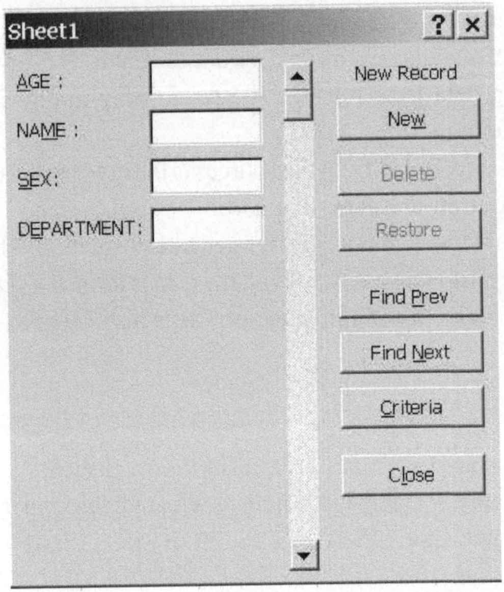

5. Click on **New**. This will add the entered record in the database.
6. To finish the entry of records, click on **Close.**

Chapter-11

Focus On Analysis And Auto-matting The Worksheet

Q1. Explain the *'what-if-Analysis'* feature of Excel with an example. What are the tools available for *'what-if-Analysis'* ?

The 'what-if-Analysis' feature of Excel is a very useful recalculation feature. Suppose, we enter values in two cells and the formula to multiply them in a third cell. Then any change in values of the first two cells automatically recalculates the result in third cell.

The 'what-if-Analysis' thus means-what would the result be, is the cell value changes.

Excel provides following tools for the 'what-if-Analysis':

1. Data Tables : Data tables provide a shortcut for calculating all the variations in one operation. A data table is a range of cells that shows the results of substituting different values in one or more formulas.

2. Goal Seek : This determines the input required to produce the desired result.

3. Solver : This helps in solving problems involving multiple variables and constraints.

4. Scenario Manger : This tool allows the user to create different set of values that produce different results.

Q2. Write short notes on:

(i) Solver **[DEC02][JAN01][JUN00]**

(ii) Goal seek **[JAN01][JUN00]**

(i) Solver : Microsoft Excel Solver is a powerful optimisation and resource allocation tool. It can help you to uncover the best uses of scarce resources so that desired goals such as profit can be maximised, or undesired goals such as cost can be minimised. Microsoft Excel Solver answers questions such as:

What product price or promotion mix will maximise profit?

How can I live within the budget?

How fast can we grow without running out of cash?

Instead of guessing over and over, you can use Microsoft Excel Solver to find the best answer. When you solve a problem using Solver, you:

1. Specify the target cell that you want to minimise, maximise, or set to a certain value.
2. Specify the changing cells that you want to be adjusted until a solution is found.
3. Specify constraint cells that must fall within certain limits or satisfy target values.
If the Solver command does not appear on the Tool menu, you need to install the Solver add-in. Add-ins are commands or functions that add special capabilities to Microsoft Excel. To install an add-in, choose the Add-ins command from the Tools menu. Once you install an add-in, its commands or functions become an integrated part of Microsoft Excel until you remove it.

To use solver follow the given steps:
1. Enter the data shown below:

C6 =PMT(C3,C4,C2)

	A	B	C
1			
2	LOAN AMOUNT		100,000.00
3	INTEREST RATE		5%
4	NO. OF PAYMENTS		240
5			
6	MONTHLY PAYMENT		5,000.04
7			

2. Choose **Tools→Solver**.....command.
3. In the **Set Target Cell** box, enter a cell reference or name for the target cell. Select:

Max option button :
If you want the target cell's value to be as large as possible.
Min option button :
If you want the target cell's value to be as small as possible.
value of option button
If you want the target cell to have a certain value.

4. In **By changing cells** box, enter the name or reference for each changing cell. If you enter more than one reference, separate the references with commas.
5. In the **Subject to the constraints** box, add any constraints you want to

apply. Constraints can be applied to the target cell, the changing cell or any cell that is directly or indirectly related to the problem.

6. Click on **Solve** button to get the results.

To see the reports, select the report from the dialog box, and click on **OK**.

Microsoft Excel 5.0c Answer Report
Worksheet: [BOOK1.XLS]Sheet2
Report Created: 16/1/97 16:06

Target Cell (Max)

Cell	Name	Original Value	Final Value
$C$6	MONTHLY PAYMENT	5,000.04	6,000.00

Adjustable Cells

Cell	Name	Original Value	Final Value
$C$2	LOAN AMOUNT	100,000.00	119,999.01
$C$3	INTEREST RATE	5%	5%
$C$4	NO. OF PAYMENTS	240	240

(ii) Goal seek : Often you know the result you want a formula to return but not the input values the formula needs to reach that result. To solve such a formula, you can use goal seek feature. With this, MS-Excel varies the value in a cell you specify until a formula dependent on that cell returns the result you want.

Goal Seek saves you from performing time-consuming trial-and-error analysis.

To seek a specific solution to a formula:-

1. Enter the data in the sheet.

2. Choose **Tools→Goal Seek...** command. The **Goal Seek** dialog box is displayed.

3. In the Set cell box, enter the reference or the name of the cell containing the formula for which you want to find a specific solution.

4. In the **To value** box, enter the value you want as the result.

5. In the By changing cell box, enter the reference of the cell containing the value to be changed in solving for the result that you want.

6. Choose the **OK** button.

Q3. Discuss the use of Scenario Manager in Excel, With an example, write the steps to create a Scenario. [DEC99]

#: Write short note on Scenario Manager. [JUN00]

In Microsoft Excel, you can create and save sets of input values that produce different results as scenarios. A scenario is a group of input vales called changing cell saved with a name you provide. Each set of changing cells represents a set of what-if assumptions that you çan apply to a workbook model to see the effects on other parts of the model. You can define up to 32 changing cells per scenario.

Following are the steps for Creating a Scenario :

Let's take an example of a condition where you are planning to buy a new vehicle. You have two choices for vehicle - one is worth Rs. 3,50,000 vehicle or Rs. 4,00,000 vehicle, with either 3 yrs, loan or 5 yrs, loan. For this,

1. First enter the given data in the blank worksheet.

2. In cell D3, enter the formula **=A3*0.8.**

3. In cell A7, enter the formula **=PMT(B3, C3*12, A3).**

4. Choose **Tools→Scenarios....**command.

5. Click on the **Add** button. **Add Scenario** box appears.

6. In the **Scenario Name** box, type the name of the scenario as **35k & 3Yrs.**

7. Select the cells or type the cell references in the **Changing Cells** box as A3 and C3.

8. If you want, edit the text in the **Comment** box.

9. If you want, select **Protection** option.

10. Click on **OK** button. **Scenarios Values** dialog box appears.

11. Enter the value for each changing cell as given in Figure.

12. Click on **OK** button.

13. To add the scenario to the list and then create additional scenarios, choose the Add button. This returns you to the Add Scenario dialog box. Type 35k & 5 Yrs, as the scenario name.

Q4. What is a template? Mention its use in MS-EXCEL and write the sequence of steps to create a template with the help of an example. [DEC02]

#: What Template is called a special workbook?

Templates are special tools Provided by MS-Excel, alongwith Macros, to automate regular tasks. Templates are reusable models that standardize the look of the worksheet. They can be used to create periodic reports.

Templates are called special workbooks because one can use their pattern to create other workbooks of the same type. Thus, one can create a Production Report workbook, save it as a template, and then create weekly production reports based on that template. Also sheets from the templates can be inserted into new workbooks. In addition to creating new workbooks based on templates, one can insert sheets from templates into the workbooks.

Templates can contain :

1. Text and graphics, such as a company name and logo.

2. Formatting and page layout, such as styles and custom headers and footers.

3. Formulas and macros.

When a template is opened Microsoft Excel creates a copy of the template to work with. This leaves the original template intact for the next time one needs it.

One can create special templates, called autotemplates, in the startup or alternate startup directory. One can then use autotemplates as the basis for all new workbooks and all new sheets inserted into workbooks. Autotemplates are just templates saved with a specific name, in a specific location.

Following are the steps to create the template :

1. Create a workbook with all the styles, formatting, text and formulas desired. One an also open an existing workbook that one wants to save as a template.

2. Choose File→Save As...command.

3. In the File Name box, type the name for the template.

4. Select the directory and drive where the template is to be saved.

5. In the Save File As Type box, select Template. MS-Excel adds the extension. XLT to the filename.

6. Finally, Click OK button.

Opening a Template : One can open the template to create the worksheet based on it by following these steps:

1. File→New...command is chosen.

2. The template on which one wants to base a new workbook is selected. MS-Excel creates a copy of the template for use and gives it a temporary name that can be changed while saving the workbook.

Q5. Explain what are macros and why these are created. [JUN01]

#: What are macros and what is the importance of creating them?

If you perform a task repeatedly in Excel, you can automate the task by using a macro. A macro is a series of commands and instructions that you group together as a single command to accomplish a task automatically. Instead of manually performing a series of time-consuming, repetitive actions, you can create and run a single macro — in effect, a custom command — that accomplishes the task for you.

Importance of creating macros:

· To speed up routine editing and formatting

· To combine multiple commands; for example, inserting a table with a specific size and borders, and with a specific number of rows and columns

· To make an option in a dialog box more accessible

· To automate a complex series of tasks

Q6. Explain what do you understand by 'Autotemplates'.

[JUN01][JAN01]

#: **What are Autotemplates?**

Autotemplates are special templates created in startup or alternate startup directory. These can then be used as basis for all new workbooks and all new sheets inserted in the workbooks.

Autotemplates are just templates saved with a specific name, in a specific location.

Q7. What are the different options that are available to run the macro?

Running the Macro means to repeat the action recorded as a macro. To run the Macro, steps are:

1. Tools→Macro...command is selected.

2. In the Macro Name/Reference box, the macro name is typed or selected.

3. The **Run** button is clicked on.

Or

Tools→Months is chosen.

Or

Ctrl + Shift + M key combination (that has been defined as the option before recording the macro) is pressed.

Q8. Define VBA.

VBA : VBA is short for Visuals Basic Application. It is a language based on Visual Basic Programming Language. MS Excel supports VBA.

Chapter-12

An Overview Of Internet & Tools For Internet Application

Q1. Explain the following :

(i) E-Commerce **[JUN02]**
(ii) E-Greetings **[JUN02]**
(iii) Telnet **[JUN03][DEC01][JUN00][JUN99]**
(iv) FTP **[JUN03][DEC01][JUN01][JAN01][JUN00][JUN99]**
(v) E-Mail **[DEC01][JAN01][JUN00][DEC99]**
(vi) FAQ **[JAN01]**
(vii) ISP **[JAN01]**
(viii) Address Book in E-Mail **[JUN00]**
(ix) Mailing Lists **[JUN00][DEC99]**
#: What is E-mail? Describe its special features. **[JUN04]**

(i) E-Commerce :- E-commerce refers to all forms of business activities conducted across the Internet. This can include E-tailing, B2B, intranets and extranets, online advertising (eg. advertising banners), and simply online presences of any form that are used for some type of communication (customer service for example). There are mainly two types of e-commerce:-

Online shopping : The scope of information and activities that provides the customer with the information he needs to conduct business.

Online purchasing : The technology infrastructure for the exchange of data and the purchase of a product over the Internet. Online purchasing is a metaphor used in business-to-business e-commerce for providing customers with an online method of placing an order, submitting a purchase order, or requesting a quote.

(ii) E-Greeting :- By E-greetings we can send a decisive message, simultaneously with our choice from a picture or animation range, to families and friends.

If you have found the perfect greeting, our next decision is to customize it, But always remember to fill out entire boxes. To check the address by the double recipient's that make sure it goes to the exact place. After we are finished, click the "Preview before sending" button. When everything looks exact, click the *"Send this greeting"* button to send it on its way. If you have to change something before sending, click the button of *"Make more changes"* which will take you to back to the screen of editing.

(iii) Telnet :- Telnet is a utility which allows us to log on to another system and use various services available on that host. We can Telnet into huge databases to do research or even telnet into libraries around the word to check if they have a certain book that we are looking for. Telnet also offers an easy entry into the world of gophers and the worldwide web for those people who may otherwise have access to these tools people who are in one location frequently want to use a computer in other location perhaps they want to look at a library catalog to see if a certain book has been published. Perhaps they want to use one of the services of the information provides such as dialog.

(iv) FTP :- FTP (File Transfer Protocol) is the primary method of transferring files over Internet. "FTP" transfers files to and from a remote network site. Some maintain Anonymous accounts on the system for retrieval of public domain software's stored on the system.
The *FTP* protocol is used to access files by FTP, the Internet's file transfer protocol. FTP has been around more than two decades. FTP servers all over the world allow people anywhere on the internet to log in and download whatever files have been placed on the FTP server. The Web does not change this; it just makes obtaining files by FTP easier.

(v) E-Mail :- Electronic Mail is a system whereby a computer user can exchange messages with other computer users or group of users via a communications network.
The backbone of an electronic mail system is a communication network that connects remote terminals to a central system or a local area network that interconnects personal computers. Users can send mail to a single recipient or they can broadcast it to any number of selected users on the systems. The method for receiving mail depends on the sophistication of the system.
Many users first encounter computer networks when they send or received electronic mail to or from a remote site. E-mail is the most widely used application service. Indeed, many computer users access networks only through electronic mail.
E-mail is popular because it offers a fast, convenient method of transferring information. E-mail can accommodate small notes or large voluminous memos with a single mechanism. One of the very useful things the Internet has is that

it allows us almost instantly exchange of electronic message (e-mail) across the world. Due to which it has become a highly popular medium of communication. We can e-mail to our friend or to researcher. Through e-mail on Internet we can be in direct touch to many of our friend colleagues.

An Internet account includes an electronic mailbox. A message meant for us is received at our Internet host computer, where it is stored in our electronic mailbox. As soon as we login in to our Internet account, one of the first thing we should do is to check our mailbox.

Some of the mail programs, which exist on Internet, are UCB mail, Elm, Prim, etc. However, one thing, which we must emphasize while selecting a mail program, is the user friendliness of that program.

(vi) FAQ :- A great resource offered by Usenet is the FAQs that is the list of frequently asked questions and responses for them for particular newsgroup. These FAQs are available on incredible number of topics; such as new Power PC to wide variety of topics.

These FAQs are generally text files or Usenet articles. FAQs can be organized as a long list of questions and answers, or as list of questions followed by answers. The second approach is better from the point of view of searching for a particular question and its answer. Some FAQs go to a distance such that they provide annotated bibliography. FAQs are very popular among Internet users. FAQs are also archieved.

Usenet serves primarily as a forum for questions by offering subscribers a documents made up of frequently Asked Question (FAQ) and their answers periodically. We must read these documents to make sure that our questions haven't already been answered. If we have a new question, people on Usenet may be extremely co-operative in helping us getting the answer. Therefore when other ask question, it becomes our responsibility to assist them. It is only the people interaction with each other that has made Usenet the amazing information resource that it is.

(vii) ISP :- Short for Internet Service Provider, a company that provides access to the Internet. For a monthly fee, the service provider gives you a software package, username, password and access phone number. Equipped with a modem, you can then log on to the Internet and browse the World Wide Web and USENET, and send and receive e-mail.

In addition to serving individuals, ISPs also serve large companies, providing a direct connection from the company's networks to the Internet. ISPs themselves are connected to one another through Network Access Points (NAPs). ISPs are also called IAPs (Internet Access Providers).

(viii) Address Book in E-Mail :- Address book feature is great for saving the e-mail addresses of people with whom we correspond. It is not easy to remember e-mail addresses, so remember instead to enter new addresses in our address book as soon as we get a message from someone new.

(ix) Mailing Lists :- E-mail provides a mechanism for groups of people who have common interests to establish and maintain contact. Such interest groups are referred to as mailing lists (lists for short), after all they are mailing list of the members' e-mail addresses. We can subscribe to any of such lists. We will receive copies of all the mail sent to the list. We can also send mail to all the subscribers of the list.

We can become a list subscribers, by contacting the list's administrator. There exist two types of list administrators: human or computer program called listserv. Our request to subscribe may sometimes be refused. Do not get disappointed, there will be plentiful more lists that will accepts your subscription.

Q2. How we will Connect Remote Machines with Telnet?

Telnet is a program that allows an Internet host computer to become a terminal of another host on the Internet. FTP opens a connection solely for transfer of files, however Telnet allows us to becomes a user on a remote machine. We can run the computer programs at remote host, browse the database or perform any desired operation of the remote machine using this facility.

Thus, Telnet provides a direct access to various services on Internet. Some of these services are available on our host, but Telnet is especially useful when these services are not available on our host. For example, if we want to use graphical interfaces designed by other users, then Telnet allows us to access their hosts and use their new interfaces. Similarly, whenever some creates a useful service on his host, Telnet allows us to access this useful service on his host. This tool is especially useful for accessing public services such as library card catalogues, the database available on the remote machine etc.

There are many databases available on the Internet. We can explore these databases using Telnet. There are many Internet services yet to be created. Every year better means of accessing the treasures of the Internet are appearing in which Telnet is the key for accessing.

Q3. Discuss in detail FTP and Telnet. Explain the usage of both on Internet.

There's an FTP client supplied with Window 98 (in our Windows folder), but it uses a command line rather than a graphic interface. Don't waste our time with it. Much better FTP clients with point-and-click or drag-and-drop capabilities are available from online sources. Each FTP application has a different screen layout, but the process of finding and downloading a file is essentially the same for all of them.

(1) Connect our client program to a FTP server.

(2) Log on to the server. Almost all public FTP servers accept the login name "anonymous," with our e-mail address as the password. If we have an account on the server, we can use our own login name and password to get access to file that may not be available to anonymous users or to upload files from our computer to the server.

(3) Move to the directory on the server that contains the file we want.

(4) Specify folder or directory on our own computer where we want to place downloaded file.

(5) Transfer the file from the server to our own computer. Some clients ask us to specify whether each file is ASCII text or binary data we start the download.

(6) Disconnect from the server.

Telnet makes our computer a remote terminal that sends commands and receives data through the Internet to and from a distant host. When we type on our own keyboard, those keystrokes go directly to the host, just like keystrokes from a keyboard plugged directly into the host. The most common uses for telnet are remote access to a distant computer where we have an account and connection to a computer that accepts access from the public, such as a library catalog. Once the connection is in place, a telnet client program should be transparent; we should be able to concentrate on the responses we receive from the host.

Because telnet makes our computer appear to a telnet host as if it's a terminal, telnet clients are also know as terminal emulation programs. Different brands and models of terminals send slightly different signal formats to host computers, so many telnet programs can be configured to emulate more than one type of terminal.

There are many Windows telnet client programs available, and most of them do at least an adequate job. In general, they fall into one of two categories:

- ✓ Single-purpose telnet clients
- ✓ Telnet clients included with general-purpose communications programs

General-purpose communication programs are usually a better choice than telnet-only applications, because they allow us to capture incoming text, send and receive files, and scroll back to read text than has disappeared off the top of our screen, among other things. The latest versions of all the popular Windows communications packages, including Pro-Comm, Crosstalk, WinComm, and Qmodem, can be used as Winsock compliant telnet clients.

Q4. What is Anonymous FTP?

FTP works in two modes, for sending a copy of a file from one computer to other computer, upload or put mode and, to retrieve file from one computer use the download or get mode. There are two methods of FTP. In the first methods, we sign on the remote host machine on which we have our own account of user identification (ID) and transfer files. Other method is to sign on as a guest or as an anonymous user, called "anonymous FTP". With anonymous FTP we are restricted by the security system of the host computer. The hosts that provide anonymous FTP do so specifically to make some files available for anybody's use. In Anonymous FTP, login name provided is anonymous, guest of ftp and the password is our e-mail address. The use of our e-mail address as password helps the FTP provider track who is interested in which materials. Thus, it provides a trace incase of a security problem.

Anonymous FTP is one of the most convenient tools for making information and other files available to the public. Many sites currently use it to provide resources; we can find the most current listing of selected sited via the Web. The easiest way to do that is to go to the Google site. http://www.google.com.

Q5. What is Internet? Describe how does it work. Describe the format of IP address. [JAN01]

#: What is Internet? How does Internet work? Discuss about the mechanism of providing addresses using the Domain Name System (DNS). [JUN00][DEC99]

#: Briefly explain IP addressing mechanism. [JUN01]

#: What is Internet? How does Internet work? Discuss tools and service available on Internet. [DEC02][DEC03,Q1(D)]

#: What are the major services and tools available to work with Internet? [JAN01][DEC99]

#: What are the various tools and services available on Internet? Explain them. [DEC02][DEC01]

#: Explain E-mail on Internet. What is an E-mail mailing list? What is the E-mail auto response?

A global network connecting millions of computers. More than 100 countries are linked into exchanges of data, news and opinions.

Unlike online services, which are centrally controlled, the Internet is decentralized by design. Each Internet computer, called a host, is independent. Its operators can choose which Internet services to use and which local services to make available to the global Internet community. Remarkably, this anarchy by design works exceedingly well.

There are a variety of ways to access the Internet. Most online services, such as America Online, offer access to some Internet services. It is also possible to gain access through a commercial Internet Service Provider (ISP).

The Internet is not synonymous with World Wide Web.

Internet Working : The Internet uses a set of rules called TCP/IP, which governs the sending ad receiving of data on the internet. TCP (Transmission Control Protocol) collectively called TCP/IP. TCP sends large block of information (text data) by dividing the data into data packets. It also adds special information i.e. the packet position in the document, error correction code etc. Such information makes it sure that these packets of the receiving end are reassembled correctly without any damage to the data. The IP puts destination address information on such packets.

Routers help to transfer information from source computer to destination computer. On Internet it is not necessary that all packets follow the same path in transfer. Router balance the load on various paths exist on the networks.

Gateway is a special hardware/software which allows different electronic network to connect to Internet under TCP/IP.

Mechanism of providing addresses using the Domain Name System (DNS) : Addresses are essential for virtually everything we go on the Internet. The IP in TCP/IP is a mechanism for providing addresses for computers on the Internet. Internet addresses have two forms:

- ✓ Person understandable which are expresses as words
- ✓ Machine understandable that are expressed as numbers also called IP addresses.

The following can be a typical person understandable address on the Internet.
username@host.subdomain.domain

Hosts are, in general, machines at a particular location. Resources of a host machine are normally shared and can be utilized by many users on the Internet. Given an account by system administrator, which allows him to use the resources of the machine.

The *username* in general, is the name of our Internet account for logging into the host machine. *Logging in* is the process of gaining access to our account on a computer, which is shared by several users.

Hosts and local network are grouped together into domains, which are grouped into one or more larger domains. For an analogy a host computer is considered as an apartment building in a housing complex and our account is just an apartment in it. Domain may be an apartment complex, a town, or even a country. Sub-domains may correspond to organization such as NASA or CompuServe. Domains are classified as non-geographic and geographic. The domain names in India comes under a larger domain ".in".

Code	**Applicable for**
.com	commercial organisations
.net	network organisations
.gov	parts of governments
.edu	organisations of higher education
.mil	non-classified military networks
.org	organisations that do not fit the commercial or educational designations

Example : www.ebay.com, www.gullybaba.com

Non-Geographic domains

Country	**Domain Name**
AUSTRALIA	.au
CHINA	.cn
GERMANY	.de
INDIA	.in
JAPAN	.jp
UNITED KINGDOM	.uk
UNITED STATES	.us

Example : www.ip**australia**.gov.**au**, www.chinaview.**cn**

Few Geographic Domains

Format of IP Address : The Internet address xyz@del2.vsnl.net.in indicates that the host computer whose name is del2 is one of the host computer in the sub-domain named Videsh Sanchar Nigam Limited (vsnl) which is a networks organisation (net) and is situated in country India (.in). The xyz is one the user group in this server/host (del2).

The 32-bit IP address is grouped 8 bits at a time, each group of 8 bits is an octet. Each of the four octets are separated by a dot, and represented in

decimal format, this is known as dotted decimal notation. Each bit in an octet has a binary weight (128, 64, 32, 16, 8, 4, 2, 1). The minimum value for an octet is 0 (all bits set to 0), and the maximum value for an octet is 255 (all bits set to 1).
The following figure shows the basic format of a typical IP address:

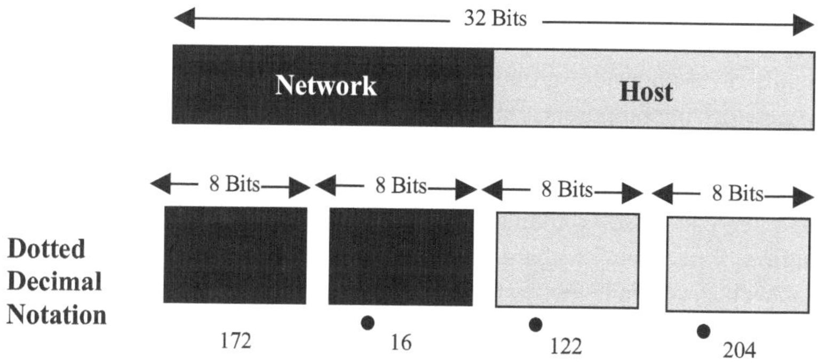

IP Address Classes : IP addressing supports three different commercial address classes; Class A, Class B, and Class C.
In a class A address, the first octet is the network portion, so the class A address of, 10.1.25.1, has a major network address of 10. Octets 2, 3, and 4 (the next 24 bits) are for the hosts. Class A addresses are used for networks that have more than 65,536 hosts (actually, up to 16,581,375 hosts!).
In a class B address, the first two octets are the network portion, so the class B address of, 172.16.122.204, has a major network address of 172,16. Octets 3 and 4 (the next 16 bits) are for the hosts, Class B addresses are used for networks that have between 256 and 65,536 hosts.

In a class C address, the first three octets are the network portion. The class C address of, 193.18.9.45, has a major network address of 193.18.9. Octet 4 (the last 8 bits) is for hosts. Class C addresses are used for networks with less than 254 hosts.

Tools and service available on Internet : To work with Internet and to utilise the information and resources available on it, we use certain tools.

Various tools and services are :
(i) Electronic Mail on Internet : One of the very useful things about the Internet is that it allows you almost instantly exchange of electronic message (e-mail) across the world instantly. For more details about it refer questions answered previously in this chapter.

Mailing Lists on Internet : For more details about it refer questions answered previously in this chapter.

(ii) Usenet and Newsgroups : There are many ways to meet people and share information-using Internet. One such way is through Usenet *newsgroups*. These are special groups set up by people who want to share common interests ranging from current topics to cultural heritage. There are currently thousands of Usenet newsgroups. The Usenet can be considered as another global network of computers and people, which is interwined with the Internet. Usenet is like a living thing: New newsgroups get added, the groups which have too much traffic get broken up into smaller, specialised groups, and the groups even can dissolve themselves. The newsgroups are really meant for interaction of people who share your interests. You can post your own questions as well as your answers to the questions of others, on the Usenet. Usenet has its own set of rules and manners, governing behaviour; most of them are based on common courtesy. Unfortunately, not everybody follow them.

What is FAQ? : A great resource offered by Usenet is the FAQ's that is the list of frequently asked questions and responses for them for particular newsgroup. These FAQ's are available on incredible number of topics, such as new Power PC to variety of dogs. FAQ's are an excellent place for sharing information about a topic. These FAQ's are generally text files or Usenet articles. FAQ's can be organised as a long list of questions and answers, or as a list of questions followed by answers. For more details about FAQ refer questions answered previously in this chapter.

(iii) Transferring Files with Ftp : Internet gives you access to all kinds of information. However, files and data are scattered all over the Internet in large and small archives. Some of these may contain text, some may contain pictures or sounds, or computer programs. A file may contain some important information for you, however it may be on a distant computer. If you want to have your own copy of the file then? For more details about ftp refer questions answered previously in this chapter.

(iv) Connecting to Remote Machines with Telnet : For more details about it refer questions answered previously in this chapter.

Many Other Tools are also available on Internet. Like **Finger** (This command allows display of the contents of the files that are associated with particular user identifier at a particular Internet site.), **Internet Relay Chat or IRC** (This allows each participant contribution displayed on the screens to all other taking part in the conversation.).

Many new services and tools are emerging on Internet with the advancement in technology. Increasing speed of Internet is also helping in increase of the number of services and tools.

Q6. Explain the various applications of Internet. [DEC02][DEC99]
#: Give ten examples of Internet use.
#: Enumerate various tasks that can be performed through access to the Internet. [JUN01]

Following are the various applications uses of internet :

- We can publish our research paper on Internet, thus making it available for others.
- We can create campus wide information systems.
- We can use it for teaching, for example tutorial for C++ can be given on Internet or college website.
- We can use it for publicity and advertisement.
- We can use it for multimedia conferencing.
- We can refer to the pictures thus making an online art gallery which is accessible 24hrs.
- We can have an electronic copy of classics such a Alice in Wonderland.
- We can have an electronic copy of journals and magazine from the Internet.
- We can meet people around the world, be in their touch.
- We can refer to job listings and requirements.
- We can get free public domain programs, we can see movies.
- We can send mail across the boundaries in no time.
- We can search for specific information.
- We can do chatting without imposing any constraint of distance..

and many other more uses of Internet are emerging with the advancement in technology.

Q7. Explain the different types of connections to Internet. [DEC01][JUN99]
#: #: Explain two ways of connecting to Internet. [DEC04,Q4(a)]
#: Explain the procedure of getting connected to Internet.
#: Explain briefly various modes of connecting to the Internet. [JUN01,Q3(b)]

For connecting to the Internet, you need to have a computer account on a host machine. For using the account, you must provide the host machine with the username and password. This process is termed as logging in. There are different types of ways of connecting to Internet which are as follows :

(i) Host/Terminal Connection : In this mode your computer behaves as if it is terminal to an Internet host or server. In general, our terminal will be remote to the host, therefore, requiring a dial-up modem to transfer information from our computer to the host and back. VSNL, Sify, etc. provide this type of connection. This type of connection may well suited when we :

- Have a limited budget
- Do not require constant connectivity
- Do not want to manage server by yourself
- Want to connect from different locations using log in facility.

In this connection only the utilities offered by host are available to the user.

(ii) Individual Computer TCP/IP Link : This connection helps a computer to act as a TCP/IP host. We can customize this computer for specific access. These links are called Serial Line Internet Protocol (SLIP) of Point to Point Protocol (PPP) Links. One can have dial-up SLIP of PPP connection. We can compress the data and send it using TCP/IP or vice-versa. Computer using such link allows Windows based applications on computer. Thus, providing a very simple user interface for connecting to Internet.
Such connection allows use of graphical Internet browsers, file transfer capability, e-mail and other PC based services.

(iii) Dial-up or On-Demand TCP/IP Link through LAN : This connection is considered to be an intermediate step between a dial-up connection and a dedicated high-speed link. It has some features of both the types This Kind of connection is established between our LAN server It may have a direct line or may dial the number of the internet server to establish a link. A regular exchange of information between the LAN server and host machine of the service provider is the exchange of e-mail messages. This type of connection is ideally suited for environments where we have very little internet traffic but many mail messages to exchange.

Using TCP/IP link one can :
perform remote login to a distant computer where you have an account
transfer files from a distant computer
find out information about people and organisations
browse the Internet using a browser

(iv) Dedicated Link Connections : This is a permanent connection, which can be set up over a telephone line using modem or a router. A router is a specialized computer, which can read the address on packet and can transmit the packet to its destination. Modems are used when the speed of transmission is low (56 kbps), whereas router are used for high speed (above 56 kbps).

Dedicated high-speed connection is best suited for larger organization, which have to serve many internal and external customers. This kind of link allows us to become information provider round the clock. This connection allows full connectivity to Internet, however, because of organizations own security, privacy or policy reasons we may choose not to use all the connectivity features.

Presently, the main Internet service provider in our country is Videsh Sanchar Nigam Limited (VSNL). They offer all security of the above, type of connections.

Q8. State the function of each the following Internet tools in at most two sentences: [JUN01,Q3(c)]

(i) Finger
(ii) Internet Relay Chat
(iii) Multi-user Dungeons (MDUs)
(iv) Multicast BackBONE (MBONE)
(v) CuSeeMe, Maven and VAT

Finger	This command allows display of the contents of the files that are associated with particular user identifier at a particular Internet site.
Internet Relay Chat (IRC)	Allows private communication between two individuals. Both parties must be connected to Internet for a session.
Multi-user Dungeons (MUDS) and Multi-user Simulation Environment (MUSEs)	This tools have rules and regulations of Information sharing. An approach for group learning
Multicast BackBONE (MBONE)	It is used to broadcast speeches, news, conferences, and other information events on Internet
CuSeeMe, Maven and VAT	These are tools for audio and video teleconferencing

Q9. What is Gopher? Explain its use with example.

Gopher displays a set of resources in the Internet in the form menus of lists or items. We go around the Internet by selecting items from these menus. We need not know the addresses and commands. We just select an-items if interest to see its content on the screen. It is based on the concept of client and servers. Here, clients are the programs that request information for a user, whereas, servers are programs that provide the information to clients. Gopher servers are scattered all over the Internet. Thus, servers site wait for requests from Gopher clients programs. One can use the Gopher client program on ones own Internet host. If Gopher program is not available on our machine we can telnet to one of the public Gopher clients available on the Internet. The people who maintain running of Gopher services create the menus. A Menu item can point to materials on that Gopher server or to materials on any other Gopher servers.

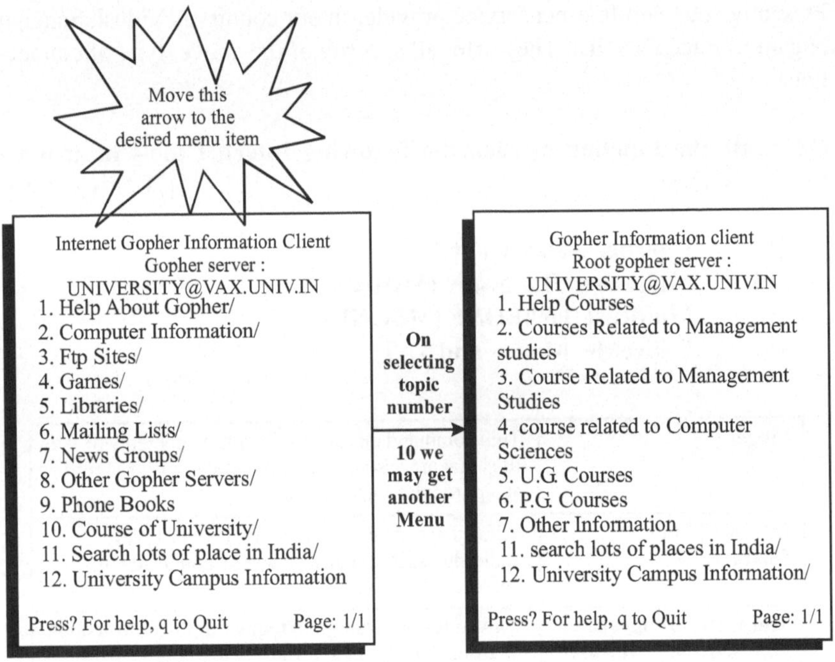

All these Gopher servers, their respective information resources we can reach are collectively referred to as Gopherspace. Have been common for Gopher users. The Internet has grown extremely fast in size, bur Gopherspace is perhaps growing even faster.

Q10. What is WWW? Explain terms hypertext, hypermedia and html. [DEC02][JAN01][JUN99]

WWW :- One of the newest media available over the Internet is the World Wide Web. The Web (or sometimes WWW or W3) is a huge collection of interconnected hypertext documents. Hypertext document can contain links to other documents, to other kind of files entirely and to other sites on the Internet with a web browser, we can jump from one like to the next following the trial of link in any direction that interests us. The World Wide Web is a system for linking up hypertext documents. Each document is a page written in HTML. A browser can display a document by establishing a TCP connection to its server, asking for the document, and then closing the connection. When a hyperlink is selected by the user, that document can also be fetched in the same way. This manner, documents all over the world are linked together in a giant web.

Hypertext :- On the Web, hypertext is simply text with links. Links are elements of the hypertext document that we can select-often presented as underlined words or icons. Click on a link and we'll be transported to the document it's linked to (or to a different part of the displayed document).

Hypermedia :- Once we start considering other media besides text, the term hypertext is replaced by the word hypermedia. But the basic idea is the same: links. An advantage of hypermedia over traditional media is that it allows us to navigate through all kinds of related documents (and other kinds of files), using one simple procedure-clicking on link.

HTML :- HTML stands for Hypertext Markup Language, and it is the code used to mark up text documents to turn them into hypertext documents. Hypertext documents on the Web generally end in the extension .html and contain funny-looking text tags, like this: <TITLE>. We can create files in HTML by using FrontPage Express or another WebPage Editor or HTML editors. Many editors are available as freeware.

Solved Papers
CS-612

CS-612 : PC SOFTWARE SKILLS
JUNE-2001

Note: Question 1 is compulsory. Answer any three questions from the rest.

Q1(a). You are given two uncalibrated jugs, one of capacity five litres and the other of capacity, three litres and an unlimited supply of water. Show a sequence of filling and emptying of the jugs and of pouring back and forth between two jugs, so that exactly four litres of water is obtained in the first jug. **[8]**

The given capacity of first jug is five litres and the given capacity of other is three litres. There are two ways of getting five litres of water in the first jug. These are:

First Method :

1. Fill the second jug (three litres of water) and pour it into the first jug of five litres capacity.

2. Now first jug is holding three litres of water. Again repeat the first step. Now one litre water is left in the second jug because out of three liters, two liter of water has been poured in the first jug and the remaining one litre is available in the second jug.

3. Empty the first jug and pour one litre water of the second jug in to the first jug.

4. Again fill the second jug having capacity of three litre

5. Pour second jug into the first jug to occupy four litre of water.

Second Method :

1. Fill the first jug having five litre capacity and pour from it to the second jug of three litre capacity.

2. Because of the capacity of three litre of second jug, two litre water is left in the first jug.

3. Empty the first jug having two litre water by pouring it in to the second jug.

4. Again, fill up the first jug.

5. Pour the water from first jug to second jug. Because of the capacity and two litre of water already existing only one litre water is poured into the second jug.

6. Only four litre water will be left in the first jug.

(b) Prove that the expressions (21n + 4) and (14n + 3) have no factors (other than 1) in common for any value of n. **[4]**

Refer to Dec03,Q1(b)

(c) Describe each of the following terms in context of internet : **[12]**

(i) Gopher

(ii) World Wide Web

(iii) Search Engine **[DEC03,Q3(a)]**

(iv) FTP **[DEC01,Q3(iv)]**

(i) Gopher - It is an information gathering tool used in Internet, which offers a smooth, menu-driven way to transverse international 'gopherspace' which these days literally means several hundred servers worldwide, offering computer programs, audio, text, movies and images. It provides a seamless, hidden programming interface with which we can transfer files, browse, databases and telnet to sites around the globe, simply and easily. We can also use the archie and ftp services from gopher.

(ii) World Wide Web

Refer to Dec04,Q4(a)

(iii) Search Engine

Refer to June04,Q1(c)

(iv) FTP

Refer to June03,Q5(c)(iii)

(d) Explain **[6]**

(i) steps required to apply 'Autoformat' to a range of cells

(ii) the recalculation features of MS-Excel

(iii) various types of charts in MS-Excel

(i) Steps required to apply 'Autoformat' to a range of cells

Refer to June03,Q2(c)

(ii) The recalculation features of MS-Excel

MS-Excel provides two ways of recalculation i.e. Automatic Recalculation and Manual Recalculation :

Automatic Recalculation – Whenever any changes are made in any cell of the worksheet, Excel automatically recalculates all formulas affected by the cell you have changed. If the worksheet is not very large, Excel normally recalculates the worksheet within a fraction of second without any delay. Manual Recalculation – When the worksheet is very large and there is not enough memory in your computer, Excel may take lot of time to recalculate the worksheet. Whenever such type of problem is faced, the worksheet can be switched on to the manual recalculation mode. In manual recalculation mode, Excel does not recalculate any formula. However, it always remind you that the worksheet needs to be recalculated by displaying 'calculate' in Status Bar.

(iii) Various types of charts in MS-Excel

Following are the types of charts provided in MS Excel :

1. Pie Chart
2. Column Chart
3. Area Chart
4. Bar Chart
5. Doughnut Chart
6. Line Chart
7. XY (scatter) Chart
8. Radar Chart
9. Surface Chart
10. Cone, cylinder and pyramid chart
11. Bubble Chart

Q2(a). Mohan and John went shopping. They had a total of Rs. 1640 between them. John had Rs. 240 more to begin with, but spent twice as much as Mohan did, and John ended up with two thirds as much money as Mohan was left with. How much money did Mohan spend? [6]

Let us suppose that Mohan has 'a' money.
Then as per question John has 'a+240 money.
So, a + a + 240 = 1640
Or, 2a + 240 = 1640
2a = 1640 – 240 = 1400
a = 700
Therefore, Mohan has Rs.700/- and John has 700+240 = Rs. 940

Let, let us suppose that Mohan spent 'b' money, therefore, as per question John spent 2b money.
John ended up with 2/3 as much money as Mohan was left with him.
940 – 2b = **2/3** (700 – b)

or 2820 – 6b = 1400 – 2b
or –6b + 2b = 1400 – 2820
or –4b = -1420
b = 1420/4 = 355
So, Mohan has spent Rs.355

(b) What is the remainder left after dividing 1! + 2! + 3! + ... 100! by 7 ? **[4]**

From 7! Onwards, every term gives as the remainder as every term contains 7 as a factor, therefore, we need to find the remainder when :
1! + 2! + ...+ 6! is divided by 7
1! + 2! +...........+ 6! = 1 + 2 + 6 + 24 + 120 + 720
1! + 2! + ...+ 6! = 873
Now

873 = 5 (mod. 7)

Hence, the remainder is 5

(c) You are given eight coins, out of which seven are of same weight, however eighth coin is slightly heavier than the others, Find the heavier coin in no more than three weighings. Explain the process. **[5]**

Generally such type of question is solved by Decision Tree. Let us suppose that we have been given eight coins as 1, 2, 3, 4, 5, 6, 7 and 8.

Steps to be followed for making Decision Tree :

1. Make two group of coins having four coins each.
2. Weigh both the groups
3. It is clear that the heavier group has heavier coin.
4. Choose heavier group and divide them in two sub groups of two coins each.
5. Again weigh both sub groups and choose heavier group. Now the heavier group has two coins.
6. Weigh both coins and ascertain the heavier coin.

The graphical representation of Decision Tree is :

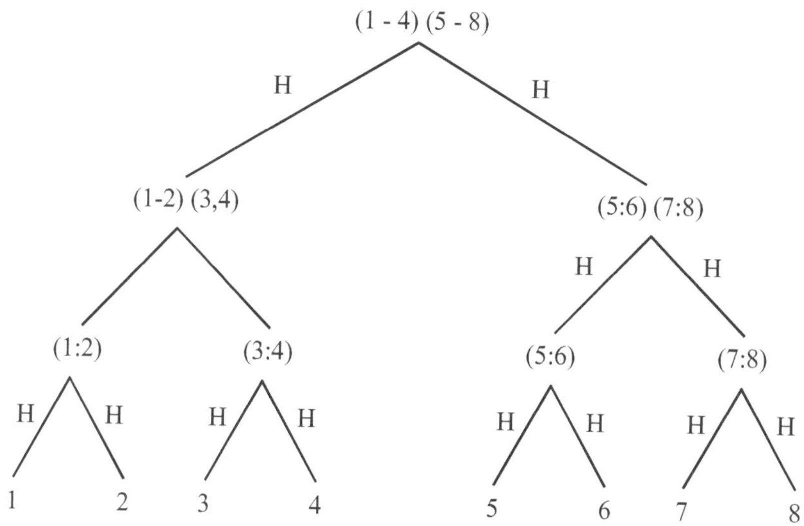

Q3(a). Enumerate various tasks that can be performed through access to the Internet. **[5]**

Refer to Chap-12, Q-6

(b) Explain briefly various modes of connecting to the Internet **[3]**

Refer to Chap-12, Q-7

(c) State the function of each the following Interest tools in at most two sentences: **[7]**

(i) Finger

(ii) Multi-user Dungeons (MUDs)

(iii) Multicast BackBONE (MBONE)

(iv) CuSeeMe, Maven and VAT

Finger	This command allows display of the contents of the files that are associated with particular user identifier at a particular Internet site.
Multi-user Dungeons (MUDS) and Multi-user Simulation Environment (MUSEs)	This tools have rules and regulations of Information sharing. An approach for group learning
Multicast BackBONE (MBONE)	It is used to broadcast speeches, news, conferences, and other information events on Internet
CuSeeMe, Maven and VAT	These are tools for audio and video teleconferencing

Q4(a). Explain what is a browser and why it is useful. Name at least three prominent browsers currently in use. Discuss any one of these browsers, including its merits and demerits vis-a-vis the other browsers. [8]

Refer to June02,Q2(a)

(b) What do you understand by 'Downloading'? Through an example, explain various steps for downloading. [4]

Refer to June04,Q5(b)

(c) Briefly explain IP addressing mechanism. [3]

Refer to June04,Q5(a)

Q5(a). Prove that the number (single number) 412,078,521,834 is not a perfect square. [3]

Refer to Chap-2, Q-12

(b) Find R_T the maximum number of regions into which a plane can be divided by a infinite straight lines, no two of which are parallel, and no three of which pass through the same point. [6]

We start by considering the number of regions formed by zero, one, two, three line etc.. According to the above consideration, when there is no line, the plane consist of one region. Mathematically : $R_0 = 1$

One line divides the plane in two regions : $R_1 = 2$ as 4(½)

Two lines divides the plane into four regions and three lines into seven as shown below :

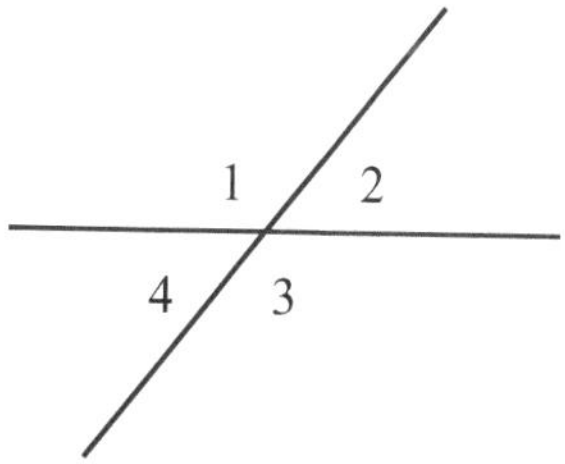

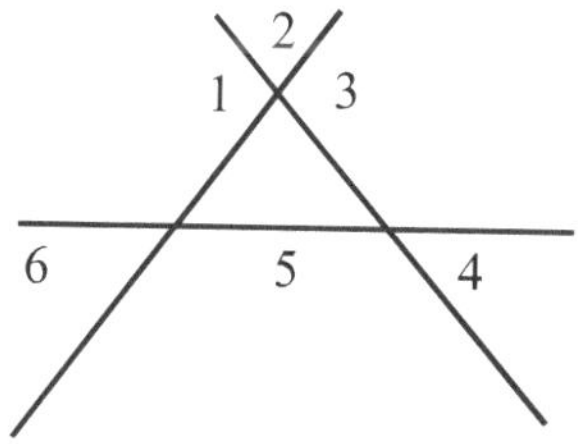

Further, four lines divide the plane into 11 regions. Therefore, we can assume a formula :

$$R_n = R_{n-1} + n \text{ for small value of n}$$

The nth line increases the number of region by n, because it **outs** the previous n-1 lines in n-1 places.
Since R_0 is 1 (It is thought of as boundary condition)
By **backwards** from R_n to these general formula in terms of n alone.

$R_n = R_{n-1} + n$
$= R_{n-1} + n$
$= R_{n-2} + (n - 1) + n$
$= R_{n-3} + (n - 2) +(n - 1) + n$
$= R_0 + 1 + 2 + 3 + \ldots\ldots\ldots\ldots + (n - 2) + (n - 1) +n$
$= 1 + S_n$

Where S_n is the sum of the first n positive integers.
Using Gauss's trick we can write :

$$S_n = 1 + 2 + 3 + \ldots\ldots\ldots\ldots + (n - 2) + (n - 1) + n$$

$$S_n = n (n + 1) /2$$
$$2S_n = n (n + 1)$$

$$2S_n = n (n + 1)$$

$$R_n = 1 + n (n +1) / 2$$

(c) A certain street contains 1000 buildings. A signmaker is contacted to number the houses from 1 to 1000. How many zeros will he need? [4]

1. All zeroes at the end of a number upto 990
= 10, 20, ……..100…….160, 170……990
= 10 x 10 = 100 zeros.

2. All zeros at the middle of the digit i.e.
= 100, 101, 102, …..200, 201…….901,
= 10 x 9 = 90 zeros

3. Three zeroes of 1,000
Total = 100 + 90 + 3 = 193 zeros are required.

(d) Explain the paradox in the following sentence: [2]
I declare 'I am lying'

The paradox in the sentence " I declare 'I am lying' " is:
The Speaker can speaks either true or false.
Case 1 : He speaks truth, since the statement says that the speaker declares that he speaks lie. One assumption that the speaker speaks truth is violated or it is clear that he is a liar.

Case 2 : He speaks false : In this case the statement says that he declares that he speaks lies actually must be speaking the truth which again contradicts our assumption that the speaker speaks lies.

Q6(a). Explain what are macros and why these are created.
[JUN03,Q1(a)] [5]

Refer to June04,Q2(a)

(b) Explain what do you understand by 'Autotemplates'.
[JAN01,Q5(b,iv)] [5]

A template is a special feature used for creating new workbooks, sheets, charts, dialog boxes and modules. You can create special templates, called auto templates, in your startup or alternate startup directory. Then you can use auto templates as the basis for all new workbooks and all new sheets you insert into your workbooks. Auto templates are the templates saved with a specific name, in a specific location. With the help of auto template, you can change the font size, column widths, page orientation and headers that will be the default for every new workbook.

(c) Enumerate various types of functions in MS-Excel and explain one type of these functions with examples. [5]
Refer to July 04,Q3(a)

CS-612 : PC SOFTWARE SKILLS
DEC-2001

Note: Question 1 is compulsory. Answer any three questions from the rest.

Q1(a). Given a 12-litre vessel filled with milk and two empty vessels with capacities of 9 litres and 5 litres. How can you divide the milk into 2 equal portions? Explain and write the sequence of steps to solve. [8]

The problem can be solved in two ways :

Let us suppose that 12 Litre vessel is X, 9 litre vessel is Y and 5 litre vessel is Z

First Method :

	X	Y	Z
STEP 1	12	0	0
STEP 2	0	7	5
STEP 3	5	7	0
STEP 4	5	2	5
STEP 5	10	2	0
STEP 6	10	0	2
STEP 7	1	9	2
STEP 8	1	6	5
STEP 9	6	6	0

Second Method :

	X	Y	Z
STEP 1	12	0	0
STEP 2	7	0	5
STEP 3	7	5	0
STEP 4	2	5	5
STEP 5	2	9	1
STEP 6	11	0	1
STEP 7	11	1	0
STEP 8	6	1	5
STEP 9	6	6	0

(b) If you are given the information that the counterfeit coin is heavier than the others, how will you pick it in only two weighings? [7]
Refer to Chap-1, Q-7

(c) Explain how the access of workbook in EXCEL can be restricted from other users. [7]
Refer to Chap-8, Q-4

(d) Explain the different types of connections to Internet. [8]
Refer to June04,Q1(b)

Q2(a). Give the shortcuts to select the following using keyboard in MS-EXCEL: [7]
(i) Current cell
(ii) Entire column
(iii) Entire Row
(iv) Entire worksheet
(v) Open a new worksheet
(vi) Open an existing worksheet
(vii) Extend selection to End of Data Block.
Refer to Chap-5, Q-3

(b) Explain the different types of data that can be entered in worksheet cells. [4]
The various kinds of entries that can be made in a cell are :
i) Text:- First select the cell in which the data has to be entered and type- in the text.
Press ENTER key to finish your entry. The data will be displayed in the active cell as well as in the formula bar. To enter digits as text (calculations cannot be done using these kind of entries) use an apostrophe(') as the first character.

ii) Number:- Numbers include digits from 0 to 9 and one special characters like:

$ % + - / ( ) , . E e

iii) Date and Time:- Date and Time entries are interpreted in a special way in Excel. They are represented as numbers for Excel given to each day from 01:01:1990 (serial number 1) to 31:12:2078(serial number 65380). Although when you type a date in the cell like 01/01/97, it will be displayed as it is.
Example Type TODAY( ) in a blank cell and press ENTER key. (This

function will display the system date and time).

iv) *Data in Series* **-** You can fill a range of cells either with the same value or with the series of values. This can be done using Autofill handle (small square on the bottom-right corner of the active cell).

Drag this handle till the last cell to create a range of cells which are to be filled-in with the values.

Example

1. Enter MONDAY in cell E20.
2. Drag the Autofill handle till the cell K20.

(The whole range will be filled with days from MONDAY to SUNDAY)

(c) Explain the 3 ways of referencing the cells in MS-EXCEL worksheet. [4]

Refer to Chap-5, Q-5

Q3(a). Explain the following : [8]

(i) WWW

Refer to Jan01,Q2(b,iv)

(ii) Telnet

Refer to Chap-12, Q-1(iii)

(iii) FTP

Refer to June01,Q1(c,iv)

(iv) E-Mail.

Refer to Chap-12, Q-1(v)

(b) Write the steps to search for a specific information on the Internet using a search engine. List any 10 search engines. [7]

Refer to June04,Q4(c)

Following are the 10 search engines listed :

01.	Google	:	www.google.com
02.	Infoseek	:	www.infoseek.com
03.	Yahoo	:	www.yahoo.com
04.	Lycos	:	www.lycos.com
05.	Excite	:	www.excite.com
06.	looksmart	:	www.looksmart.com
07.	webcrawler	:	www.webcrawler.com
08.	Dogfile	:	www.dogfile.com
09.	AstalaVista	:	www.astalavista.com

10. Altavista : www.altavista.com

Q4(a). Prove that there is atleast one prime between K^2 and $(K+1)^2$ for all integers K satisfying $1 \leq K \leq 20$. **[6]**

Refer to Chap-2, Q-1

(b) What is the remainder left after dividing **[4]**
$1! + 2! + 3! + \dots\dots + 100!$ by 7 ?

Refer to Dec05,Q3(b)

(c) Find a prime divisor of the form 4K+3 for the integer $4(3\times7\times11\times19) - 1$. **[5]**

Refer to Chap-2, Q-9

Q5(a). What are custom controls? Explain their use on the worksheet. Write the sequence of steps for creating controls on the worksheet.
[JUN00,Q1(d)] [8]

Refer to Dec03,Q2(b,i)

(b) List and explain different tools and services available on internet.
[JUN00,Q3] [7]

Refer to Dec03,Q1(d)

Q6(a). Determine all 3 digit numbers N such that N is divisible by 11, and N/11 equals the sum of the squares of the digits of N. **[7]**

Refer to Chap-3, Q-10

(b) Prove that for any positive $x<1$, the series $1+x+x^2+x^3+\dots\dots+x^n$ converges to $1/(1-x)$ as n tends to infinity. **[8]**

Refer to Dec04,Q2(b)

CS-612 : PC SOFTWARE SKILLS
JUNE-2002

Note: Question 1 is compulsory. Answer any three questions from the rest.

Q1(a). Prove that for any prime $p \geq 5$, $p^2 + 2$ is composite. **[8]**

Here, p>= 5 and as P is a prime, therefore, P must not be divisible by 3.

⇨ P = 3k + 1 or 3k + 2 for some integer k
⇨ Either (P – 1) or (P + 1) is divisible by 3.
⇨ (P – 1) (P + 1) is necessarily divisible by 3.

Now,

$P^2 + 2 = (P^2 - 1) + 3 = (P - 1)(P + 1) + 3$
$= 3k' + 3 = 3(k' + 1)$

–> $(P^2 + 2)$ is divisible by 3 and hence, $(P^2 + 2)$ is composite.

(b) Determine all positive integers for which 2^n+1 is divisible by 3. **[7]**

The given expression is $2^n + 1$. We wish to determine all positive integers for which $2^n + 1$ is divisible by 3.

i.e. n < 1, 2, 3, ……………………n

Now for	n = 1	$2^n + 1 = 3$
	n = 2	$2^n + 1 = 5$
	n = 3	$2^n + 1 = 9$
	n = 4	$2^n + 1 = 17$
	n = 5	$2^n + 1 = 33$
	n = 6	$2^n + 1 = 65$
	n = 7	$2^n + 1 = 129$

It is observed that whenever n is a odd positive integer i.e. 1, 3, 5, 7, ……. $2^n + 1$ is divisible by 3 and for odd n, we can rewrite the given expression as : $2^n - (-1)^n$

This expression of the form $a^n - b^n$ is always favorable. One of its factor is, therefore, for all positive odd n integers, the expression $2^n + 1$ is always divisible by 3.

(c) What is an address book in context of E-mail? How is it useful? Also explain the procedure to give reply to an arrived E-mail. [7]

Address Book in context of E-mail is a convenient place where contact information for retrieval by programs i.e. Microsoft Outlook Express are stored. Normally every mail reader allows address book facility to maintain a database of regularly used addresses. All addresses can be categorized in different groups of receivers like address book we maintain manually. It is used because :

1. In the address book, you get a place to store email addresses, home and work addresses, phone and fax numbers, conferencing information, instant messaging addresses and personal information such as date of anniversaries and birthdays.

2. It supports lightweight Directory Access Protocol for using Internet directory services.

3. Group of contacts can be created to make it convenient to send email to a set of people, such as relatives, friends and business associates.

4. It can be shared with other users.

5. You can import your personal address book from numerous popular email programs.

6. Send and receive business cards

7. Print all or part of your Address Book for your record in office as well as residence.

Following procedure is to be followed for giving reply to an arrived email :

1. First of all you have to open your email account and then click on Inbox button.

2. In the message list, double click the message you want to reply.

3. Click on Reply button

4. Write the message in the box for replying.

5. Click on to send button.

If the message is served to the destination server, it return message sent otherwise return error message.

(d) What is Function Wizard in EXCEL ? Explain how to use it. [8]

Refer to Dec03,Q1(c, ii)

Q2(a). Explain the features of the browser. What are the different menu options available in Internet Explorer ? Discuss. [8]

Browsers are software applications used to locate and display web pages. There are two types of Browsers i.e. text browsers and graphical browsers. The text browsers are those browsers which allow only to see the text from web sites, whereas Graphical Browsers display graphics as well as text. The Netscape Navigator and Microsoft Internet Explorer are graphical browsers. In addition, most modern browsers can present multimedia information including sound and video, though they require plug-ins for some formats. Text browsers does not need to transfer images and multimedia effects, which needs much data to be transferred, hence text browsers are faster than graphical browsers.

The main features of Browser are :

Popup Controls help you to stop pop-ups, which are small windows that are served by various web sites and are often unsolicited, from taking over our browsing experience. The feature can be turned on from the tools menu. Additional settings in Preferences give you personalized control, so we can 'allow' Pop-ups that may be needed by an individual web site.

Tabbed Browsing in Netscape 7.1 lets you browse faster by allowing you to open up more pages at once, and switch back and forth between those pages. To use Tabbed Browsing, click on the Tab icon in the left hand corner next to the first Tab or right mouse click on a tab or go to the File menu and choose New Navigator Tab. We can also open hypertext links within a new tab by right clicking on the link.

Images Fit to Screen to view large images in its entirety. We can also zoom out and view the image in its original size.

Find option or feature from the menu can be selected to find the text you want to search in a webpage. If you are looking for something specific on a web page, just type the text in the Find dialog box displayed when Find option is selected and see the selection(it is the text you want to find), if it is not available on this webpage then not found message will be displayed.

Web Site Icons : we easily keep track of where we are on the web. These icons are shown in the URL field and are also handy within Tabbed Browsing.

Full Screen Mode : we see more of a web page when we need to and maximize screen space. This is great for viewing web content on laptops or smaller desktop screens.

Downloading and Saving Files :

Multiple files can be downloaded at once and reliably pause and resume download if our Internet connection is interrupted or need to use telephone to make a phone call. Download Manager keeps track of our downloads from one place, in addition view information on the status of our download, percentage complete, download location, source, time remaining and more.

Save a complete web page – Initially several steps have to be followed to download and save a complete web page, but now takes only one. In a single action, save a page with all its graphics files. No need to individually download each file to capture all contents on the page.

Search – Search from URL field - We can easily start a web search on any word in a web page without having to leave the page. Simply select the word with our mouse, right click and choose Web Search for that word. The results appear within a second in a separate browser window and also in My Sidebar.

Printing – Printing Preview and Page Set-up tools give you greater control over the output, sizing, margins, scale and even headers and footers of a printed document.

Following are the different menu options available in Internet Explorer :

File, Edit, View, Go, Favourites, Tools and Help.

File ...

Create Shortcut: Create a shortcut to the current web page. So, whenever we click on this shortcut, the Internet Explorer will be automatically opened and connects to this site.

Delete: deletes a document from the local memory.

Rename: renames the document.

Properties: It has the following submenus:

History: shows the URL's of the recently browsed web pages.

Browse Offline: show web pages without fetching from the host server.

Close: closes the browser.

Edit ...

Cut: stores the highlighted text in the clipboard.

Copy: copies the data in the clipboard to the position of cursor.

View ...

Toolbar: shows or hides toolbar

Status bar: shows or hides the status bar.

Refresh: reloads the current document from the host server.

Options: enables us to change the settings of Internet Explorer.

Go ...

Back: loads the previous page onto the screen.

Forward: load the page, which has been viewed after the current page previously will be loaded onto the screen.
Up one level: goes up by one level i.e. closes a window, which is open.
Home Page: opens the home page of the web sites whose URL has been set in the configuration which will be loaded as the start page of the browser.
Search: opens and closes the search bar.
Best of the web page: opens the best site like top 100 sites.
Mail: opens the e-mail window of Microsoft Exchange of Microsoft Outlook from where we can send e-mail.
News: opens the Internet's newsreader program. From here, we can switch onto the icon, which represents the sites of new corporations.
Contacts: opens the address book, which is the part of Microsoft Outlook.
Calendar: opens the calendar so that we can fix our own schedules.
Tasks: lists the appointments.
Internet Call: connects to the Internet.

Favourites ...
It lists the bookmarks we added when we are browsing the Internet.

Tools ...
Find: switches on to the search sites and prompts for the search string.
Map network drive: maps the drive to another drive.

Help ...
It contains the information about Internet Explorer.

(b) Write the sequence of steps for downloading a file from Internet. [7]

Downloading is a process through which one can copy different types of files like movies, songs, software, games, texts etc. from web sites on Internet to his own computer's hard disk.

Following steps are to be taken for downloading a file :
1. Open any Internet Browser
2. Open topic related web site from where you want to download
3. Go to that specified page
4. Click on 'download'
A dialog box will appear and ask you to define place of copying.
5. Enter or select where do you want to copy and click OK.
6. Wait for download complete 100% (a message box will be displayed with message download complete)

Q3(a). Explain the two ways to create database in MS-EXCEL.
[DEC2002,Q2(b)] [7]

Refer to Dec03,Q2(a)

(b) Explain the following : [8]
(i) Auto filter
(ii) Chart wizard
(iii) Pivot table
(iv) Macro

1. Auto filter – It enables you to specify criteria and the Excel temporarily hides those rows in the database which do not meet the criteria. For example – You have stored the data of all the employees of your firm. The query can be made on the database to view the details of all those employees who have been working with the organization for more than 2 years. This would be your criteria for searching and finding all those records.
After selecting command, Data then Filter then AutoFilter, MS Excel inserts drop down arrow to each column label in the list. Click on that arrow, it displays a drop-down list which contain following bars:

- **ALL :** shows all record
- **CUSTOMS :** To specify two criteria for a column
- **TOP 10 :** To display top 10 records

2. Chart Wizard – Generally a worksheet contains large numeric data that it becomes very difficult to accurately analyze it and take a correct decision. In this type of cases, the facility to represent data in the form of charts becomes very handy, because charts convey the message clearly and quickly. They play a very important role in the business world. Excel permits you to view graphs on the screen as well as to print them on a printer. It supports many types of chart such as Bar, line, Stacked bar, Pie, XY, Area, 3-D Bar, Radar, Doughnut etc. In Excel, creating chart is very simple. To create a chart, all you need to do is to select the range that you want to include in the chart and use a wizard called chart-wizard. Chart Wizard asks a series of questions and creates a chart for you.

3. Pivot table
Refer to Dec03,Q1(c,iv)

4. Macro
Refer to Chap-11, Q-5

Q4(a). Prove that for every integer n >2, $(n!)^2 > n^n$. **[8]**
Refer to June03,Q4(b)

(b) Prove that for any 3 consecutive integers, the cube of the largest cannot be the sum of the cubes of the other two. **[7]**
Refer to June04,Q6(b)

Q5(a). Mention the functions for the following in MS-EXCEL. **[8]**
(i) Add cells specified by a given criteria – SUMIF(range, criteria, sum_range)**Where** range is the range of cells you want to evaluate. Criteria is the criteria in the form of a number, expression or text that defines which cell will be added. Sum_range is the actual cells to sum.

(ii) To find the exponential of a number – EXP(number)

(iii) To find the absolute value of a number – ABS(number)

(iv) Compares 2 text strings and returns TRUE if they are exactly the Same otherwise FAILS – EXACT(text1,text2)
Here text1 is the first text and text2 is second text.

(b) Explain the following: **[7]**
(i) E-Commerce
In E-Commerce, the word commerce is derived from a Latin word. It covers the range of online business activities for products and services both business to business and business to consumers through the Internet. All orders are accepted through web sites. After accepting orders bill is raised to the client and goods or services requested are provided to the client. Online payments are also accepted for the goods purchased in the form of credit card and transaction ID. The whole process is performed electronically, therefore, it is called E-Commerce. There are mainly two types of e-commerce i.e. Online shopping and online purchasing. Some of the components of E-commerce include : Electronic presentation of goods and services (catalogue), online ordering and payment processing, automated customer account inquiries and receipt generated and online bill/account presentation. E-commerce is an attractive mode of transactions. Now thousands of Internet users are doing purchasing online in even smaller cities.

(ii) E-Greeting
E-Greeting stands for Electronic Greeting. By E-Greetings, decisive messages are sent by one people to another with choice of his picture from available

picture range. These messages are colorful, beautifully designed with attractive pictures, animation video, audio and text. E-Greetings are sent as an attachment to Email from one user computer to the other for whom the greeting is prepared to send. Various email packages contain special E-Greeting making options. With the help of these options, many interesting greetings can be made on various occasions like anniversaries, wedding, birthday, new year, deepawali and other festivals; besides all these festivals there are greetings available for almost every occasion like mothers day, fathers day, women day, friendship day etc.

Q6(a). Given 13 coins, one of them heavier than the rest. How can you determine it in no more than 3 weighings using decision tree? [7]

Refer to Chap-1, Q-8

(b) Let $a_1, a_2, a_3, ...a_n$ be an arbitrary arrangement of the number 1, 2, 3, ...n. Prove that, if n is odd, the product $(a_1 - 1) ' (a_2 - 2) ' (a_3 - 3)....(a_n - n)$ is even number. [8]

The number of factors in the following product $(a_1 - 1) \times (a_2 - 2) \times (a_3 - 3) ....(a_n - n)$ is odd.

Since the given n is odd.

By inspection, the sum of all the factors is 0. This, is impossible if each of the factors was odd, because an odd numbers cannot sum to an even number, zero.

Hence, atleast one factor in the product is even. Hence the product $(a_1 - 1) \times (a_2 - 2) \times (a_3 - 3) ....(a_n - n)$ is an even number.

CS-612 : PC SOFTWARE SKILLS
DEC-2002

Note: Question 1 is compulsory. Answer any three questions from the rest.

Q1(a). Prove that for every integer (n > 2) **[7]**
$(n!)^2 > n^n$
Refer to June02,Q4(a)

(b) Given 13 coins, one of them heavier than the rest, how can you determine it in no more than 3 weighings using decision tree. **[8]**
Refer to June02,Q6(a)

(c) Explain the various applications of Internet. **[7]**
The various applications of Internet are :
1. It can be used for publicity and advertisement.
2. It can be used for multimedia conferencing.
3. It can be used to search for specific information.
4. Mails can be sent across the boundaries in no time.
5. We can refer to job listings and requirements.
6. We can get free public domain programs and can see movies.
7. We can meet various people around the world, be in their touch.
8. We can get an electronic copy of journals and magazine from the Internet
9. We can get an electronic copy of classics such as Alice in Wonderland.
10. We can refer to the pictures of the art gallery.
11. We can use it for teaching, for example we can teach languages using WWW.
12. We can create campus wide information system.
13. We can publish own research paper on Internet, thus making it available for others.

(d) Explain the various access restriction mechanisms related to the worksheet in MS-EXCEL. **[8]**
Refer to Chap-8, Q-4

Q2(a). Explain different charts components. Using chart wizard, explain the sequence of steps to create a chart. **[7]**

Refer to Chap-9, Q-2

(b) Explain the concept of Filtering a Database in MS-EXCEL using Autofilters and using Advanced filters.

[DEC03,Q2(a);JUN02,Q3(a)] [8]

Refer to Chap-10, Q-4

Q3. What are the various tools and services available on Internet? Explain them. **[15]**

Refer to Chap-12, Q-5

Q4(a). Explain the following : **[8]**

(i) WWW **[JAN01,Q2(b,iv)]**

(ii) Domain Name Service (DNS) **[DEC03,Q5(a,(i))]**

(i) WWW – The term WWW stands for World Wide Web. It is a network of interconnected hyper-documents, which contains hypertext or hypermedia. The hypertext or hypermedia is a text or photo that links to another part of document or another document. This type of links are called hyperlinks. We can jump from one link to another following a trail of link in any direction of our interest. The web grew out of the need to have these large teams of internationally researchers collaborate using a constantly changing collection of reports, blueprints, drawing, photos and other documents. The world wide web is an architectural framework for accessing linked documents spread out over crores of machines all over the Internet. It is based on a client-server system. In this the documents are known as pages. Each page may contain links to other related page anywhere in the world. These pages are viewed with the program called browser. A browser can display a document by establishing a TCP connection to its server, asking for the document and then closing the connection. When a hyperlink is selected by the user, that document can also be fetched on the same way. In this manner, documents all over the world are linked together. At present, any type of information you desire can be obtained through web sites.

(ii) Domain Name Service (DNS)

Refer to June04,Q2(b)

(b) What is a template? Mention its use in MS-EXCEL and write the sequence of steps to create a template with the help of an example. **[7]**

Refer to June04,Q6(a)

Q5(a). Find the smallest number such that if its leftmost digit is placed at its right end, the new number so formed is precisely 50% larger than the original number. **[8]**

Let us suppose that n+1 digits comprising the number beginning from the left d_0, d_1, d_2, ……, d_n, where d_0 is different from 0, and d_1, d_2, …., d_n are in [0 – 9]. Then the condition of the problem is :

$$d_1, d_2, d_3 \ldots\ldots\ldots\ldots d_n d_0 = (3/2) \times d_0, d_1, d_2 \ldots\ldots\ldots\ldots d_n$$

By explicitly stating the 'weight' of each digit as determined by its position, we rewrite the above equation:

$$2 \times (d_1 \times 10^n + d_2 \times 10^{n-1} \times d_3 \times 10^{n-2} + \ldots\ldots\ldots\ldots + d_0)$$
$$= 3\ (d_0 \times 10^n + d_1 \times 10^{n-1} + d_2 \times 10^{n-2} + d_3 \times 10^{n-3} + d_4 \times 10^{n-4} \ldots\ldots\ldots\ldots + d_0)$$

By transposing the term involving d_0 to right hand side of the equation and the other term to its right side, we find :

$$17 \times (d_1 \times 10^{n-1} + d_2 \times 10^{n-2} + d_3 \times 10^{n-3} + \ldots\ldots\ldots\ldots + d_0)$$
$$= 3 \times 10^{n-2}\ d_0$$

In accordance with the fundamental theorem of Arithmetic, it is obviously clear that 17 must be a factor of right hand side of the above equation. Now as per problem we must find the smallest number.

Since d_0 is the first digit of the number and the smallest number will have the least value of d_0. Now, it is reasonable to set d_0 equals to I. We must now find the least n such that $3 \times 10^{n-2}$ is divisible by 17.

That number is 2999999999999998 of the quotient obtained on dividing this number by 17 is 176470588235294, therefore, d_1 is 1, d_2 is 7, d_3 is 6 ……………… D_{15} is 4 and the 16 digits number obtained is : 1176470588235294.

(b) For any prime p > = 5, prove that $p^2 + 2$ is composite. **[7]**

Refer to June02,Q1(a)

Q6(a). Prove that the expressions 3x + 7y and 9x + 4y are divisible by 17 for the same set of integral values of x and y. **[8]**

To prove that if 3 x + 7y is divisible by 17 for some integer, values of x and y, then, for the same values of x & y, 9x + 4y is divisible by 17 and this also holds vice-versa.

First, let us suppose that for some set of integer values of x & y, 3x + 7y is divisible by 17 i.e.

Let,

$3x + 7y = 17k$

$\Rightarrow 3x = 17k - 7y$

$\Rightarrow 9x = (51k - 21y)$

$\Rightarrow 9x + 4y = 51k - 21y + 4y = 51k - 17y$

$\Rightarrow 17(3k - y)$ (multiple of 17)

9x + 4y is also divisible by 17 for the same set of integer values of x & y. Now, vice-versa, let

$9x + 4y = 17k$

$$\Rightarrow 3x = \left(\frac{17k - 4y}{3}\right)$$

$$\therefore 3x + 7y = \left(\frac{17k - 4y}{3}\right) + 7y$$

$$\Rightarrow 3x + 7y = \left(\frac{17k - 4y + 21y}{3}\right)$$

$$= \left(\frac{17k - 17y}{3}\right) = 17\left(\frac{k - y}{3}\right) (multiple\ of\ 17)$$

$\Rightarrow$ 17 divides (3x + 7y)

($\because$ 17 does not divide by 3 and 17 is a prime number)

Hence, 3x + 7y is divisible by 17 for the same for integer values of x & y for which 9x + 4y is divisible by 17.

(b) Write short notes on : **[7]**

(i) Pivot table

(ii) Function wizard

(iii) Solver **[JUN00,Q2(i);DEC03,Q2(b,ii)]**

(i) Pivot table

Refer to Chap-10, Q-3(i)

(ii) Function wizard

Refer to Dec03,Q1(c,ii)

(iii) Solver

It is a powerful optimization and resource allocation tool in MS-Excel. Whenever your forecasting problem contains more than one variable, you need to use the solver add-in utility to analyze the scenario. Whenever you use solver to solve a problem, you have to :

(a) specify the target cell that you want to minimize, maximize or set to a certain value.
(b) specify the changing cells that you want to be adjusted until a solution is found.
(c) specify constraint cells that must fall within certain limits or satisfy target values.

If the Solver command does not appear on the Tool menu, it means that the Solver has not been installed. Choose Add-in from the Tools menu and select the solver Add-in option in the Add-in dialog box. It is an Add-in utility, therefore, you should verify that it is installed on your system before you get started. Once you install an add-in, its commands or functions become integrated part of Microsoft Excel until you remove it. For using this option, following steps are to be followed:

1. Enter the data.
2. Choose Tools, Solver Command
3. In the Set Target Cell box, enter a cell reference or name for the target cell. Select :
Max option button – if you want the target cell's value to be as large as possible.
Min option button – if you want the target cell's value to be as small as possible.
Value of option button – if you want the target cell to have a certain value.

4. In by changing cells box, enter the name or reference for each changing cell. If you enter more than one reference, separate the references with commas.
5. In the Subject to the constraints box, add any constraint you want to apply. Constraints can be applied to the target cell, the changing cell or any cell that is directly or indirectly related to the problem.
6. Click on Solve button to get the results

To view the reports, select the report from the dialog box, and click on OK.

CS-612 : PC SOFTWARE SKILLS
JUNE-2003

Note: Question 1 is compulsory. Answer any three question from the rest.

Q1(a). Discuss the Konigsberg Bridges problem using the graph method. **[7]**

Refer to Chap-1,Q-1

(b) Prove that for all n > = 4, $2^n > n^2$. **[7]**

For n> = 4

$2^n > n^2$

or we can say that

$2^4 >= 4^2$ this shows equality (By putting value of n = 4)

for n = 5,

$2^5 > 5^2$ it is also true as above true for n = 4

So, for any values which are greater than or equal to 4.

Let the given statement is true for n = x,

Where x is an integer.

$\Rightarrow 2x >= x^2$ ------------(i)

Further, we have to proof, for consecutive number from n = x+1 will also be true.

$\Rightarrow 2^{x+1} >= (x+1)^2$

or, $2^x \geq \frac{(x+1)^2}{2}$ -----------(ii)

or, $x^2 - \frac{(x+1)^2}{2} = \frac{2x^2 - (x^2 + 2x + 1)}{2}$

or, $\frac{x^2 - 2x - 1}{2} = \frac{(x-1)^2 - 2}{2}$ ------------(iii)

Now x = 0 (n =1) x = 1 (n = 2)

x = 2 (n=3) the expression does not true

but x = 3 (n = 4), x = 4(n = 5) the given expression (iii) is positive

$\Rightarrow x^2 \geq \frac{(x+1)^2}{2}$ for x = 3, 4 ....(or, n = x+1 as 4, 5, 6 ....)

By equation (i)

$2^x >= x^2$

$\Rightarrow 2x \geq \frac{(x+1)2}{2} \Rightarrow 2^{x+1} \geq (x+1)^2$ will also true hence proved.

(c) What are Macros in EXCEL? Write the sequence of steps to record a macro, run a macro and delete a macro. **[JUN01,Q6(a)]** **[8]**

Refer to June04,Q2(a)

(d) Write the sequence of steps to send an attachment (file) through an E-mail account. **[8]**

The sequence of steps to be followed for sending an attachment (file) through E-mail account are as under :

1. First of all, we have to log on to the email account.
2. Then Click Mail button. An another page is displayed indicating details of mail in your Inbox account. Then click on to the Compose button to open compose editor.
3. Now click the button 'Attach'. A dialog box for selecting or typing name of a file will appear.
4. Click on to the Browse button and select the file which you have to send and click OK. If the file is lengthy then it will take some time to attach the same.
5. After selecting it will come back to the compose page displaying the file to be sent under column 'Attach'. Click on send button and wait for a while. It will display message sent.

Q2(a). Discuss about the Save and Protect Workbook in MS-EXCEL. **[4]**

Any matter typed first of all stored in the RAM (Random Access Memory) of your computer. As the RAM is volatile i.e. it loses its contents if the power connected to PC is failed or switched off or the computer is reset. Therefore, whatever matter typed must be saved as a disk file in the hard disk or the floppy disk. Once the matter has been saved in a disk, it can be retrieved any time in future. In Excel, worksheet can be **saved** in three different ways :

1. By pressing Save button on toolbar
2. By pressing the Save command from the File Menu.
3. By pressing ^S (it is the shortcut key used for Save command)

In MS-Excel, it may be necessary to **protect** the data from being seen or used by unauthorized persons. To resolve this issue a password facility is available and following steps should be followed :

1. Open the workbook to be saved and protected, if it is not opened.
2. From the File option, select the Save As command. A dialog box appear, click on to Option button. Excel displays the Save Options dialog box. In this dialog box, the first text box is used to define the password required for opening the workbook and the second password required to modify the file. Either or both passwords can be defined.
3. Type text in the Protection Password text box. Remember that Excel does not display the password in text box. Then click OK button. Excel displays the Confirmed Password dialog box.
4. Type the same text in the Re-enter Protection Password text box in Confirm Password dialog box.
5. Press Enter or Click OK and Excel displays a message box for replacing the existing file.
6. Click the NO button.

To restrict the access to a workbook by other users, there are three different ways, which are Protection Password, Write Reservation Password and Read-only Recommendation. Under Protection Password type the password required to open the workbook. The password can be upto 15 characters long, can include alphabets, number and special characters. Then Excel will ask to re-enter the password for confirmation. Enter the password and click Ok. Under Write Reservation Password changes in the existing workbook are made and then workbook is used. This prevents unauthorized users to make any modification in the workbook. Password rules are same as indicated above. If the Read-only Recommendation option is selected then no changes can be made by any user. This option is generally used to discourage the other users from making any changes by mistake or want to prevent the changes to be made by more than one users simultaneously.

(b) What is a fill-handle and explain its use in EXCEL? **[3]**

Fill handle is a small black square on the bottom right corner of the active cell in MS-Excel, whenever anybody point to the fill handle, the pointer changes to a black cross. It is used to copy contents to adjacent cells or to fill a series of data like week days, months, dates etc. This handle is dragged till the last cell to create a range of cells which are to be entered with the values. For example if you enter January in active cell A-12 and drag the Autofil handle till G-12, the cells A-12 to G-12 will be filled with name of months from January to December. Similarly if you drag the fill handle to the left of a selection and stop in the selected cells without going past the first column or the top row in the selection, MS-Excel deletes data within the selection. The Autofill saves not only the time but also energy of the user.

(c) Explain the terms: **[8]**
(i) Auto Format
(ii) Format Painter
(iii) Auto Fit
(iv) Alignment and its options **[JAN01,Q4(b)]**

(i) Auto Format : It is a built-in table design used to format an entire list or a large range of cells. It includes the formatting of font, colour, numbers, border alignment etc.. It uses distinctive formats for the various elements of the table. It is a very useful feature provided in MS-EXCEL, which can help you to quickly format list entered in the worksheet. To apply Autoformat option to a range of cells following steps are to be followed :

1. Select the range of cells to be formatted
2. Select Autoformat option from the Format Menu.
3. Choose the appropriate format from the list of Table Format.
4. Click OK.

(ii) Format Painter : Format Painter button is available in the formatting toolbar by default. In MS-Excel, this feature provides the facility to copy the formats from selected cells or document easily and quickly by clicking on the Format Painter tool button. After copying the formats, they can be pasted into any cells in the worksheet for Excel or MS-Word document.

Following are the steps to be followed for using Format Painter in Excel :
1. Select a cell or range, whose formats you want to copy.
2. Click Format Painter on the formatting toolbar.
On clicking the mouse on Format Painter, the Excel changes the shape of mouse pointer by attaching a paintbrush with it.
3. Select the cell or range where you want to copy the copied formats.

(iii) Auto Fit : It is a command available in Format Menu. It helps in deciding the width or height of a column in MS Excel. It adjusts the size of selected column or row according to their existing contents. Manually setting the width or height of a row or column becomes difficult when working on larger sheets. To autofit the column width select the specified column and press Ctrl + Spacebar or open format menu, choose column and then select autofit option.

(iv) Alignment and its option : Aligning or adjusting data in a cell is known as alignment. There are various types of options available in excel for horizontal and vertical alignments, they are :

Horizontal :

1. General – The text is left aligned and the numbers are right aligned. This is default status.
2. Left – Aligns the contents of cell to the left of the cell.
3. Center – Aligns the contents of the cell in the center of the cell.
4. Right – Aligns the contents of the cell to the right of the cell.
5. Fill – Fills the selected cells with the single character.
6. Justify – This option is selected with multiple lines of text as it wraps the contents from left to right.
7. Center Across Selection – This option centers the text across multiple columns.

Vertical :

1. Top – Aligns the text of the cell to the top of the cell.
2. Center – Places the text in the center of the cell.
3. Bottom – Aligns the text of the cell to the bottom of the cell.
4. Justify – Wraps the text of the cell from top to bottom of the cell.

Q3(a). Explain the features of any Graphical Browser. Also discuss the different menus and options available on them. List any 3 browsers. [8]

Browsers are software applications used to locate and display web pages. There are two types of Browsers i.e. text browsers and graphical browsers. The text browsers are those browsers which allow only to see the text from web sites, whereas Graphical Browsers display graphics as well as text. The Netscape Navigator and Microsoft Internet Explorer are graphical browsers. In addition, most modern browsers can present multimedia information including sound and video, though they require plug-ins for some formats. Text browsers does not need to transfer images and multimedia effects, which needs much data to be transferred, hence text browsers are faster than graphical browsers.

The main features of Browser are :

Popup Controls help you to stop pop-ups, which are small windows that are served by various web sites and are often unsolicited, from taking over our browsing experience. The feature can be turned on from the tools menu. Additional settings in Preferences give you personalized control, so we can 'allow' Pop-ups that may be needed by an individual web site.

Tabbed Browsing in Netscape 7.1 lets you browse faster by allowing you to open up more pages at once, and switch back and forth between those pages. To use Tabbed Browsing, click on the Tab icon in the left hand corner next to the first Tab or right mouse click on a tab or go to the File menu and choose New Navigator Tab. We can also open hypertext links within a new tab by right clicking on the link.
Images Fit to Screen to view large images in its entirety. We can also zoom out and view the image in its original size.

Find option or feature from the menu can be selected to find the text you want to search in a webpage. If you are looking for something specific on a web page, just type the text in the Find dialog box displayed when Find option is selected and see the selection(it is the text you want to find), if it is not available on this webpage then not found message will be displayed.
Web Site Icons : we easily keep track of where we are on the web. These icons are shown in the URL field and are also handy within Tabbed Browsing.
Full Screen Mode : we see more of a web page when we need to and maximize screen space. This is great for viewing web content on laptops or smaller desktop screens.

Downloading and Saving Files :
Multiple files can be downloaded at once and reliably pause and resume download if our Internet connection is interrupted or need to use telephone to make a phone call. Download Manager keeps track of our downloads from one place, in addition view information on the status of our download, percentage complete, download location, source, time remaining and more.

Save a complete web page – Initially several steps have to be followed to download and save a complete web page, but now takes only one. In a single action, save a page with all its graphics files. No need to individually download each file to capture all contents on the page.

Search – Search from URL field - We can easily start a web search on any word in a web page without having to leave the page. Simply select the word with our mouse, right click and choose Web Search for that word. The results appear within a second in a separate browser window and also in My Sidebar.

Printing – Printing Preview and Page Set-up tools give you greater control over the output, sizing, margins, scale and even headers and footers of a printed document.

The three browsers are :

1. Internet Explorer
2. Netscape Navigator
3. NCSA MOSAIC

(b) Explain the terms : **[7]**
(i) IRC (Internet Relay Chat)
(ii) Web Cast
(iii) Messengers

(i) IRC (Internet Relay Chat) – IRC stands for Internet Relay Chat. As is apparent, it is a chatting package available on the net. First of all we have to register ourselves and then logon the net and select the topics for discussion. The persons related with that topic is allowed a separate room, where they can chat. An IRC is having a number of rooms on different topics from music groups to literatures to politics. Once you joined a channel, you can communicate with the other people thereby simply by typing what you want to convey. IRC allow each participants combination displayed on the screens to all other taking part in the conversation.

(ii) Web Cast – Whenever we receive any information about anything through Internet, it comes to us under web cast. In other words, every casting send or receive through web is known as web cast. There are three categories of web cast indicated below :

Texture Web cast – Under this category, we can only get and send texture documents on Internet e.g. email and written chat etc.
Audio Web cast – It provides facility to send and receive our sound and sound related things e.g. verbal chat, listening and downloading sound and speech files.

Audio-video web cast – It provides the facility of receiving and sending pictures as well as sound and text e.g. sending, receiving and viewing picture, movie etc.. It plays a very vital role in education.

(iii) Messengers – It is a software which has the facility to store the address of many users. If one log in, it automatically prompts the other about the other user logged on. It enables you to find and communicate with all your friends, whether they are signed on to the same web sites which provides that messenger. Now even you can send offline messages (when the other person is not logged in), these messages are displayed whenever that user log in. Examples: are Yahoo Messenger, MSN Messenger etc.

Q4(a). Determine all the digits numbers N such that N is divisible by 11 and N/11 equals the sum of the squares of the digits of N. [8]

Some three digit numbers which are divisible by 11 are :

110, 121, 132, 143, 154, 165 .... etc.

Let any number can be N and written as N = n1 n2 n3

According to question :-

$$\mathbf{N / 11} = n1^2 + n2^2 + n3^2$$

So, we check it again and again

$\mathbf{110 / 11} = 1^2 + 1^2 + 0^2$

$10 \,!= 2$

$\mathbf{121 / 11} = 1^2 + 2^2 + 1^2$

$11 = 1 + 4 + 1$

$11 \,!= 6$

....

$\mathbf{550 / 11} = 5^2 + 5^2 + 0^2$

50 = 25 + 25 + 0 (undefined terms)

if we ignore undefined terms the number will be 550.

$\mathbf{803 / 11} = 8^2 + 0^2 + 3^2$

73 = 64 + 02 + 9

73 = 73

the number will be 803

$990 / 11 = 9^2 + 9^2 + 0^2$

$= 81 + 81$

$90 \,!= 162$

There are only two numbers 550 and 803 which will be divisible by 11 and the square of its digit will be equal to N / 11.

(b) Prove that for every integer n > 2

$(n!)^2 > n^n$. [7]

We are given that n>2, where n is an integer. We have to prove that

$(n!^2) > n$

Now, the expansion for (n!) can be written as the product

$1 \times n \times 2 \times (n - 1) \times 3 \times (n - 1) \times .... \times (n - 1) \times 2 \times n \times 1$

In this set of products, each of the terms, $1 \times n$, $2 \times (n - 1)$, $3 \times (n - 2)$, etc. is greater than or equal to n.

The fist and the last terms are $(1 \times n)$. These are smaller than others. Each of the other terms is of the form $(K + 1) \times (n - K)$ and exceeds, because

$$(K + 1) \times (n - K) = K (n + K) + (n - K)$$
$$= K + (n - k)$$
$$= n$$

And there are n such products. Therefore,

$(n!)^2 > n \times n \times n \times \ldots\ldots\ldots \times n$ (n terms) = n

$\Rightarrow (n!)^2 > n^n$

Q5(a). Explain with a suitable example how to enter formula and edit a formula on a worksheet. [5]

Refer to Chap-8, Q-1

(b) Explain the use of the following functions : [4]

(i) SUMIF (num 1, num 2, ...)

(ii) FACT (num)

(iii) RAND ( )

(iv) EXACT ( )

(i) SUM IF (num 1, num 2, ...) – It adds the specified cells by a given **SYNTAX : ** SUM IF (range, criteria, SUM range),

where range is the range of cells which you want to evaluate.

criteria is the criteria in the form of number, expression or text that defines which cells will be added.

sum-range are the actual cells to sum.

Example : SUMIF(C2:C10,">50",D2:D10)
SUMIF-(D5:D15"<75",F5:F15)

(ii) FACT(num) – It returns the factorial of a number, equal to
1* 2 * 3 * ……… * Number

SYNTAX : FACT(num)

Example = FACT(4)

The result will be 24

(iii) RAND( ) – It returns an evenly distributed random number greater than or equal to 0 and less than 1. A new number is returned every time the worksheet is calculated. If anybody wants to use RAND to generate a random number but don't want the numbers to change every time the cell is calculated, one can enter

=RAND( ) in the formula bar and press F9 to change the formula to a random number.

Example – To generate random number greater than or equal to 0 but less than 100 : RAND( ) * 100 is entered in the formula.

SYNTAX : RAND( )

(iv) EXACT ( ) - It compares two text strings and returns TRUE, if they are exactly the same number otherwise FALSE. It is case sensitive but ignores formatting differences.
SYNTAX : EXACT(Text 1, Text 2)
Example : EXACT ("Book", "Book")

The result will be TRUE and in case it is written as EXACT("Book", "Bok") the result will be FALSE.

(c) Explain the terms: **[6]**
(i) TCP/IP
(ii) Telnet **[JUN03,Q5(c(i)]**
(iii) FTP

(i) TCP/IP
Refer to July04,Q1(b)

(ii) Telnet
Refer to July04,Q1(d)

(iii) FTP
Refer to Chap-12, Q-1(iv)

Q6(a) Prove that for any prime P > = 5. **[6]**
$p^2 + 2$ is composite
Here, p>= 5 and as P is a prime, therefore, P must not be divisible by 3.
⇨ P = 3K + 1 or 3 K + 2 for some integer k
⇨ Either (P – 1) or (P + 1) is divisible by 3.

Now, $P^2 + 2 = (P^2 - 1) + 3 = (P - 1)(P2 + 1) + 3 = 3k' + 3 = 3(k' + 1)$
⇨ $(P^2 + 2)$ is divisible by 3 and hence, $(P^2 + 2)$ is composite.

(b) Determine all positive integers n for which $2^n + 1$ is divisible by 3. **[6]**

The given expression is $2^n + 1$. We wish to determine all positive integers for which 2^n+1 is divisible by 3.

i.e. $n \geq 1, 2, 3, \ldots\ldots.n$

Now for $n = 1$ $\quad 2^n + 1 = 3$

$n = 2$	$2^n + 1 = 15$
$n = 3$	$2^n + 1 = 9$
$n = 4$	$2^n + 1 = 17$
$n = 5$	$2^n + 1 = 33$
$n = 6$	$2^n + 1 = 65$
$n = 7$	$2^n + 1 = 129$

It is observed that whenever n is a odd positive integer i.e. 1, 3, 5, 7,.....$2^n + 1$ is divisible by 3. And for odd n, we can rewrite the given expression as

$2^n - (-1)^n$

This expression for the form $a^n - b^n$ is always factorable. Therefore, for all positive odd n integers, the expression $2^n + 1$ is always divisible by 3.

(c) Write short notes on Minimum Spanning Circles. **[3]**

Refer to Dec03,Q6(b)

CS-612 : PC SOFTWARE SKILLS
DEC-2003

Note: Question 1 is compulsory. Answer any three question from the rest.

Q1(a). Prove that the product of four consecutive natural numbers cannot be the square of an integer. **5**

Let four consecutive natural numbers are n, n+1, n+2 and n+3

Here, we have given : $n(n + 1) (n + 2) (n + 3)$

$$n(n + 1) (n + 2) (n + 3) = \{ n (n + 3) \} \times \{(n + 1) (n + 2)\}$$
$$= (n^2 + 3n) (n^2 + 3n + 2)$$

Let $n^2 + 3n = x$, so we have $= n(n + 1) (n + 2) (n + 3) = x (x + 2) = (x^2 + 2x)$

Now, let us suppose $\exists$ an integer t

$n(n + 1) (n + 2) (n + 3)$ is equal to t^2

$= x^2 + 2x = t^2$

$= (x + 2)^2 = t^2 + 4$

$t^2 + 4$ must be a perfect square.

Also, $x = n(n + 3)$ => x is an even number

=> x + 2 is also an even number

=> $(x + 2)^2 = 4y^2$ for some integer y.

Therefore, we are having : $4y^2 = t^2 + 4 \Rightarrow 4y^2 - t^2 = 4$

=> $(2y - t) (2y + t) = 4$

Also, t is an even number

Therefore, both $2y - t$ and $2y + t$ are even numbers

The only solution possible is $2y - t = 2y + k = 2$

Where k = 0, which is absurd.

Hence, our assumption is incorrect and it is proved that the product of four consecutive natural numbers cannot be the square of an integer.

(b) Prove that the fraction (21n + 4) / (14n + 3) cannot be reduced for any n. **5**

Let n = 1,

$21n + 4 = 21 \times 1 + 4 = 25$

and $14n + 3 = 14 \times 1 + 3 = 17$

There is no any common factor between both equation.

Again, if we put n = 2

$21n + 4 = 21 \times 2 + 4 = 46$

and $14n + 3 = 14 \times 2 + 3 = 31$

No any common factor between them.

Now, given n = 3,

$21n + 4 = 21 \times 3 + 4 = 67$

and $14n + 3 = 14 \times 3 + 3 = 45$

There is no any number factor.

Thus, we can say that both expression have no factors in common for any value of n.

(c) Explain the terms : **10**

(i) VLOOP UP : It searches for a value in the left most column of a table and then returns a value in the same row from a specified column in the table. In VLOOPUP, V stands for Vertical.

The Syntax is : VLOOKUP (LOOK UP_Value, Table_array, col_index_num, range_lookup)

For example : VLOOKUP (1, A2 : C10, 2)

(ii) Function Wizard **[JUN02,Q1(d)]**

Function Wizard : Excel provides built-in function through Function Wizard. It guides us through all the steps of writing and its arguments. It provides the textual help to understand the function as well as the option where data is to be entered. Following are the ways of opening the Function Wizard :

1. On Standard Toolbar, Click on the Function Wizard.

2. Click on function bar on Insert Menu.

3. Press shift plus F3 keys on the keyboard.

(iii) Filters

It is one of the powerful features available in MS-Excel. It is used to view the selected information from a large database, rather than seeing all the records in the table. This is being done by using filters. This command is available in DATA menu. There are two types of filter; Autofilter and Advance filter. After selecting header row of a table, the filter command can be applied by clicking on :

DATA then Autofilter or DATA then Advance filter

After clicking a drop down box will appear at every header column. After clicking drop down box, it shows some data according to that you filter your database.

(iv) Pivot table **[DEC02,Q6(b,i);JUN02,Q3(a,iii)]**

It is a most sophisticated data-management feature available in MS-Excel. An organization analysis tool displays the fields and records in your list in new and potentially useful combinations. Pivot table made it easy and is available in the Data Menu. A pivot table report is an interactive table that can be used for quick summarization of large amount of data. Its rows and columns can be rotated to see different summaries of the source data, filter the data by displaying different pages or display the details of your interest. A pivot table report can be created from MS-Excel list.

(d) What is Internet? How does Internet work? Discuss the tools and services available on Internet. **[DEC01,Q5(b);JUN00,Q3]** **10**

Refer to Chap-12, Q-5

Q2(a). Write sequence of steps to create a database, add records into it, delete records and modify the records in MS-EXCEL. **7**

[DEC02,Q2(b);JUN02,Q3(a)]

There are various kinds of data in any company e.g. all the details of the employees, sales details, client data, products data. The purpose of storing and maintaining data is to retrieve it later for day-to-day transactions and management planning.

The data, which is collected from the sources is the raw data. Various operations can be carried out on the data, like sorting, searching and totalling. This is processed and manipulated now and termed as Information. The system which helps us to perform all these activities on the data is termed as DBMS. Database is an organized collection of information. It is also referred to as a list or a table. There are two kinds of databases:

Internal Database - Databases created in the worksheet.
External Database - Database which is created through other DBMS or RDBMS packages like MS-ACCESS, FOXPRO, dBASE, SQL Server, ORACLE.

In MS-Excel, database can be created in two simple ways:
1. Enter the data in the form of table in the worksheet.
2. Use **Data Form** command.

To create database using Data Form command, the steps are:
1. Enter the given details:

In Cell	*Enter*
A1	AGE
B1	NAME
C1	SEX
D1	DEPARTMENT

2. Choose **Data, Form** command while keeping one of the field name active.
3. The dialog box is displayed, warning you for taking the row of the selected cell as the header row of the database. Click on OK.
4. Another dialog box is displayed, which shows one record at a time. Fill-in the appropriate details in the box against each field name.

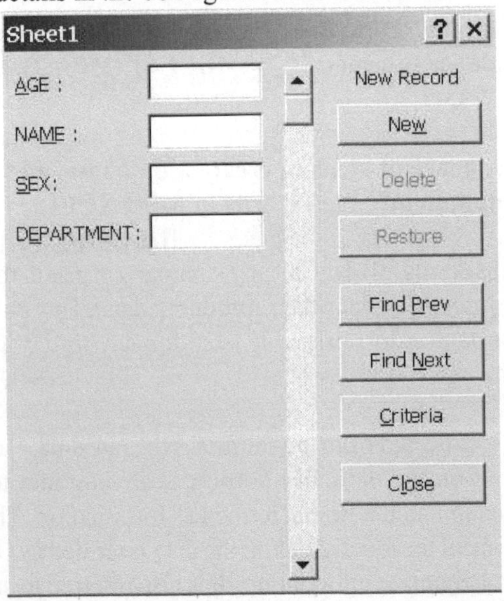

5. Click on **New**. This will add the entered record in the database.
6. To finish the entry of records, click on **Close.**

Following steps are to be followed for deleting records in database :
1. The records can be deleted by simply selecting the records or cell(s) to be deleted and press Delete Key. Another way of deleting the record is as under
a) Activate any cell from the database list.
b) Choose Data, Form command.
c) Get the record to be deleted by clicking on the Find Prev or Find Next button.
d) Click on the Delete button.

Modifying records : The records once entered in the database can be easily modified. This can be done by selecting the cell and retyping the data. Another way of doing this is by Data Form :
a) Scroll up or down to select the record to be modified.
b) Edit the field value.
c) Click on New button to update the modification in the record.
d) Click on Close once you have finished the task of modification of records.

(b) Explain the terms: **8**
(i) Custom Controls **[DEC01,Q5(a);JUN00,Q1(d)]**
A software routine that adds some enhancement or feature to an application. Custom controls are written to provide as little as a few graphical interface improvements to as much as providing full imaging, spreadsheet and text editing extensions to the application. Depending on the development system, custom controls are either linked into the application when it is written or maintained as independent executable files that are called at runtime. DLLs, VBXs and OCXs are examples.
Example : instead of typing-in the response, you can select the appropriate option from the drop-down list. The tool buttons that are used to draw control objects are found on the **Forms Toolbar**. To display this toolbar -
Choose **View -> Toolbars**.

Some of the custom controls are: lable(text), edit box, group box, check box, option box, list box, drop down list box, list box link to edit control, combination of edit control and drop-down, scroll bar control and spinner control. Following is the picture of all the tool buttons and the short description.

	label (text)		edit box
	group box		button
	check box		option box
	list box		drop-down list box
	list box link to edit control		combination of edit control & drop-down
	scrollbar control		spinner control

The edit control, list box linked to edit control, and combination of edit control & drop-down tool buttons cannot be linked to worksheet cell. These controls can be used inside dialog box only. One control can be linked to only one cell. But one cell can have many controls linked to it.

(ii) Goal Seek **[JUN00,Q2(i)]**

Generally, you know the result you want a formula to return but not the input values the formula needs to reach that result. To arrive at a formula, you can use goal seek. When goal seeking, MS-Excel varies the value in a specified cell until a formula that is dependent on that cell return the result you want.

The formula of cell will not be destroyed. Goal Seek saves you from performing time consuming trial and error analysis. Whenever the Goal Seek from Tool Menu is clicked, a dialog box will appear with three text boxes :

(a) In Set Cell text box you put formula cell reference

(b) In To value text box you put value which referred to the formula cell.

(c) In On changing cell you put variable cell reference in which variation take place.

(iii) Solver **[JUN00,Q2(ii)]**

It is a very powerful optimization and resource allocation tool. It helps you to uncover the best uses of scarce resources, so that goals such as profit can be maximized, or undesired goals such as cost can be minimized. Whenever the forecasting problem contains more than one variable, you need to use the solver add-in utility to analyze the scenario. Instead of guessing time and again, you can use MS-Excel Solver to find the best answer. Whenever you Solver is used to solve the problem, you have to :

(a) Specify the target cell that you want to minimize, maximize or set to a certain value.
(b) Specify the changing cells that you want to be adjusted until a solution is found and
(c) Specify constraint cells that must fall within certain limits or satisfy target value.
If the solver command is not on your Tools Menu, choose Add-in from the Tools Menu and select the solver Add-in option in the Add-in dialog box.

(iv) Scenario Manager **[JUN00,Q2(iii)]**

In MS-Excel, you can create and save sets of input values that produce different results as scenarios. A scenario is a group of input values called changing cell saved with a name you provide. Scenario dialog box open after selecting Scenario from Tools menu. It is a set of values that MS-Excel saves and can substitute automatically in your worksheet. Up to 32 changing cells per scenario can be defined.
If the solver command is not on your Tools Menu, choose Add-in from the Tools Menu and select the solver Add-in option in the Add-in dialog box.

Q3(a). Explain the features of any search engine. (Example: YAHOO, LYCOS, GOOGLE) **[JUN01,Q1(c(iii))]** **[7]**

Refer to Jun04,Q1(c)

(b) Discuss the different components available in an email software. **[8]**

Refer to Dec04,Q5(a)

Q4(a). For all n, prove that $2^n >= 2n$. **[5]**

We will prove it by mathematical induction:

$2^n \geq 2n$

$n = 1$

$2^1 \geq 2.1$

$2 = 2$ which is true.

Let it is true for $n = r$, then

$2^r \geq 2r$

Multiplying both sides by 2

$2^{r+1} \geq 2r.2$

$= 4r$

(b) For all n>= 10, prove that 2^n>= 100n. **[5]**

Given that n>10

First we take, $n = 11$

$$2^{11} = 2 \times 2 \times 2 \times 2 \times 2 \times 2 \times 2 \times 2 \times 2 \times 2 \times 2 = 2048$$

and $100.11 = 1100$

we know that $2048 > 1100$

so, $2^{11} > 100.11$ ....(I)

now, we take, $n = 12$

$$2^{12} = 2 \times 2 \times 2 \times 2 \times 2 \times 2 \times 2 \times 2 \times 2 \times 2 \times 2 \times 2 = 4096$$

and $100.12 = 1200$

we know that $4096 > 1200$

so, $2^{12} > 100.12$ ....(II)

Again, we take, $n = 13$

$$2^{13} = 2 \times 2 \times 2 \times 2 \times 2 \times 2 \times 2 \times 2 \times 2 \times 2 \times 2 \times 2 \times 2 = 8192$$

and $100.13 = 1300$

we know that $8192 > 1300$

so, $2^{13} > 100.13$ ....(III)

after observing condition (I), (II) and (III), we can say that 2^n>100n for n>10.

Also solved that

Let, formula is correct for $n = k$

$\therefore \quad 2^k \geq 100k$

or, $\quad 2^k.2 \geq 200k$

or, $\quad 2^{k+1} \geq 100k + 100k$

or, $\quad 2^{k+1} \geq 100k + 100$

or, $\quad 2^{k+1} \geq 100(k + 1)$

so, formula is correct for $n = k + 1$

Hence, by the mathematical induction, we have proved that. $\boxed{2^n \geq 100n}$ for $n \geq 10$.

(c) Given 13 coins, one of them heavier than the rest, how can you determine it in not more than 3 weighings? Draw the decision tree. [5]

Refer to Chap-1, Q-8

Q5(a). Explain the following terms: [8]

(i) Domain Name Service [DEC02,Q4(a,ii)]

Refer to June04,Q2(b)

(ii) Hypermedia

It is known as a combination of hypertext and multimedia. Present computer browser can also display multiple colors, geometric shapes and diagrams as well as still or moving pictures and can emit audio and reproduce the sound of human speech or music.

A hypermedia system can embed references to non-textual information as well as references to textual information in a document.

(iii) IP Address

IP address is an address used by every host and router on the Internet, which encodes its network number and host number. It is similar to that of an address of a human being to identify in the locality. The IP in TCP/IP is a mechanism for providing addresses for computers on the Internet. Internet addresses are of two kinds, which are :

(a) Person understandable which are expressed as words

(b) Machine understandable which are expressed as numbers also called IP address.

The combination is unique. Two machines are not having the same IP address. All IP addresses are 32 bits long and used in the source address and Destination Address fields of IP Packets. Network numbers are assigned by the NIC (Network Information Centre) to avoid conflicts.

(iv) Modem

Or called **Mod**ulator **Dem**odulator. It is a sort of communication device that converts binary electrical signals into acoustic signals for transmission over telephone lines and converts these acoustic signals back into binary at the receiving end. Conversion to acoustic form is known as modulation; conversion back to binary form is known as demodulation .

(b) What is a function? Explain different categories of functions in MS-EXCEL along with the syntax and an example for each. [7]

Refer to Chap-8, Q-2

Q6(a). Prove from lemma 2, the sum

$1+\frac{1}{2}+\frac{1}{3}+\frac{1}{4}+...+\frac{1}{n}$ **(Harmonic series) tends to infinity with n. [8]**

The sum: $1 + 1/2 + 1/3 + 1/3 + ...1/n$
tends to infinity with n. (This series of terms is called the Harmonic series).

Proof:
With four terms we find:

$$1 + 1/2 + 1/3 + 1/4 > 1 + 1/2 + 1/4 + 1/4 = 2$$

while with eight terms:

$$1 + 1/2 + 1/3 + 1/4 + 1/5 + 1/6 + 1/7 + 1/8 + 1/8 + 1/8 + 1/8 + 1/8 = 5/2.$$

With sixteen terms:

$$1 + 1/2 + 1/3 + ...+ 1/16 > 5/2 + 1/16 + ...1/16 = 5/2 + 1/2 = 3.$$

Thus, with a sufficiently large number of terms, the series can be made to exceed any preassigned number, however larger. In other words, the sum of the series approaches infinity, as the number of terms in it becomes infinite.

Euler's Proof **:**
Suppose that the number of primes is finite, say N. Let these primes be p_1, p_2, p_3....p_n. Then the product:

$$1/(1 - 1/p_1) \text{ x } 1/(1 - 1/p_2).....1/(1 - 1/p_n)$$

must also be finite.
By Lemma 1, this product is written as

$$\left(1+\frac{1}{p1}+\frac{1}{(p1)^2}+.........\frac{1}{(pn)^2}+.........\right)\left(1+\frac{1}{p2}+\left(\frac{1}{p2}\right)^2+.........\left(\frac{1}{p2}\right)^{1/n}+.........\right)$$

$$\left(1+\frac{1}{pN}+\frac{1}{(pN)^2}+.........\right)$$

By Lemma 2 the harmonic series has an infinite sum. Therefore the number of primes cannot be finite.

(b) Explain the concept of Minimum Spanning Circles and Jung's Theorem. [DEC03,Q6(b)] [7]

The minimum spanning circle is the smallest circle enclosing a set of points. It is valuable in the analysis of artificial boundaries such as legislative districts.

We can understand both concepts by taking the Example : Consider a finite set of *n* points in the plane; then the set of distances between any two points is also a finite set, which has a largest number, say *d*, called the *span* of the set of points. Clearly, if a set of points has span *d*, then it is possible to draw a circle of radius *d* that encloses all the points.

But it is possible to draw a smaller circle that still encloses the entire set: first locate a pair of points, *P* and *Q*, whose distance from each other is *d*. (If there are several such pairs, we may choose any one.) Construct two circles of radius *d* with centres at *P* and *Q* (Fig.).

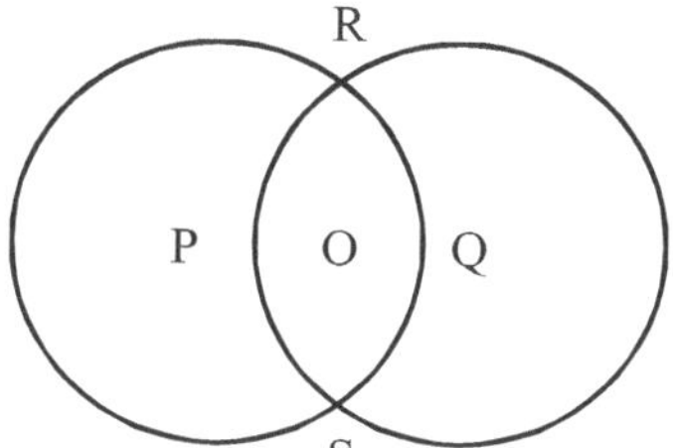

PQ = d, OP = d/2, PS = d, maximally

The circle centred at *P* passes through *Q*, while the circle centred at *Q* passes through *P*. These circles intersect at *R* and *S*. The entire set of *n* points lies within each circle. Therefore it must lie within their intersection, But the intersection itself is enclosed within die circle which has *RS* for its diameter. Since *PS* is maximally *d*, the radius of *this* spanning circle, by Pythagoras' Theorem, is d $3^{1/2}$ /2, (why?) a bound lower than the one we had started with. This bound lean be further improved, and this is **Jung's Theorem:** Every finite set of points of span *d* has a spanning circle no greater than d 3 $^{1/2}$/3, a still better bound. Though smaller spanning circles are possible for certain finite sets of points, there are some which require the spanning circle to be at least this large.

CS-612 : PC SOFTWARE SKILLS
JUNE-2004

Note: Question 1 is compulsory. Answer any three questions from the rest.

Q1(a). A boatsman must ferry across a river a wolf, a sheep and a bundle of fodder. His boat is too small to carry more than himself and one of the "passenger" at a time. He cannot leave the wolf alone with the sheep, or the sheep alone with the fodder. Explain how he can cross without any detriment to either sheep of fodder, using the graph method by representing the states. **10**

Let the status in which there are 'W' wolf, 'S' sheep and 'F' bundle of fodder be represented by symbol (W, S and F).

The status of eight possible sets is indicated in the below mentioned table :

	(1)	(2)	(3)	(4)	(5)	(6)	(7)	(8)
Left bank	(W,S,F)	(O,S,F)	(W,O,F)	(W,S,O)	(O,O,F)	(W,O,O)	(O,S,O)	(O,O,O)
Right bank	(O,O,O)	(W,O,O)	(O,S,O)	(O,O,F)	(W,S,O)	(O,S,F)	(W,O,F)	(W,S,F)

The way to cross the river without any detriment to either sheep or fodder is indicated below :

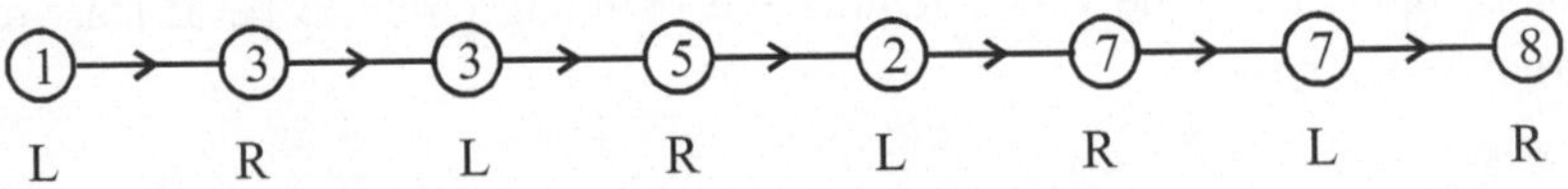

Where, L denotes left bank, R denotes right bank of the river and no under circle denotes the situation.

(b) What is Internet? Explain the protocol used in the working of Internet. Discuss two services available on Internet **10**

The Internet is a connection amongst the people, who are connected through computer cables by telephone lines, modems and satellite links, making communication possible with each other. It is also called network of networks. The Internet permits computer users to share computer equipment programs, messages and information available on sites. Information should be in the form of files of data stored in a computer. For communication two things are necessary. One is address of the destination to be communicated and a safe method of transferring data in the form of electronic signals. Internet is also a treasure of knowledge.

Protocol used in working of Internet : A key communication protocol used in the Internet is called, the Internet Protocol. The Internet uses a set of rules called TCP/IP, which governs the sending and receiving of data on the Internet. TCP stands for Transmission Control Protocol whereas IP stands for Internet Protocol. They are collectively known as TCP/IP. The TCP helps in sending large block of information (text data) by dividing the data into data packets. It also adds special information i.e. the packet position in the document, error correction code etc. The IP puts destination address information on such packets. IP software allows a computer to send and receive data. IP does not handle all the problems that can arise. A computer using the Internet also needs TCP software to provide reliable, error free communication whereas Routers help to transfer information from source computer to destination computer. On Internet it is not necessary that all packets follow the same path in transfer. Routers balance the load on various paths that exist on the network.
To make better utilization of Internet we use certain tools like Telnet, Gopher etc.. Telnet is a tool, utilized for logging on remote computers on the internet. Its specification is part of the TCP/IP documentation. The Telnet protocol specifies exactly how a remote login client and a remote login server interact. An information services allow an individual to conveniently obtain and display information that is stored on a remote computer. A browser can obtain textual information, recorded sounds or graphics images from a variety of sources on remote computers. One of the earliest services was known as Gopher. Gopher popularized a menu driven approach to information browsing.

There are several types of services provided by Internet. Some of them are :-

ftp : Short form of File Transfer Protocol. It is a protocol which transfers computer files from one place to another over internet. User invokes File Transfer Protocol, connects to a remote machine, list the contents of the main directory on that machine, list the contents of subdirectory and then obtains a copy of file.

E-mail on Internet : It is a popular way of communication of electronic matter. Through email on Internet we can be in direct touch to many of our friends and colleagues. We can send a single message to many recipients including graphics, video or voice.

(c) State two function of each of the following Internet tools: **6**

(i) Finger

This command allows display of the contents of the files that are associated with particular user identifier at a particular Internet Site or it contacts a server on a remote machine to obtain information about a specific user or all users on that machine. Usually, when someone invoke finger, they are the identifier of a user .

(ii) Multi-user Dungeons

MUD is the abbreviated form of Multi-user Dungeon. Allows private communication between two individuals. Both parties must be connected to Internet for a session. It allows a group of users to establish a game-playing session analogous to the way a group can establish a teleconference. MUD uses text, not graphics. When a user join a multi-user dungeons game, they explore a large labyrinth and possibly encounter other users.

(iii)Talk

It provides interaction between a pair of users. When two users agree to communicate, the talk service established a connection between their computer and divides their display screen in half. This tool has rules and regulations of information sharing. It is an approach for group learning.

(d) Explain the process of connecting of two remote machines, using Talent. Also explain two commonly used options on Telnet. **4**

Telnet is a program, which allows an internet host computer to become a terminal of another host on the internet. FTP opens a connection solely for transfer of files, however, Telnet allows us to become a user on a remote machine. We can run the computer programs at remote host, browse the database or perform any desired operation of the remote machine using this facility.

It provides direct access to various services on Internet. Some of these services are available on our host, but Telnet is especially useful when these services are not available on our host. For example, if we want to use graphical interfaces designed by other users, then Telnet allows us to access their hosts and use their new interfaces. Similarly, whenever someone creates a useful service on his host, Telnet allows us to access this valuable information resources. This tool is especially useful for accessing public services such as library card catalogues the databases available on the remote machine etc.

It is very simple to use, suppose we are working as a faculty member of XYZ University. We have a typical account FACULTY-1 on the UNIVERSITY computer and that is one of the hosts of the Internet. We are selected for Academic exchange scholarship to USA. We will get a user account in USA. However, all our colleagues know only us from UNIVERSITY account. Thus using Telnet we can always log on to our account in India for our papers etc. There are many databases available on the Internet. We can explore these databases using Telnet. There are many Internet services yet to be created. Every year better means of accessing the treasures of the Internet are appearing in which Telnet is the key for accessing. To run :

Step1 : Run telnet application.

It provides command prompt like :

login :_

Step 2 : Enter account of computer where you want to enter.

After entering right login name and another prompt is appeared.

Password : _

Step 3 : Enter password. After accepting password nothing appears on the screen. After successfully logging into a time sharing system, a user can enter command to invoke application program.

Two commonly used options on telnet are:

(i) **Close**, to close current connection.

(ii) **Open**, to connect to a site. This can be abbreviated to "o".

Q2(a). What is the significance of formulae in calculations? Give three basic properties of formulae 7

Formulae play a very significant role in calculations. It is an equation, which are widely used to perform simple mathematical operations like addition, subtraction, multiplication or division and also complex computations. They provide the power to analyze data in depth. Formulas can be entered by referring to the values of other worksheets of the workbook, or by referring to the values stored in other workbook. In the following example 50 has been added to the value in cell C2 and then multiplied with sum of the values in cells A3 and B3 :

Following are the basic properties of formula :

(1) A formula may consist of operators, cell references, range names, values and functions.

(2) A formula always start with an equal to (=) sign.
(3) When a formula is entered in the cell, after the Enter key is pressed, only the calculated result is displayed in the cell and not the formula.
(4) If we make a cell, containing formula, as an active cell, through it still shows the value, but in the formula bar, the formula is displayed.

Following are the sequence of steps to enter a formula and to edit it also :
The formula is entered as shown below.
1. In the cell D5, enter the formula as: =(40%)*C5
2. Copy this formula in cells D6 to D9.
3. In the cell E5, enter the formula as: =(20%)*C5
4. Copy this formula in cells E6 to E9.
5. In the cell F5, enter the formula as :=C5 + D5 + E5
6. Copy this formula in cells F6 to F9.
Formulas can be entered by referring to the values of other worksheets of the workbook, or by referring to the values stored in other workbook.

Example

	A	B	C	D	E	F
1						
2			MADE EASY WEB SOLUTIONS			
3						
4	NAME	AGE	BASIC	HRA	DA	GROSS
5	ANITA	23	1500			
6	VIJAY	24	1450			
7	SANJAY	25	1700			
8	RAJESH	23	1400			
9	PARVEEN	22	2000			

By referring to other worksheet cell =Sheet2! B3 + A2
(Sheet 2! B3 refers to the value stored in the cell B3 of Sheet 2 while user is working in Sheet1.)
By referring to the cell of other workbook = 100([Employee.xls] Sheet1!$D$2)
(In the formula given above, [Employee.xls] Sheeta!$D$2 refers to the cell D2 of Sheet1 of workbook Employee.xls.)

This also creates a link between worksheets and workbooks. Therefore, while making changes in these linked worksheets and workbooks one has to be careful as the change will affect the dependent and linked cells also.

Editing Formula :

The formulas can be edited in the similar way as you have been editing text or number entries.

- You can edit the formula by pressing F2 key, and make changes directly in the cell.
- Type the changes in the formula bar.
- Double-click on the cell containing the cell and make changes as the formula is displayed in the cell.

(b) What is the twelve-coin problem? Solve this problem. **8**

Solving of twelve coin problem is based on the decision trees. When alternative choices are made based on discrete answers – usually true or false to question and then further choices are made based on those answers, the graphical representation of the situation result in a special kind of a graph called a decision tree. Such graphs are known as tree because they look like inverted trees. Top level is known as root and the down levels are branches. Let us suppose that 12 coins are name by their number 1 to 12. This results in the tree below :

DECISION TREE

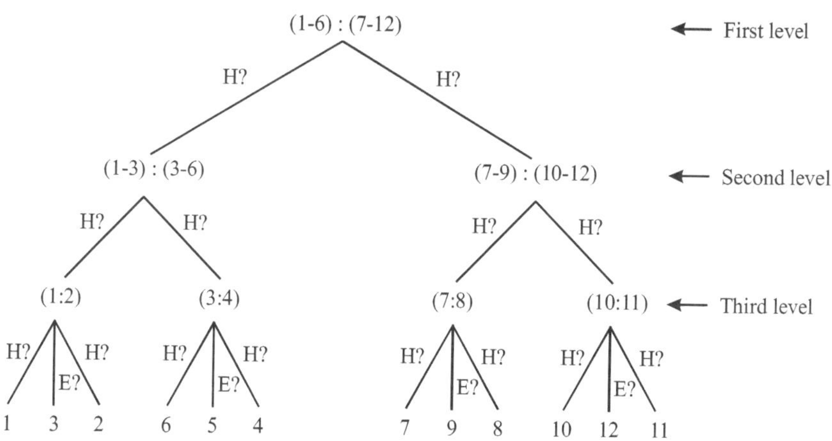

Where H is heavier and E is equal to.

For weighing :

1. First of all you create two group of 6 – 6 coins.
2. Weight both the groups and select the heavier one.
3. Further divide the selected group in two part of 3 – 3 coins.
4. Again weight both newly created groups and pick heavier one.

5. Now, you have obtained 3 coins, you pick 2 coins out of them.
6. Weight both coins comparatively, if both coins are equal, then third coin is heavier otherwise one of both.
In this counterfeit coin is obtained in three steps weighing.

Q3(a). What does 'function' mean in MS-EXCEL? How are functions used in solving problems? Briefly explain the use of any six function available in MS-EXCEL? 8

In MS-EXCEL, a function is a tool, which performs a predefined calculation or operation. Each function has a name and many arguments as the operands of the calculation. Excel has many in-built functions for specific categories of applications. Excel includes a collection of over 200 functions in several useful categories. For example, you can use the PMT (payment) function from the Financial category to calculate the periodic payment for a loan based on the interest rate charged, the number of payment desired, and the principal amount. Each function must be entered with a particular syntax, or structure, so that Excel can process the results correctly. For example, the PMT function has a function syntax that looks like PMT (rate,nper,pv,fv,type). The abbreviated words shown between the parentheses are called arguments of the function that are given values and return the result that is displayed in the same cell where the function was entered. The use of functions also shortens the formula. These functions are used for simple mathematical calculations of number data. For example, to use the PMT function to calculate the loan payment on a Rs.1,000 loan at 19 percent annual interest over 48 months, you could type the following formula :

= PMT(19%/12,48,1000)

Use of any six functions available in MS-EXCEL are :

1. DATABASE FUNCTION : Database functions are used for calculation and queries on the data entered in a database in a worksheet, DCOUNT function comes under it. It counts the numbers containing cell in the field or column of records in the database that match the conditions you mention.

Syntax: DCOUNT(database, field, criteria)
Here, database represents the cells that make up the list or database, field represents the column which is used in function and criteria represents the range of cells that contains the condition you specify. e.g. DCOUNT(A1:E10, 2, basic =

4000), it return the number of record of given criteria.

2. TEXT FUNCTION : These functions are used to manipulate the text data entered in the worksheet. UPPER is a text function. It takes argument as text and gives output in upper case.

Syntax: UPPER(text)
e.g. = UPPER("gullybaba"), it returns GULLYBABA

3. MATH & TRIGNOMETRIC FUNCTION : These functions are used to perform mathematical operation for numeric data. One of them is MOD function. This function calculates the modules of two values.
Syntax: MOD(number, divisor)
e.g. =MOD(50,6), it gives result 2.

4. LOOK UP & REFERENCE FUNCTION : These functions are used to enable you to retrieve specified data from the worksheet. One of them is COLUMN function. This function returns the column number of given reference.

Syntax: COLUMN(reference)
Here, reference is column number.
e.g. COLUMN(C10) it returns 3

5. FINANCIAL : It consists of functions related to finance like bank, account, sales etc.
RATE function

Syntax : RATE(nper, pmt, pv, fv, type, guess)

Nper is total number of payment
pmt is payment mode each period
pv is the present value of total amount that a series of future payments is worth now.
fv is the future value at the end of the last payment (optional)
type indicate payment is due or not (optional)
guess is your guess for what the rate may be (optional)

e.g. = RATE(36,-4000, 100000) is a cell, it displays result 2%

6. STATISTICAL FUNCTION : Excel supports more than 70 statistical function. One of them is COUNT function. It counts the number of non-blank numeric cells in list.

Syntax : COUNT(spos : epos)

Here

spos is starting position of the list

epos is ending position of the list.

e.g. =COUNT(B2:D10) is a range, it displays non-blank cells in the range specified.

(b) Explain the processes involved in the two different types of connections to Internet. Also mention two advantages of each type over the other. 7

Two different types of connections to Internet are Broadband Connection and Integrated Services Digital Network Dial-up connection.

Broadband connection : It is a high-speed Internet connection, which makes surfing the Web more enjoyable. It also easily accommodates the audio, video or complex graphics that are becoming common place on the Internet. It is a type of data transmission through which a single medium wire can carry several channels or communication paths at once. Therefore, the broadband cable connections are able to transmit both television signals and Internet data at the same time. Broadband telephone connections like DSL (Digital Subscriber Line) are able to transmit both voice and data over the same line at same time. For most average users, a broadband connection will mean accessing the Internet by either a cable modem provided by their local cable company or a DSL modem and DSL telephone line provided by their local telephone service provider. It is a high speed and trouble free Internet connection.

Advantages

(i) No telephone line is needed. Can provide very high speed sometimes needed to play 3D games etc.

(ii) Broadband connections always remain on. This means that when your computer is on, you will be automatically connected to the Internet without any dialing of telephone but in ISDN dial-up is must.

Integrated Services Digital Network – Dial-up connection : It is a high speed dial up connection and requires a special type of dedicated digital telephone line. This type of connection improves speed because the signals received are already in a digital format, but it is a costly affair. It is considered to install only when broadband connections are not available. For a while dial-up connection were the only way to access the Internet. Now, however, broadband connections are available in many parts or the country as telephone and cable companies install new lines to accommodate Internet connection. It is also a high speed connection.

Advantages

(i) Less expensive than broadband and provides high speed.

(ii) No extra modem is to be installed like in broadband, the tradition modem works well.

Q4(a). Given a set A consisting of 10 numbers between 1 and 100, prove that there exist two distinct subsets of A whose elements sum to the same number. **8**

A = { 1, 2, 3, 4, 5, 6, 7, 8, 10, 12 }

Now, A_1 and A_2 are two subset of A whose elements are :

A_1 = { 1, 4, 5, 7, 12 }

A_2 = { 2, 3, 6, 8, 10 }

Again

Sum of element of A_1 = 29

Sum of element of A_2 = 29

So, A_1 and A_2 are the subset of A and its elements sum are the same numbers.

(b) Write the steps for creating a scenario in MS-EXCEL. **2**

For creating a scenario in MS-Excel, following steps are taken:

1. Choose Scenarios from the Tools menu. On clicking, the Scenario Manager dialog box appears.

2. For creating your first scenario, click the Add button. On clicking, the Add Scenario dialog box appears.

3. Type Best Case in the Scenario Name text box, and press the Tab key.

4. In the Changing Cell text box, specify the variable cells that you want to modify in your scenario. You can type cell names, highlight a cell range, or hold down the Ctrl Key and click individual cells to add them to the text box. If you hold down the Ctrl Key, Excel automatically places commas between the cells that you click.

5. Click OK to add your scenario to the Scenario Manager. On clicking, Scenario Values dialog box appears, asking you for your model's variables. The default values are the numbers that were already in the cells.

6. Click Add to create a second scenario. Type Worst Case, and then click OK to display the Scenario Values dialog box.

7. Type values in the variable cells, and then click OK. (These values represent our guess at the worst case). The Scenario Manager dialog box appears and lists the Best Case and Worst Case scenarios. Now you are ready to view the results of your forecasting models.

8. Click Close to close the Scenario Manager dialog box.

(c) What is a search engine? List five search engines. Example the process of using any search engine
5

A large amount of information is available on Webs. It is very difficult to find the required information easily. For the convenience of the users to find the required information at once, several researchers have written programs to index the Web in various ways. The programs used to search the Web is called the search engine. Search engines are basically the programs that accept a string as input and will output entire URL's (Universal Resource Locators) whose pages contained the related information to string. There are a number of search engines, a few of them are:

01.	Google	:	www.google.com
02.	Infoseek	:	www.infoseek.com
03.	Yahoo	:	www.yahoo.com
04.	Lycos	:	www.lycos.com
05.	Excite	:	www.excite.com

A variety of searches can be performed through two of Microsoft's pages:
(i) Best of the Web : Click the Best of the Web button on the Links Toolbar, or choose that command from the Favourites-Links menu.
(ii) Search the Web : Choose Go – Search the Web.

The general way to search the Web is by entering keywords : Show me all pages that contain the words "discoveries of India". Note : if the search string/phrase is placed within inverted comma then the webpages containing that complete phrase will be displayed, only. Within a second, you will be presented with a list of links to pages that contain these words. At many sites we can search the Web or newsgroups by keywords and following process is used:
1. Select the name of search site we want in our browser window or open the home page for that site.
2. Enter the keywords you are searching in a data entry field.
3. Click the Go or Search button or press enter.
4. Wait a second or two the search site scans through its database and displays the required information. For most search sites, each result includes a title for the page (based on the page's HTML title), which is actually a link right to that page and a short description of the page.
5. Click one of the result links to open that page.

Q5(a). Explain the steps involved in the process of IP addressing **5**

Each computer in a TCP/IP network has a unique IP address to identify a system's location on the network. IP address is just like a street number used to identify a house in a city block. The IP address must be globally unique and have a uniform format. Each network ID (also known as a network address) identifies the systems that are located on the same physical network bounded by IP routers. All systems on the same physical network must have the same network ID. The network ID must be unique to the internet. The host ID (also known as a host address) identifies a work station server, router or TCP/IP host within a network. The address for each host must be unique to the network ID. Network ID refers to any IP network ID, whether it is a class-based, a subnet or a supernet. The subnet mask determines the network where the computer is located. This is especially important in larger networks. Large networks are frequently divided into several subnets. The direct cable connection also forms a network of its own.

An IP address consists of 32 bits but it is a common practice to segment the 32 bits of an IP address into four 8-bit fields called octets. Each octet is converted to a decimal number (the base 10 numbering system) in the range 0-255 and separated by a dot. This format is called dotted decimal notation. A small LAN can be configured with private IP address. Whenever you approach Internet Service Provider (ISP), he gives you your Internet IP address when you dial in.

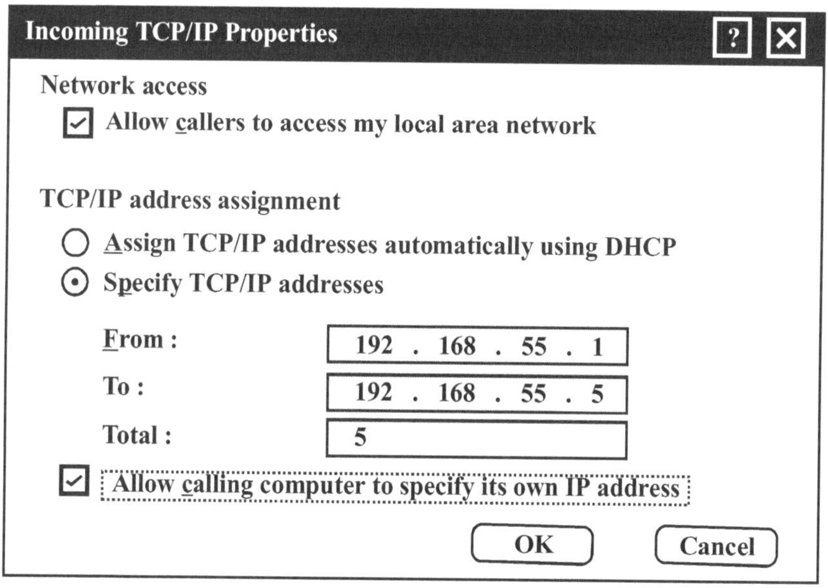

From 169.254.0.1 to 169.254.255.254 is the range of IP addresses for Auto-

matic Private IP Addressing, which enables your computer to have a valid TCP/IP configuration even if it does not have a fixed IP address or in larger networks, if a DHCP server cannot be found. The standard subnet mask for this address range is 255.255.0.0. During a direct cable connection it is replaced by subnet mask 255.255.255.255 because the respective remote party is the only computer that must be reached.

The address pool also allows users to use a fixed address for the guest computer. To use a fixed address, following steps are required to be taken :

1. When you configure the pool, click to select the Allow calling computer to specify its own IP address check box.

2. Configure a fixed IP address on the guest computer, right-click the connection and then click Properties.

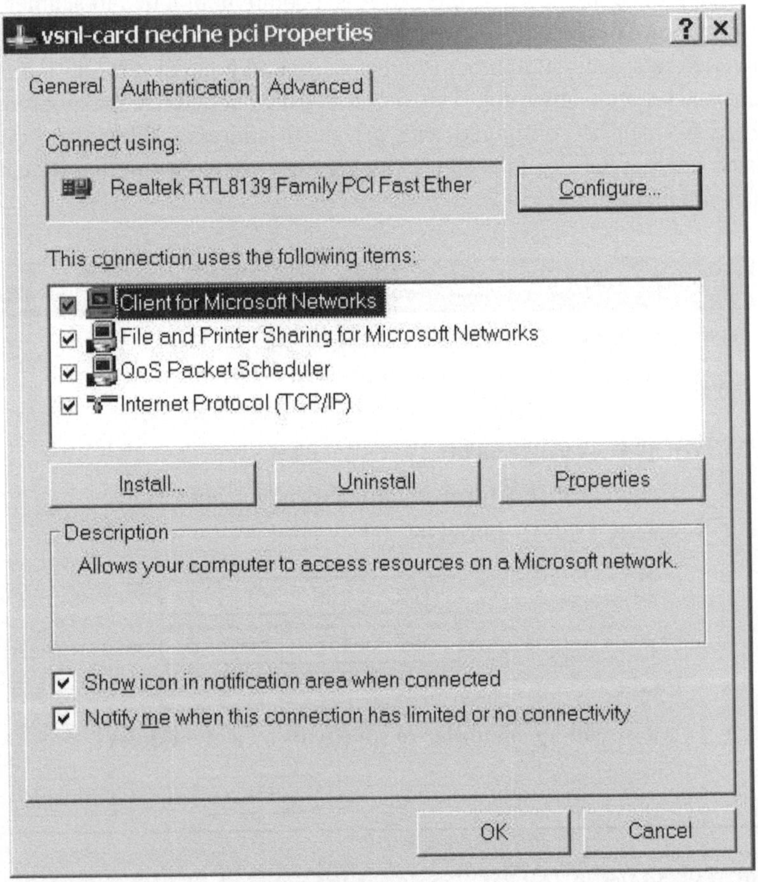

3. Click the Networking tab, click Internet Protocol(TCP/IP), and then click Properties.
Click OK.

(b) What is "Downloading" ? Explain the procedure of downloading information from the Internet. **5**

Downloading is the process of copying a file like software, movies, songs, games etc. from websites on Internet to own computer's hard disk. In another words, it is just like copying a file from a floppy disk to your computer's hard drive.

Following are the steps to be taken for downloading purposes :

Downloading file or software from a website (here, we will download JAVA DEVELOPMENT KIT from one of the sites of SUN MICROSYSTEMS using Internet Explorer) It is illustrated with the following steps and figures.

Step 1: Enter the string "download jdk" or "java development kit download" using one of the search engines and start search. Here, we are taking Google as our search engine.

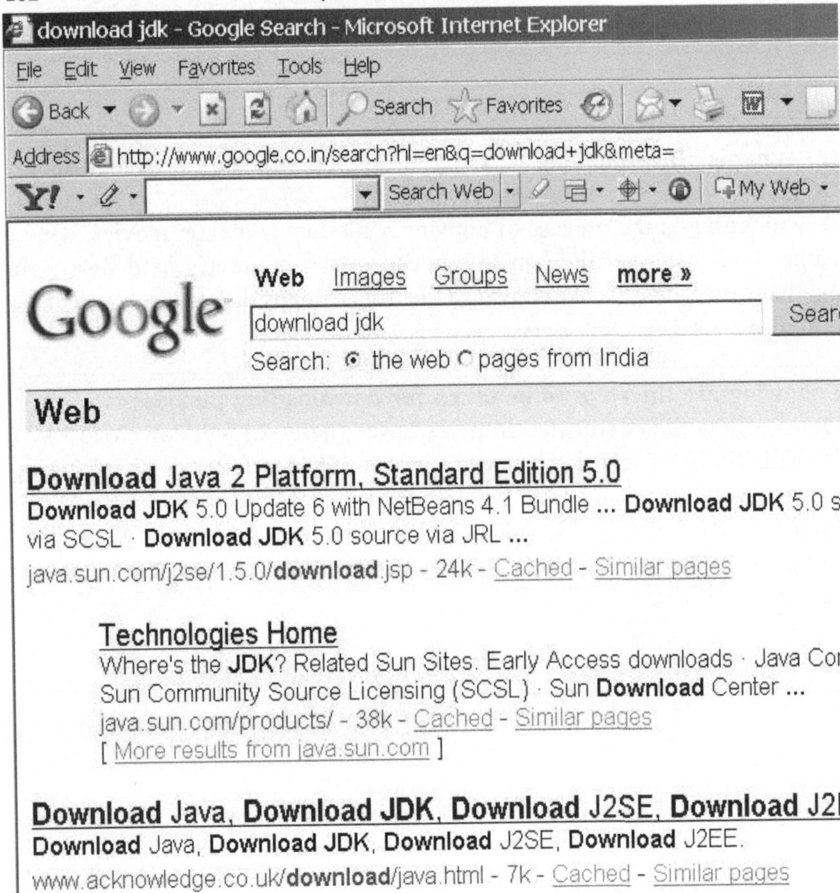

Step 2: Now, the search engine listed the sites related to the downloading of the Java Development Kit.

Step 3: Let us choose the link of Download Java 2 Platform Standard Edition 5.0. Now, the browser displays the webpage of Sun Microsystems(having url java.sun.com).

Step 4: Here, two versions are provided for us to download. Let us click on JDK for Windows 95/NT. Then, it prompts for the filename with which the software has to be stored. Then, let us enter the filename as "java" and click on save.

Step 5: Now, the process of downloading starts and one dialog box is displayed. From the information given on the dialog box, we learn that it takes nearly nine and half hours more to complete the process of downloading JDK and it has already downloaded 16k of 79MB software. In this way, you can download any software from any site with the help of any search engine. Of course, there are other ways to download. But, this is the most preferred way. One more information about downloading simple utilities, softwares, shareware, freeware and software with trial versions; we can visit to www.download.com, and follow the same steps.

(c) Find the smallest number n which has the following properties:
(i) Its decimal representation ha s 6 as the last digit.
(ii) If the last digit 6 is erased and protocol in format of the remaining digits, the resulting number is four times as great as the original number n. **5**

Let number is n, digit 6 of n is preceded by x

$\therefore$ $n = 10x + 6$ ....(i)

We have given that

$$6 \times 10^y + x = 4(10x + 6)$$

or $6 \times 10^y + x = 40x + 24$

or $36x = 6 \times 10^y - 24$

$$\therefore \quad x = \frac{6 \times 10^y - 24}{39}$$

Since the number is smallest. So, we put the value of y from 0 to above and check overall reminder, till reminder will not 0.

If $y = 2$

$\therefore$ $x = \dfrac{6 \times 10^2 - 24}{39}$ reminder no equal to 0.

If $y = 3$

$\therefore$ $x = \dfrac{6 \times 10^3 - 24}{39}$ reminder not equal to 0.

If $y = 4$

$\therefore$ $x = \dfrac{6 \times 10^4 - 24}{39}$ reminder not equal to 0.

If $y = 5$

$\therefore$ $x = \dfrac{6 \times 10^5 - 24}{39}$ reminder is 0.

$= 15384$

Putting the value of x in equation (1)

$n = 10 \times 15384 + 6$

$\therefore$ $n = 153846$

Q6(a). Explain what a template is. Give the sequence of steps involved in creating a template in EXCEL. Write two advantages of it. 7

Templates are the special tools provided by MS-Excel along with Macros to automate regular tasks. They are reusable models that standardize the look of the worksheet. They can be used to develop periodic reports. Templates are also known as special workbooks because one can use their pattern to create other workbooks of the same type. Thus, one can create a Production Report workbook, save it as a template, and then create weekly production reports based on that template. Also sheets from the templates can be inserted into new workbooks. In addition to creating new workbooks based on templates, one can insert sheets from templates into the workbooks. Templates can accommodate:

1. Text and graphics, such as a company name and logo.
2. Formatting and page layout, such as styles and custom headers and footers.
3. Formulas and macros

When a template is opened, Microsoft Excel creates a copy of the template to work with. This leaves the original template intact for the next time use. One can create special templates which are called auto-templates, in the startup or alternate startup directory. One can then use auto-templates as the basis for all new workbooks and all new sheets inserted into workbooks. Auto-templates are just templates saved with a specific name, in a specific location.

To create the template following steps are taken :

1. Create a workbook with all the styles, formatting, text and desired formulas. One can also open an existing workbook that one wants to save as template.
2. Choose File à Save as ….. command
3. In the File Name box, type the name for the template
4. Select the directory and drive where the template is to be saved
5. In the Save File as Type box, select Template. MS-Excel adds the extension .XLT to the filename.
6. Click on OK button.

Opening a Template : One can open the template to create the worksheet based on it by following the below mentioned steps :

01. File, New …. Command is chosen.

02. The template on which one wants to base a new workbook is selected. MS-Excel creates a copy of the template for use and gives it a temporary name that can be changed while saving the workbook.

Advantages :

(i) if we have to create same form for different person, then we need not to create form's format again and again.

(ii) Another advantage is template provides uniform look and time saver utility.

(b) Prove that for any 3 consecutive integers, the cube of the largest cannot be the sum of the cubes of the other two.

8

Let us suppose that three consecutive integers are n, n+1, n+2

Now according to the question we have to prove that : $(n+2)^3 = n^3 + (n+1)^3$

We assume that $(n + 2)^3 = n^3 + (n + 1)^3$

=> $n^3 + 6n^2 + 8n + 8 = n^3 + n^3 + 2n^2 + 2n + 1$

=> $n^3 + 4n^2 - 6n - 7$

=> $n(n^2 - 4n - 6) - 7$

Equation is not true for any integer. Therefore, the cube of the largest number among any 3 consecutive integers cannot be the sum of cubes of the other two.

CS-612 : PC SOFTWARE SKILLS
DEC-2004

Note: Question 1 is compulsory. Answer any three question from the rest.

Q1(a). What is a Search Engine? List four different Search engines.
Refer to Dec05,Q3(a)

(b) What is a gopher? Compare it with WWW.
Surfing the Internet is just like channel surfing on your cable television. You have very little idea what is on or even what you want to see. You just flip through channels seeing what's on, and move to the next when you lose interest in what you are watching. Gopher and World Wide Web make surfing a simple and enjoyable pastime. Beware it is easy to lose track of time while exploring the Internet!
Gopher is a system that pre-dates the World Wide Web for organizing and displaying files on Internet servers. A Gopher server presents its contents as a hierarchically structured list of files. With the ascendance of the Web, many gopher databases were converted to Web sites which can be more easily accessed via Web search engines. Gopher was developed at the University of Minnesota and named after the school's mascot. Two systems, Veronica and Jughead, let you search global indices of resources stored in Gopher systems.

Comparison between Gopher and WWW :
Some individuals and groups have taken up task of creating special subject-specific listings and archives. These are available through both Gopher and World Wide Web. These listings are just like libraries that specialise in material on one subject.
While both of these information presentation systems are client-server based, they differ in terms of their model of data. In gopher, data is either a menu, a document, an index or a telnet connection. In WWW, everything is a (possibly) hypertext document which may be searchable. In practice, this means that WWW can represent the gopher (a menu is a list of links, a gopher document is a hypertext document without links, searches are the same, telnet sessions are the same) and WAIS (a WAIS index is a searchable page, returning a document with no links) data models as well as providing extra functionality.
World Wide Web usage grew far beyond Gopher usage in the last few months, according to the statistics-keepers of the Internet backbone. (Of course, World

Wide Web browsers can also access Gopher servers, which inflates the numbers for the latter.) WWW has long since reached critical mass, with new commercial and noncommercial sites appearing daily.

(c) Prove that the sum of the cubes of the first n natural numbers is $\left(\frac{1}{2}n(n+1)\right)^2$.

The sum S_n of the first n cubes obeys the formula :

$S_n = \left[\frac{1}{2}n(n+1)\right]$ **power 2**

We prove this formula by the method of induction as follows. The formula is certainly true for n=1 called the base case, since

$$1^3 = \left[\frac{1}{2}(1+1)\right]^2$$

We now establish the inductive case, namely that if the formula is true for n=k, then it is true also for n = k+1;

Assume that for some fixed k,

$S_k = (1/2k\,(k+1)^2$

$S_{k+1} = [1/2(k+1)(k+1+1)2]^2 = 1/2k(k+1)^2+(k+1)^3$

$= (k+1)^2\,(k+1+(1/2k))^2$

$= (k+1)^2(1/2(k+2))^2$

$= (1/2(k+1)(k+2))^2$

Thus, if the formula is true for some k then it is true for k+1. In particular, if the formula is true for k=1, it is necessarily true for k=2. But we know by direct testing that the formula does hold for k=2. Therefore it holds for k=3. Therefore for k=4. And similarly for any k. This is the method of induction.

(d) Prove that the product of four consecutive natural numbers cannot be the square of an integer.

Examine the product of the consecutive numbers.

$1 \times 2 \times 3 \times 4 = 24$

$2 \times 3 \times 4 \times 5 = 120$

$3 \times 4 \times 5 \times 6 = 360$ and so on.

In each case we find that the product is one less than a perfect square. Thus 24 is 5^2-1, 120 is 11^2-1, 360 and so on.

Now consider the product of four consecutive integers.

$n(n + 1)\,(n + 2)\,(n + 3)$

where n is arbitrary. We will prove the result after rewriting this product in the form f(n)

1. Where f(n) is a perfect square expression on n, we first note that the term n (n + 2) in the product looks "almost" like a perfect square.

$n(n+2) = n^2 + 2n$
$= n^2 + 2n + 1 - 1$
$(n+1)^2 - 1$
$(n+1)(n+3) = n^2 + 4n + 3$
$= n^2 + 4n + 4 - 1$
$= (n+2)^2 - 1$

$\therefore$ $n(n+1)(n+2)(n+3) = [(n+1)^2 - 1]$, which is an expression not like that we are looking for. Lets therefore experiment with a different order of expansion:

$[n(n+3)][(n+1)(n+2)] = (n^2 + 3n + 2)$
$= (n^2 + 3n)^2 + 2(n^2 + 3n)$
$[n(n+3)][(n+1)(n+2)] = (n^2 + 3n) + (n^2 + 3n) + 1 - 1$
$= (n^2 + 3n + 1)^2 - 1$

(e) In Excel, what is the significance of formulae in calculations ? Give the basic properties of formulae. Write a step-by-step procedure to enter a formula and perform calculations, with the help of an example.

Refer to Chap-8, Q-1

Q2(a). What is a function? Give two examples of arithmetic and logical category of functions. Also explain what is the function Wizard in Excel.

Refer to Chap-8, Q-2

(b) Prove that for any positive x < 1, the series 1 + x + x^2 + x^3 + ...+xn converges to 1/(1-x) as n tends to infinity.

Let $S = 1+x+x^2+x^3+.....+x^n$ (i)

Then $xS = x+x^2+x^3+.......+x^{n-1}$ (ii)

From (i) - (ii)

$S - xS = (1+x+x^2+x^3.......+x^n) - (1+x+x^2+x^3.......+x^{n-1})$

$S(1-x) = 1-x^{n+1}$

And $S = \dfrac{1-x^{n+1}}{1-x}$

$= \dfrac{1}{1-x} - \dfrac{x^{n+1}}{1-x}$

Now, as $n \rightarrow \infty$, $x^{n+1} \rightarrow 0$, hence, the second term of S tends to zero as

$n \rightarrow \infty$, hence S converges to $\frac{1}{1-x}$ as $n \rightarrow \infty$

i.e. $1+x+x^2+x^3+....+x^n$ converges to $\frac{1}{1-x}$ as n tends to infinity.

Q3(a). What are the uses of charts in excel? Mention different types of charts. Explain any two of them in the context of their use.

Refer to Dec05,Q4(c)

(b) Explain the concept of Minimum spanning circles with the help of a suitable example.

The minimum spanning circle is the smallest circle enclosing a set of points. It is valuable in the analysis of artificial boundaries such as legislative districts.

Example : Consider a finite set of *n* points in the plane; then the set of distances between any two points is also a finite set, which has a largest number, say *d*, called the *span* of the set of points. Clearly, if a set of points has span *d*, then it is possible to draw a circle of radius *d* that encloses all the points.

But it is possible to draw a smaller circle that still encloses the entire set: first locate a pair of points, *P* and *Q*, whose distance from each other is *d*. (If there are several such pairs, we may choose any one.) Construct two circles of radius *d* with centres at *P* and *Q* (Fig.).

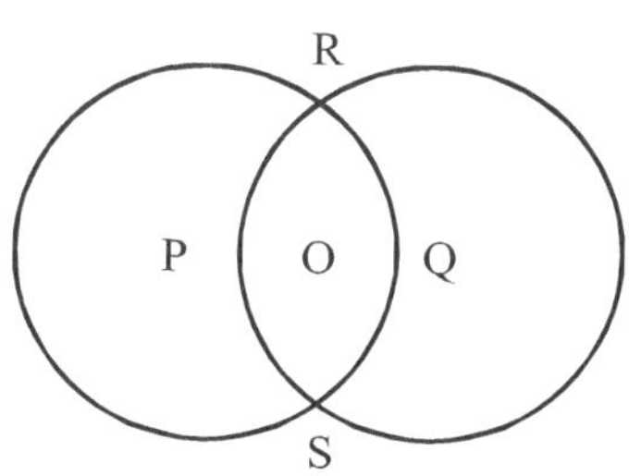

PQ = d, OP = d/2, PS = d, maximally

The circle centred at *P* passes through *Q*, while the circle centred at *Q* passes through *P*. These circles intersect at *R* and *S*. The entire set of *n* points lies within each circle. Therefore it must lie within their intersection, But the intersection itself is enclosed within die circle which has *RS* for its diameter. Since *PS* is maximally *d*, the radius of *this* spanning circle, by Pythagoras' Theorem, is d $3^{1/2}$ /2, (why?) a bound lower than the one we had started with. This bound lean be further improved, and this is *Jung's Theorem:* Every finite set of points of span *d* has a spanning circle no greater than d 3 $^{1/2}$ /3, a still better bound. Though smaller spanning circles are possible for certain finite sets of points, there are some which require the spanning circle to be at least this large.

Q4(a). Explain two ways of connecting to Internet.

Refer to Chap-12, Q-7

(b) What is Scenario Manager? Write step-by-step procedure to create a, display and edit the scenario.

Scenario Manager : In Microsoft Excel, you can create and save sets of input values that produce different results as scenarios. A scenario is a group of input vales called changing cell saved with a name you provide. Each set of changing cells represents a set of what-if assumptions that you can apply to a workbook model to see the effects on other parts of the model. You can define up to 32 changing cells per scenario.

Following are the steps for Creating a Scenario :

Let's take an example of a condition where you are planning to buy a new vehicle. You have two choices for vehicle - one is worth Rs. 4,50,000 vehicle or Rs. 5,00,000 vehicle, with either 3 yrs, loan or 5 yrs, loan. For this,

1. First enter the given data in the blank worksheet.
2. In cell D3, enter the formula **=A3*0.8.**
3. In cell A7, enter the formula **=PMT(B3, C3*12, A3).**
4. Choose **Tools→Scenarios....**command.
5. Click on the **Add** button. **Add Scenario** box appears.
6. In the **Scenario Name** box, type the name of the scenario as **45k & 3Yrs.**
7. Select the cells or type the cell references in the **Changing Cells** box as A3 and C3.
8. If you want, edit the text in the **Comment** box.
9. If you want, select **Protection** option.
10. Click on **OK** button. **Scenarios Values** dialog box appears.
11. Enter the value for each changing cell as given in Figure.
12. Click on **OK** button.
13. To add the scenario to the list and then create additional scenarios, choose the

Add button. This returns you to the Add Scenario dialog box. Type 45k & 5 Yrs, as the scenario name.

Following are the steps involved in displaying a Scenario Manager :

1. Choose **Tools->Scenarios**... command.

2. In the **Scenario Manager** dialog box, select the scenario that you want to display.

3. Choose the **Show** button. The changing cell values for the selected scenario appear in the changing cells on the worksheet. The worksheet is recalculated to reflect the new values.

4. Repeat steps 2 and 3 to display other scenarios.

5. Choose the **Close** button.

Following are the steps involved in editing a Scenario Manager :

The need may arise to modify the scenarios that have been created. The changes could be in the name given to the scenario, the cell references or the values of the changing cells. To make modifications in the scenarios, follow the given steps :

1. Choose **Tools->Scenarios...** command.

2. In the **Scenario Manager** dialog box, select the scenario you want to edit.

3. Click on the **Edit** button. The **Edit Scenario** dialog box appears.

4. In the **Scenario Name** box, type the new name, if you want.

5. Edit the **Changing cell** references, if you want.

6. Edit text in the **Comment** box, if you want.

7. Click on the OK button. The **Scenario Values** dialog box appears. Make the required changes.

8. To save the changes made to your scenario, choose the **OK** button.

(c) What is a database ? What a step-by-step procedure to create a database in MS-EXCEL using Data Form Command.

Refer to Chap-10, Q-5

Q5(a). What are the different components of E-mail ? Example any three components.

The main components of E-mail are addressing, composing, sending and reading. The key to successful E-mail exchange is mastery of these components. Here, we are taking example of Pine (a software which provide complete Email management), to explain these components. Note : the way Pine manages the Email or components of Email is almost same in all Email Management softwares, so learning anyone of them will make you aware with almost all the softwares available.

Compose a Message : When you select C Compose Message**, you'll see:**
To :

Cc :
Attachment:
Subject:

You can move from one line to another by using the TAB key or the arrow keys. Note: while you can TAB down the lines, you can't TAB back up. To go to a previous line, you'll have to use the up-arrow key.

The first line (**To:**) is the addressee (such as dinesh@gullybaba.com or gph@degreewala.com). Use a comma to separate multiple addresses.

The second line (**Cc:**) is the address of the person that you'd like to receive a copy of your message.

The third line (**Attachment:**) is the file (if any) that you'd like to accompany the message.

This file may be of any type (binary, text, etc.), but if it is not a text file, things get a little complicated (this is where MIME comes in. The **^J** key combination brings up a message on the dialog line: **File to attach:** Here you can type in the name of the file you want to attach or type a **^T** to see a list of files in your home directory. If the file you want to attach isn't there, you can type **G** (not ^G) to change to the directory where the file you want to attach is located.

The fourth line (Subject :) is where you'll type a short description of the message you're sending.

After you've filled out the Header Information (above), you can start typing your message. The lines will wrap automatically (you don't have to put a <return> at the end of each line.) You can use the arrow keys to position your cursor and make corrections. Pine includes a spelling checker (**^T**).

Send a Message : When you're finished writing and editing your message, you type ^X to Send it. A message on the dialog line asks: Send message?[y]: You type a y and off it goes. After the message is sent, you are returned to the Main Menu. If you've made a mistake, a ^C will cancel a composed message, but nothing can cancel a sent message. Once you've entered ^X, your message is on its way.

Read Messages : The I Folder Index is the Main Menu choice that allows you to read incoming E-mail messages. When you have new mail, Pine's Main Menu will notify you in two places.

The first is the **Status Line**, the top reversed line (white type on black background), at the right corner. You should see **Folder : INBOX n Messages.** The **n** is the number of messages in your **INBOX**.

The second notification is right under the copyright line, also in reversed type, and enclosed in brackets [ ]. It should read **[Folder "INBOX" opened with n messages]**.

Pine lets you access this mail through the "INBOX" folder.
When you select the **I Folder Index - View messages in current folder** from the Main Menu of Pine, you will get a list of all the messages (if any) waiting for you to read. You can read them by highlighting the message (using arrow keys) and pressing <return>. The highlighted message will appear on your screen.

Disposing of Read Messages : If you read the first message but not the second in your INBOX and then go back to the Main Menu and QUIT Pine, you get a series of questions on the Message Line at the bottom of the Pine screen. The first says Really quit pine? Y [yes] N No to quit, type y. The first dialog line message says: Save the 1 read message in "readmail"? Y [yes] N No: If you type a Y here, Pine will save your message in a special read-mail folder where you can retrieve the message later.

(b) What is the process of downloading ? How would you download a file or s/w from a web-site Explain with an example.
Downloading is the process of copying software from a remote server to your machine's secondary memory.

Downloading file or software from a website (here, we will download JAVA DEVELOPMENT KIT from one of the sites of SUN MICROSYSTEMS using Internet Explorer) It is illustrated with the following steps and figures.

Step 1: Enter the string "download jdk" or "java development kit download" using one of the search engines and start search. Here, we are taking Google as our search engine.

Step 2: Now, the search engine listed the sites related to the downloading of the Java Development Kit.

Step 3: Let us choose the link of Download Java 2 Platform Standard Edition 5.0. Now, the browser displays the webpage of Sun Microsystems(having url java.sun.com).

Step 4: Here, two versions are provided for us to download. Let us click on JDK for Windows 95/NT. Then, it prompts for the filename with which the software has to be stored. Then, let us enter the filename as "java" and click on save.

Step 5: Now, the process of downloading starts and one dialog box is displayed.

From the information given on the dialog box, we learn that it takes nearly nine and half hours more to complete the process of downloading JDK and it has already downloaded 16k of 79MB software. In this way, you can download any software from any site with the help of any search engine. Of course, there are other ways to download. But, this is the most preferred way. One more information about downloading simple utilities, softwares, shareware, freeware and software with trial versions; we can visit to www.download.com, and follow the same steps.

Q6(a). Explain the process of transferring the files with FTP. What is the purpose of compressing a file before uploading? Also, list four commonly used programs (s/w) to compress a file.

Internet gives you access to all kinds of information. However, files and data are scattered all over the Internet in large and small archives. Some of these may contain text, some may contain pictures or sounds, or computer programs. A file may contain some important information for you, however it may be on a distant computer. If you want to have your own copy of the file then?

There exist a standard tool on Internet for transferring copies of files. This program is called ***ftp***, that is, *file transfer protocol*. Ftp can be used to copy any file from one Internet host to other. However, for such transfer you need an account on a remote host. The ftp program will make a connection with the remote host, which will allow you to browse the directories and specify files at the remote host for transfer. However, you cannot look at the contents of these remote files by using ftp. You have to transfer the copy and then look at it, once it is on your own account.

What will happen if you do not have an account on a remote Internet host? For such cases ftp recognises a special account name called anonymous. Thus by using anonymous ftp you can access public archives on the Internet and copy a file from there.

The basic **purpose of compressing file** before uploading is that these files require less storage space, and less time to transmit from site to site on Internet. Some of the common **programs used for file compression** are Winzip, Stuffit, PKZip, or Compactor are used to compress a file before using ftp.

(b) Explain the way to restrict the access of a workbook from other users.

Restrict the access of the Workbook : Your data can be very confidential which has to be saved from unauthorised people.

Click on Options... button from the **File -> Save As** dialogue box.

You can restrict the access of that workbook from other users in 3 different ways:

Protection Password

1. Type the password which will be required to open the workbook. The password can be upto 15 characters long, can include alphabets (upper case or lower case), numbers and special characters. It is case sensitive also.
2. You will be asked to re-enter the same password.
3. Click on OK.

Write Reservation Password

This password will be required when you make changes in the existing workbook and then try to save that workbook. This prevents the unauthorised users to make any modifications in the workbook. The rules to give the password are same as Protection Password.

Read-only Recommended

If this option is checked, the following dialogue box will be displayed every time you try to open the workbook

(c) Give the syntax for the following built-in functions with the help of an example of each:

(i) ROUND

(ii) FIND

Refer to Chap-8, Q-2

CS-612 : PC SOFTWARE SKILLS
JUNE-2005

Note: Question 1 is compulsory. Answer any three question from the rest.

Q1(a). What are the two ways to create a database in MS Excel? Explain the step involved in any one of these ways. 5

There are various kinds of data in any company e.g. all the details of the employees, sales details, client data, products data. The purpose of storing and maintaining data is to retrieve it later for day-to-day transactions and management planning.

The data, which is collected from the sources is the raw data. Various operations can be carried out on the data, like sorting, searching and totalling. This is processed and manipulated now and termed as Information. The system which helps us to perform all these activities on the data is termed as DBMS. Database is an organized collection of information. It is also referred to as a list or a table.

There are two kinds of databases :

Internal Database - Databases created in the worksheet.

External Database - Database which is created through other DBMS or RDBMS packages like MS-ACCESS, FOXPRO, dBASE, SQL Server, ORACLE.

In MS-Excel, database can be created in two simple ways:

1. Enter the data in the form of table in the worksheet.

2. Use **Data Form** command.

To create database using Data Form command, the steps are:

1. Enter the given details:

In Cell	*Enter*
A1	AGE
B1	NAME
C1	SEX
D1	DEPARTMENT

2. Choose **Data, Form** command while keeping one of the field name active.
3. The dialog box is displayed, warning you for taking the row of the selected cell as the header row of the database. Click on OK.
4. Another dialog box is displayed, which shows one record at a time. Fill-in the appropriate details in the box against each field name.

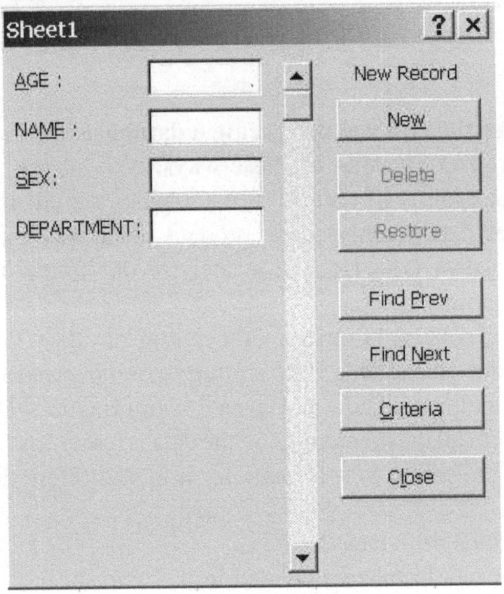

5. Click on **New**. This will add the entered record in the database.
6. To finish the entry of records, click on **Close.**

(b) What is a Search Engine? How is it useful? Mention any four popular search engines and four general characteristics of a search engine. 7

Search Engine : A program that searches documents for specified keywords and returns a list of the documents where the keywords were found. Although search engine is really a general class of programs, the term is often used to specifically describe systems like Alta Vista and Excite that enable users to search for documents on the World Wide Web and USENET newsgroups.

Typically, a search engine works by sending out a spider to fetch as many documents as possible. Another program, called an indexer, then reads these documents and creates an index based on the words contained in each document. Each search engine uses a proprietary algorithm to create its indices such that, ideally, only meaningful results are returned for each query.

Search engine is **useful** to search for content meeting specific criteria (typically those containing a given word or phrase) and retrieves a list of references that match those criteria. OR **search engine is useful when :**

(i) you are searching for a specific web site

(ii) your subject is very narrow or obscure

(iii) the information you are searching for is best found inside millions of full text documents

(iv) you wish to find a very large amount of documents

(v) you are just curious about something

Now follows the **list of famous search engines** : Google,Lycos, Excite, Hotbot, Infoseek, Alta Vista, The Scout, Infoseek.

Characteristics of search engines:

(i) huge databases and a large amount of material

(ii) good functionality, if the search is well presented in a few words

(iii) upheld by 'robots': the results are often irrelevant to your search

(iv) the databases are updated at a variable rate

(v) emphasise quantity over quality

(c) Explain the concept of Minimum Spanning Circles and find the radius of the Spanning Circle of the vertices of an equilateral triangle of side d. **5**

The minimum spanning circle is the smallest circle enclosing a set of points. It is valuable in the analysis of artificial boundaries such as legislative districts.

We can understand both concepts by taking the Example : Consider a finite set of *n* points in the plane; then the set of distances between any two points is also a finite set, which has a largest number, say *d*, called the *span* of the set of points. Clearly, if a set of points has span *d*, then it is possible to draw a circle of radius *d* that encloses all the points.

But it is possible to draw a smaller circle that still encloses the entire set: first locate a pair of points, *P* and *Q*, whose distance from each other is *d*. (If there are several such pairs, we may choose any one.) Construct two circles of radius *d* with centres at *P* and *Q* (Fig.).

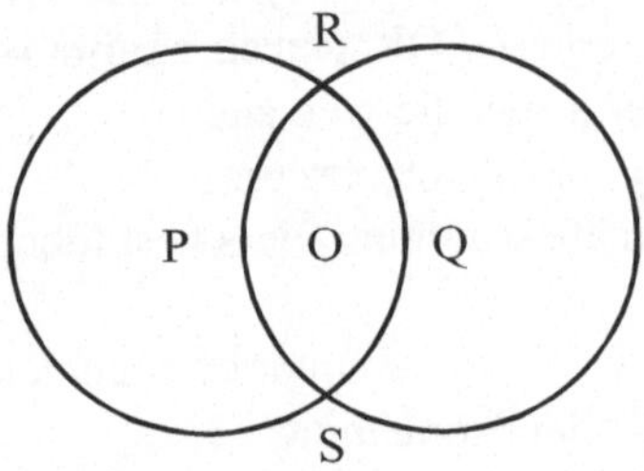

PQ = *d*, *OP* = *d*/2, *PS* = *d*, maximally

The circle centred at *P* passes through *Q*, while the circle centred at *Q* passes through *P*. These circles intersect at *R* and *S*. The entire set of *n* points lies within each circle. Therefore it must lie within their intersection, But the intersection itself is enclosed within die circle which has *RS* for its diameter. Since *PS* is maximally *d*, the radius of *this* spanning circle, by Pythagoras' Theorem, is d $3^{1/2}$ /2, (why?) a bound lower than the one we had started with. This bound lean be further improved, and this is **Jung's Theorem:** Every finite set of points of span *d* has a spanning circle no greater than d 3 $^{1/2}$ /3, a still better bound. Though smaller spanning circles are possible for certain finite sets of points, there are some which require the spanning circle to be at least this large.

Radius of the Spanning Circle of the vertices of an equilateral triangle of side d is given below :

Let the radius of the circle be R.

R^2 = [(1/2)d]^2 + {[sqrt(3)/6]d}^2

R^2 = (1/4)(d^2) + (1/12)(d^2)

R^2 = (1/3)(d^2)

R = [sqrt(3)/3]d

(d) List the differences between the following : **3*3=9**

(i) Work book and a Work sheet

(ii) SLIP and Dial up connection to Internet

(iii) Prime and Odd numbers

(i) Following are the differences between a work book and a work sheet :

1. A workbook is the MS Excel file in which you enter and store related data. A worksheet (also known as a spreadsheet) is a collection of cells on a single

"sheet" where you actually keep and manipulate the data.
2. Each workbook can contain many worksheets. But reverse is not possible. (It's a lot like a book. One book contains an entire story. Each page of the book contains part of the story.)
3. Often one workbook has a single theme, such as a personal budget. Each worksheet would then have a part of the theme, such as the budget broken down by month.

(ii) There are two types of dialup connections: online accounts or dialup IP links. Dialup IP links are usually described by the particular protocol they are running: either Serial Line Internet Protocol (SLIP) or the more advanced Point to Point Protocol (PPP). Both types of connections can give you a lot of things to do on the network. If you are starting your Internet adventure as an individual, an online account is easy to access and less expensive. If your usage is heavy, or if you have several people on a local area network (LAN), a SLIP or PPP connection becomes necessary. If you have an online account, you connect from your own computer using a telephone line and a modem, just as you would connect to a bulletin board. An online account is one step removed from full Internet connectivity, though, and has some important limitations. If you have a SLIP or PPP account, you also connect through a modem over a phone line, but your computer runs TCP/IP software to talk the TCP/IP protocol. A SLIP or PPP actually puts your computer on the network, and gives you full Internet access.

(iii) Prime number : The numbers which are divisible by one(1) or itself only, called prime numbers. These are told as rude numbers as given below 2, 3, 5, 7, 11, 13, 17, 19, 23, 29, 31, 37, 41, 43, 47, 51 etc.
Odd numbers : The numbers which are divisible by 3 only are called odd numbers. These numbers are not divisible by 2.
e.g. 3, 6, 9, 12, 15, 18, 21, 24, 27, 30, 33,36, 39, 42, 45 ... etc.

(e) What is a Pivot table? Explain the use of a Pivot table, with an example.4

It is a most sophisticated data-management feature available in MS-Excel. An organization analysis tool displays the fields and records in your list in new and potentially useful combinations. Pivot table made it easy and is available in the Data Menu. A pivot table report is an interactive table that can be used for quick summarization of large amount of data. Its rows and columns can be rotated to see different summaries of the source data, filter the data by displaying different pages or display the details of your interest. A pivot table report can be created from MS-Excel list.

Example showing Use of Pivot table :

To create the Pivot Table from an internal Database, follow the given steps :
First, set up a create some data, in A1:D50, like this, with 4 or 5 different names, 4 or 5 different activities and a little variety of week numbers and expenses:
Add as many rows as you can stand -- around 50 will do.
Now choose any cell in this table and choose Pivot Table wizard in the Data menu. Excel asks for the data source and suggests this table. Click OK.
Next question is the data range. Excel suggests the table. If you expect to add data in the future, set the data range to include as many rows as you think you will ever need. Rather than A1:D50, you may want to specify $A$1:$D$500.

Now comes the layout wizard, show below.

Who	Week	What	Amount
Joe	3	Beer	18
Beth	4	Food	17
Janet	5	Beer	14
Joe	3	Food	12
Joe	4	Beer	19
Janet	5	Car	12
Joe	3	Food	19
Beth	4	Beer	15
Janet	5	Beer	19
Joe	3	Car	20
Joe	4	Beer	16
Beth	5	Food	12
Beth	3	Beer	16
Joe	4	Food	17
Joe	5	Beer	14
Janet	3	Car	19
Joe	4	Food	17
Beth	5	Beer	20
Janet	3	Food	18
Joe	4	Beer	14
Joe	5	Food	12
Janet	3	Beer	18
Janet	4	Car	17
Janet	5	Food	12

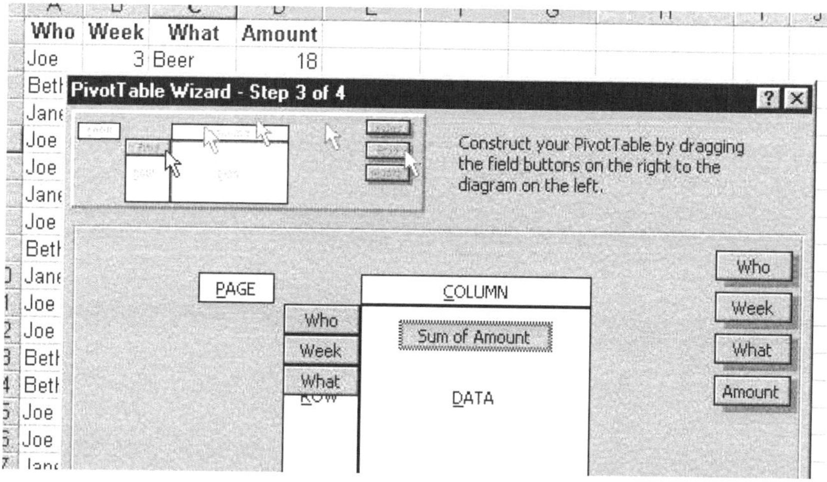

Drag the headers Who, Week and What into the ROW area, and the Amount header into the Data area. (Leave the Column area blank for now.) If the Amount tag does not show "Sum of Amount", double-click it and choose the Sum option. Finally Excel asks if the table should be placed in a new worksheet. Click OK.

Now you have your table, and it looks very much like a sorted version of the original data list, except from the automatic subtotals. Now comes the cool stuff:

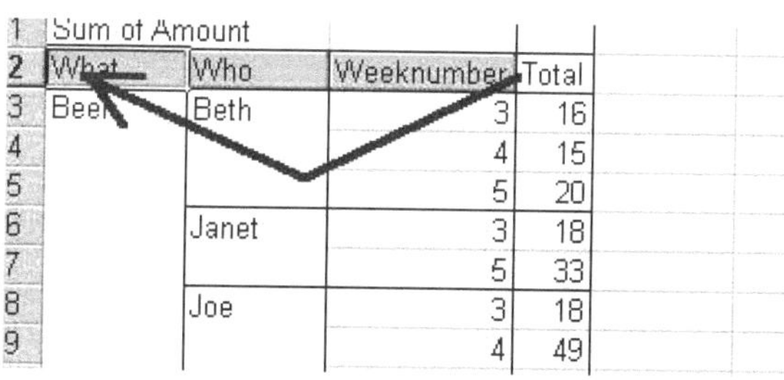

Grab the What header in the table and drag it all the way to the left. When you drop it here, the table re-sorts and re-sums; you have a table of beer costs by person instead. Now drag the Week header to the left and you have a weekly report.

Double-clicking the headers gives options of showing/hiding specific data (like Empty and Beer, may come in handy) and removing subtotaling for this column. Right-clicking gives other options, among them Hide and Show Detail for reading totals only.

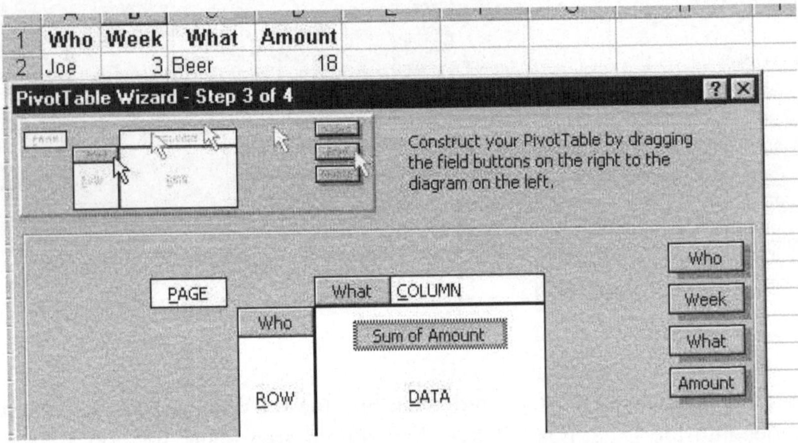

Here comes another useful pivot, made from the same list. Select any item in the original data list and choose Pivot Table wizard again. This time, drag Who into the Row field, What into the Column field and Amount into the Data field. This table is -among other things- very useful for graphing.

The only tricky thing is this: You have to update the table manually from the Data menu. A Pivot table does not update itself. If this becomes boring, here is some macro code that makes the tables update on selecting the worksheet:

```
Sub Auto_Open()
Application.OnSheetActivate = "UpdateIt"
End Sub

Sub UpdateIt()
Dim iP As Integer
Application.DisplayAlerts = False
For iP = 1 To ActiveSheet.PivotTables.Count
  ActiveSheet.PivotTables(iP).RefreshTable
Next
Application.DisplayAlerts = True
End Sub
```

Q2(a). What is a function? List three different categories of functions in MS-EXCEL along with the syntax and an example for each. 7

Refer to Chap-8, Q-2.

(b) What is Format Painter? Explain the use of Format Painter with an example. 5

This feature of Excel provides the facility to copy the format of cell(s) to the selected cells easily and quickly by clicking on the Format Painter tool button(picture given below) on the Standard Toolbar.

Use of Format Painter by an Example : Here, we are considering a situation of a user who was working on a spreadsheet like the one shown in Figure A, only her file contained dozens of columns and hundreds of rows. Her end users complained that it was difficult to follow a single row of data. She had the brilliant idea to use the Formatting toolbar's Fill Color tool to shade every other row in the spreadsheet as light green, creating a "green-bar" stripe effect. The result was that the spreadsheet, both on-screen and in printed form, was easier to read. Unfortunately, the user was formatting those rows the slow and difficult way. She was selecting every other row, one at a time, and clicking the Fill Color tool on each row.

Figure A

DemoStripes.xls

	A	B	C	D	E	F	G	H	I
1	Acct	Jan-01	Feb-01	Mar-01	QTR1	Apr-01	May-01	Jun-01	QTR2
2									
3	ID001	6.74	8.83	57.13	72.71	12.00	12.00	12.00	36.00
4	ID002	8.08	31.00	31.00	70.08	31.00	31.00	31.00	93.00
5	ID003	22.00	22.00	22.00	66.00	22.00	22.00	22.00	66.00
6	ID004	11.00	11.00	11.00	33.00	11.00	11.00	11.00	33.00
7	ID005	8.60	8.60	8.60	25.80	8.60	8.60	8.60	25.80
8	ID006	22.00	22.00	22.00	66.00	22.00	22.00	22.00	66.00
9	ID007	0.72	12.77	7.98	21.46	13.33	12.80	15.51	41.64
10	ID008	4.55	9.32	12.37	26.24	19.21	1.89	11.41	32.51
11	ID009	12.34	4.76	3.99	21.09	15.06	18.12	5.09	38.28
12	ID010	10.41	18.99	18.62	48.02	21.88	16.19	1.14	39.21
13	ID011	17.32	2.51	14.75	34.58	6.26	6.94	15.75	28.95
14	ID012	19.64	2.07	15.42	37.14	17.04	18.13	18.48	53.66
15	ID013	9.94	0.43	1.67	12.05	3.51	12.57	0.43	16.52
16	ID014	19.35	7.70	5.56	32.60	14.80	5.06	4.32	24.18
17	ID015	19.23	0.53	13.62	33.39	17.16	18.37	20.49	56.02
18	ID016	1.29	13.99	20.33	35.61	17.20	13.09	19.28	49.57
19	ID017	15.97	7.73	20.42	44.12	2.44	19.01	14.94	36.39
20	ID018	21.33	8.16	1.39	30.88	13.81	6.80	18.60	39.21
21	ID019	9.62	10.68	14.58	34.87	18.16	1.54	4.56	24.26
22	ID020	9.51	8.69	19.19	37.39	11.25	11.20	17.66	40.12

DummyData

Some readers have trouble keeping track of rows and columns of data in densely packed spreadsheets like this one.

The **solution**: **The intelligent Format Painter**
Now format the first row as light green, select that row, and double-click the Format Painter. Then, to "paint" additional rows, all we had to do was click on the row's number, and the Format Painter copied the "light green fill" attribute onto the target row. Because the Format Painter is smart enough to recognize patterns when you've selected two or more rows, we were able to format every other row in her spreadsheet with one swipe of the mouse.

First, we selected two rows—the first, plain row of data and the row that had been formatted with a light green fill. Next, we clicked the Format Painter once, and clicked on the first row number below our selection, and dragged down the column. Figure B shows what the sheet looked like while we were copying. (Notice the paintbrush icon near the bottom of the range we were formatting.) Figure C shows the final result.

Figure B

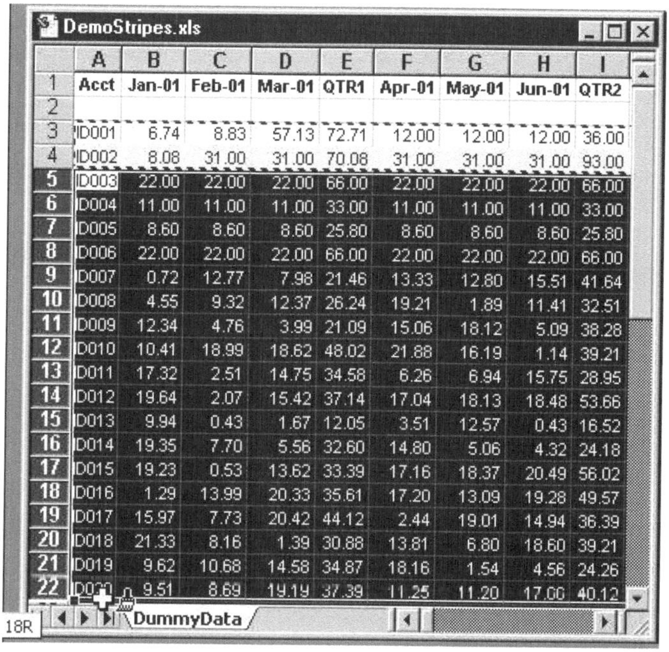

DemoStripes.xls

	A	B	C	D	E	F	G	H	I
1	Acct	Jan-01	Feb-01	Mar-01	QTR1	Apr-01	May-01	Jun-01	QTR2
2									
3	ID001	6.74	8.83	57.13	72.71	12.00	12.00	12.00	36.00
4	ID002	8.08	31.00	31.00	70.08	31.00	31.00	31.00	93.00
5	ID003	22.00	22.00	22.00	66.00	22.00	22.00	22.00	66.00
6	ID004	11.00	11.00	11.00	33.00	11.00	11.00	11.00	33.00
7	ID005	8.60	8.60	8.60	25.80	8.60	8.60	8.60	25.80
8	ID006	22.00	22.00	22.00	66.00	22.00	22.00	22.00	66.00
9	ID007	0.72	12.77	7.98	21.46	13.33	12.80	15.51	41.64
10	ID008	4.55	9.32	12.37	26.24	19.21	1.89	11.41	32.51
11	ID009	12.34	4.76	3.99	21.09	15.06	18.12	5.09	38.28
12	ID010	10.41	18.99	18.62	48.02	21.88	16.19	1.14	39.21
13	ID011	17.32	2.51	14.75	34.58	6.26	6.94	15.75	28.95
14	ID012	19.64	2.07	15.42	37.14	17.04	18.13	18.48	53.66
15	ID013	9.94	0.43	1.67	12.05	3.51	12.57	0.43	16.52
16	ID014	19.35	7.70	5.56	32.60	14.80	5.06	4.32	24.18
17	ID015	19.23	0.53	13.62	33.39	17.16	18.37	20.49	56.02
18	ID016	1.29	13.99	20.33	35.61	17.20	13.09	19.28	49.57
19	ID017	15.97	7.73	20.42	44.12	2.44	19.01	14.94	36.39
20	ID018	21.33	8.16	1.39	30.88	13.81	6.80	18.60	39.21
21	ID019	9.62	10.68	14.58	34.87	18.16	1.54	4.56	24.26
22	ID0[illegible]	9.51	8.69	19.19	37.39	11.25	11.20	17.06	40.12

18R DummyData

When you select two or more rows and click the Format Painter, the program copies the formatting from each row.

Figure C

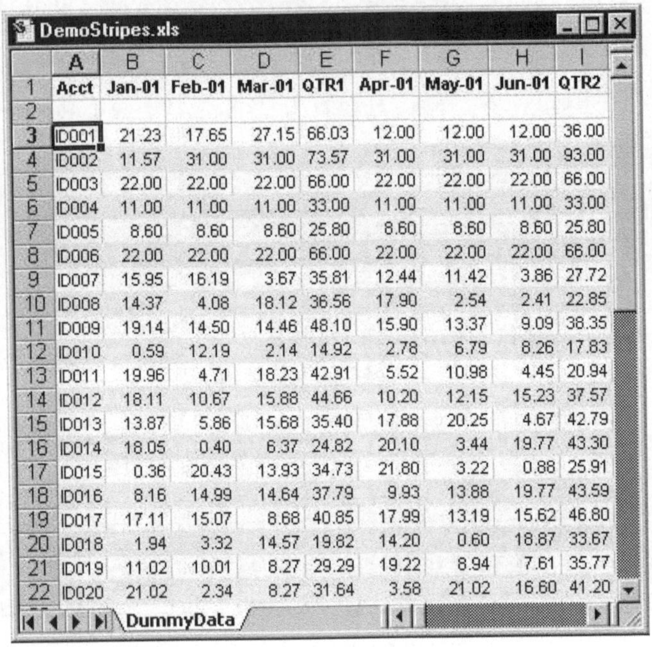

	A	B	C	D	E	F	G	H	I
1	Acct	Jan-01	Feb-01	Mar-01	QTR1	Apr-01	May-01	Jun-01	QTR2
2									
3	ID001	21.23	17.65	27.15	66.03	12.00	12.00	12.00	36.00
4	ID002	11.57	31.00	31.00	73.57	31.00	31.00	31.00	93.00
5	ID003	22.00	22.00	22.00	66.00	22.00	22.00	22.00	66.00
6	ID004	11.00	11.00	11.00	33.00	11.00	11.00	11.00	33.00
7	ID005	8.60	8.60	8.60	25.80	8.60	8.60	8.60	25.80
8	ID006	22.00	22.00	22.00	66.00	22.00	22.00	22.00	66.00
9	ID007	15.95	16.19	3.67	35.81	12.44	11.42	3.86	27.72
10	ID008	14.37	4.08	18.12	36.56	17.90	2.54	2.41	22.85
11	ID009	19.14	14.50	14.46	48.10	15.90	13.37	9.09	38.35
12	ID010	0.59	12.19	2.14	14.92	2.78	6.79	8.26	17.83
13	ID011	19.96	4.71	18.23	42.91	5.52	10.98	4.45	20.94
14	ID012	18.11	10.67	15.88	44.66	10.20	12.15	15.23	37.57
15	ID013	13.87	5.86	15.68	35.40	17.88	20.25	4.67	42.79
16	ID014	18.05	0.40	6.37	24.82	20.10	3.44	19.77	43.30
17	ID015	0.36	20.43	13.93	34.73	21.80	3.22	0.88	25.91
18	ID016	8.16	14.99	14.64	37.79	9.93	13.88	19.77	43.59
19	ID017	17.11	15.07	8.68	40.85	17.99	13.19	15.62	46.80
20	ID018	1.94	3.32	14.57	19.82	14.20	0.60	18.87	33.67
21	ID019	11.02	10.01	8.27	29.29	19.22	8.94	7.61	35.77
22	ID020	21.02	2.34	8.27	31.64	3.58	21.02	16.60	41.20

When you use the Format Painter to apply formatting from two or more rows, Excel formats subsequent rows using the same patterns. (In this case, the pattern is one plain row followed by one shaded row.)

Works for columns, too

Of course, this same shortcut applies to formatting columns. Suppose you want to format every four columns of data using the same color scheme, like in Figure D.

To copy the attributes associated with two or more columns in a row, just select them and click the Format Painter. Then click and drag on the letters of the target columns. When you release the mouse, Excel will format those columns using the same pattern as the one whose attributes you copied.

Figure D

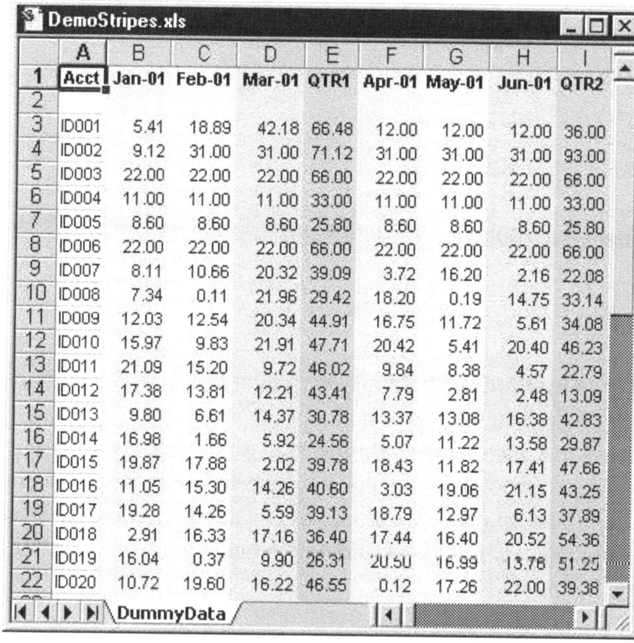

	A	B	C	D	E	F	G	H	I
1	Acct	Jan-01	Feb-01	Mar-01	QTR1	Apr-01	May-01	Jun-01	QTR2
2									
3	ID001	5.41	18.89	42.18	66.48	12.00	12.00	12.00	36.00
4	ID002	9.12	31.00	31.00	71.12	31.00	31.00	31.00	93.00
5	ID003	22.00	22.00	22.00	66.00	22.00	22.00	22.00	66.00
6	ID004	11.00	11.00	11.00	33.00	11.00	11.00	11.00	33.00
7	ID005	8.60	8.60	8.60	25.80	8.60	8.60	8.60	25.80
8	ID006	22.00	22.00	22.00	66.00	22.00	22.00	22.00	66.00
9	ID007	8.11	10.66	20.32	39.09	3.72	16.20	2.16	22.08
10	ID008	7.34	0.11	21.96	29.42	18.20	0.19	14.75	33.14
11	ID009	12.03	12.54	20.34	44.91	16.75	11.72	5.61	34.08
12	ID010	15.97	9.83	21.91	47.71	20.42	5.41	20.40	46.23
13	ID011	21.09	15.20	9.72	46.02	9.84	8.38	4.57	22.79
14	ID012	17.38	13.81	12.21	43.41	7.79	2.81	2.48	13.09
15	ID013	9.80	6.61	14.37	30.78	13.37	13.08	16.38	42.83
16	ID014	16.98	1.66	5.92	24.56	5.07	11.22	13.58	29.87
17	ID015	19.87	17.88	2.02	39.78	18.43	11.82	17.41	47.66
18	ID016	11.05	15.30	14.26	40.60	3.03	19.06	21.15	43.25
19	ID017	19.28	14.26	5.59	39.13	18.79	12.97	6.13	37.89
20	ID018	2.91	16.33	17.16	36.40	17.44	16.40	20.52	54.36
21	ID019	16.04	0.37	9.90	26.31	20.50	16.99	13.76	51.25
22	ID020	10.72	19.60	16.22	46.55	0.12	17.26	22.00	39.38

You can also use the Format Painter to copy formatting to two or more columns at a time.

(c) What is macro in MS-EXCEL. Explain the importance of macros.
Refer to Chap-11, Q-5. 3

Q3(a). Define FTP. Explain the different methods of FTP. Further, list six commonly used FTP commands. 8

FTP (File Transfer Protocol) is a standardized method of transferring files between computers, regardless of the platform or operating system the computers are running. FTP is a protocol or method of transferring files. The FTP client is a program that runs on your local computer and interacts with your Web server's FTP service. There are many FTP client programs that make FTP very easy to use. Most have a graphical interface that make it easy to transfer and manipulate files. If you don't have an FTP client, you can download them from the Internet for free. The following list of FTP clients are just a sample of those available for download from the Internet:

· Microsoft Internet Explorer FTP

· CuteFTP

· SmartFTP

· WS_FTP (30-day trial)

· FTP Commander

· Crystal FTP 2000

For instructions on installing and configuring these clients, please refer to the documentation that accompanies the product.

There are two methods of FTP access available to a web site. Depending on your account type, you may have both options available to you. The two types of FTP access to your site are Administrative FTP and Anonymous FTP. Regardless of the type of FTP access you use to your site, it is important to know that you can upload, download, overwrite and delete files on your account. For this reason, it is good practice to backup any material before overwriting or deleting it!

Administrative FTP

The Administrative FTP comes by default with your account. When you access your site by FTP using your primary user name and password, you are doing so as an Administrative FTP user. The term 'Administrative' is used since you have full control of your site, including directories not accessible with the FrontPage client. Many Webmasters and web site Administrators will use Administrative FTP to gain an overall understanding of a web site's structure.

To access your web site using Administrative or Anonymous FTP, you will need to refer to your site with the 'ftp' prefix. That is because FTP is a protocol, similar to HTTP. It is a different way of accessing your site. You may use either of the below methods to access your site by FTP on the Internet:

ftp://www.mydomain.com/

ftp://ftp.mydomain.com/

If you wish to login as the Administrative FTP user, you will be required to enter your 'user name' and 'password'. If you wish to login as the Anonymous FTP user, you may be prompted for a user name of 'anonymous' and your email address as a password. This is for logging purposes. Depending on the type of FTP login, you will see the directories to which you have access. The Administrative FTP user has control over the www & ftp directories. The Anonymous FTP user will have restricted access to the contents of the ftp directory.

Anonymous FTP

Anonymous FTP is very similar to Public FTP. It is FTP access, where no password is validated upon login. Some FTP clients ask for a user name of 'anonymous' and an 'email address' for a password. This means, any user on the Internet can login as the Anonymous FTP user, if the service is enabled. For this reason, your account Anonymous FTP service is setup with restricted access to one directory (/ftp). Many web site administrators and webmasters will use the Anonymous service to share content, inviting others to upload their material to this directory. As a result, this service acts as a shared drive for you and the public to use. Note: Anonymous FTP cannot be configured to allow simultaneous uploads and downloads to the same directory. Note: Anonymous FTP cannot be configured to allow simultaneous uploads and downloads to the same directory.

Six Commonly Used FTP commands :

Command	**Action**
(i) ls-l, dir	lists the current directory of the site you are connected
(ii) dir (directory name)	list the files in directory
(iii) cd (directory name)	change directory
(iv) ascii	prepare to download text file
(v) binary or image or bin	prepare to download non text file
(vi) get filename	get the contents of a file (called down load)

(b) Explain the different components of a URL with an example. Write down the steps involved in accessing a Web-site by typing its address. 7

The **URL** is the address of a resource, or file, available on the Internet. The URL contains the protocol of the resource (e.g. http:// or ftp://), the domain name for the resource, and the hierarchical name for the file (address). For example, a page on the internet may be at the URL http://www.gullybabapublishinghouse.com/define/u/url.shtml. The beginning part, http:// provides the protocol, the next part www.gullybabapublishinghouse.com is the domain, the main domain is gullybabapublishinghouse.com, while www is a pointer to a computer or a resource. The rest, /define/u/url.shtml is the pointer to the specific file on that server.

The URL could point to other things, CGI programs, Java programs, graphic files, or other resources available on the Internet. Abbreviation of Uniform Resource Locator, the global address of documents and other resources on the World Wide Web. The first part of the address indicates what protocol to use, and the second part specifies the IP address or the domain name where the resource is located. **For example**, the two URLs below point to two different files at the domain gullybabapublishinghouse.com. The first specifies an executable file that should be fetched using the FTP protocol; the second specifies a Web page that should be fetched using the HTTP protocol:

· ftp://www.gullybabapublishinghouse.com/orderbooks.exe

· http://www.gullybabapublishinghouse.com/index.html

Steps to access a Website :

(i) Fist open the Browser.

(ii) Then, in browser address bar type the name of the website you want to access.

(iii) After typing name press enter key, then wait for the website to come. It will be dispalyed by the browser after sometime depending upon the speed of Internet Connection. Note : to access a website Internet must be connected otherwise all the steps listed will not be fruitful.

Q4(a). What is a chart? Explain three types of charts in MS-EXCEL, with an example of each.

7

Refer to Chap-9, Q-1

(b) Prove that if n is a composite integer, then n has a prime divisor less than or equal to $\sqrt{n}$.

5

Let n be a composite number and its root is $\sqrt{n}$

Let n = 1

P(1) : 1 is divisible by 1 or $\sqrt{1}$ which is true

p(1) is true

Let n=2

P(2) : 2 is divisible by $\sqrt{2}$

Since $2 \div \sqrt{2} = 1.414$ (which is $\sqrt{2}$)

$2 \div 2 = 1$

$2 \div \sqrt{2} = \sqrt{2}$ and $2 \div 1 = 2$

$\therefore$ Let P(k) is true i.e. P(k) : k is divisible by k or (k+1) is divisible by (k+1) or $\sqrt{k+1}$

so k = K some value or $\sqrt{k}$. some value

$\therefore$ (k + 1) = (k + 1) some value or ($\sqrt{k+1}$) some value

= k($\sqrt{k+1}$) some value or ($\sqrt{k+1}$) some value

= which is divisible by k or which is divisible by 1

$\therefore$ So we conclude that p(k+1) is true.

Hence, we can say that n is divisible by prime divisor.

(n / or $\sqrt{n}$. Hence Proved)

(c) Based on Euler's theory, draw a configuration of 2 houses and 2 utilities such that each house is connected to each utility, but with no crossover. **3**

Let Houses are defined by H and utilities by U

then H = $\{h_1, h_2\}$

and U = $\{u_1, u_2\}$

Since each house is connected to each utility with no cross over the other. It is one-one mapping between them and this may be also called injective type mapping, it can be shown by the figure below :

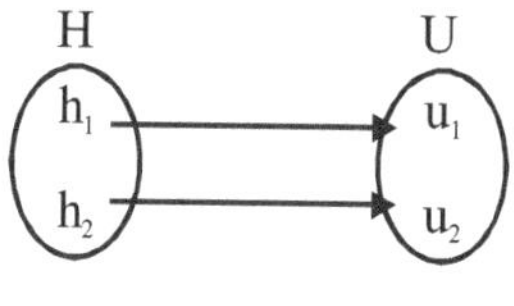

Q5(a). Explain the importance of Splitting and Freezing Window Panes. Explain the steps involved in sequence in this process. **6**

Importance of Splitting and Freezing Window Panes

While working on a very large worksheet with row and column headings, when you move right, the row headings scroll off to the left. When you move down to see the data the column headings scroll up. To fix these headings, you can split the active window into two, with row or column headings in one window and the data on the other window.

Steps in sequence in this process :

1. Select the entire row or column where you want to split the windows.

or

2. Select a single cell to split the window immediately above and to the left of the cell.

3. Choose **Window -> Split** command.

4. The different regions are separately scrollable.

To freeze the heading row or column window(s), choose **Window -> Freeze Panes**.

This command will allow you to scroll only the current section of the window. The rest of the section(s) will be freezed or locked.

To unfreeze the panes, choose **Window -> Unfreeze Panes**.

To remove the splits, choose **Window -> Remove Split** command.

(b) List two tools and four services available on the Internet.

Refer to Chap-12, Q-5

3

(c) What is the difference between browsing and searching the Internet for information? Mention an advantage and a disadvantage of each. **6**

To follow links in a page, to shop around in a page, exploring what's there, a bit like window shopping. The opposite of browsing a page is **searching** it. When you search a page, you find a search box, enter terms, and find all occurrences of the terms throughout the site. When you browse, you have to guess which words on the page pertain to your interests. Searching is usually more efficient, but sometimes you find things by browsing that you might not find because you might not think of the "right" term to search by.

Advantage of Browsing is : no need to think the right term to search by.

Disadvantage of Browsing is : it provides very limited webpages.

Advantage of Searching is : a large amount of webpages are displayed matching our searched term.

Disadvantage of Searching is : it requires use of search engine. Efficiency in using a search engine leads to finding of exact information within less time.

CS-612 : PC SOFTWARE SKILLS
DEC-2005

Note: Question 1 is compulsory. Answer any three questions from the rest.

Q1(a). Three married couples are to cross a river in a boat which can hold only two persons, one of whom must row the boat. Each of the three husbands is a jealous man who will not allow his wife to be left in the company of other men, unless he is also present. Show how the jealous husbands and their wives can accomplish the trip by labeling all the states on the left and right banks of the river. **8**

There are three husbands and three wives, who are initially on the left bank of a river and want to cross the river. The only available boat can hold only two persons at a time and one of them must row the boat and the condition is that the husbands are doubtful and jealous by nature, who never allow their wives with others. For this condition we will apply Cannibals and Missionaries Concept of crossing river.

Let husbands are denoted by H and wives by W. (H, W) is a pair. Some states like (3, 2) on left bank or (1, 2) on the right bank. So there are only 16 possible states :

Table for possible states

Left bank	1	2	3	4	5	6	7	8	9	10	11	12	13	14	15	16
(H, W)	3,3	3,2	3,1	3,0	2,3	2,2	2,1	2,0	1,3	1,2	1,1	1,0	2,3	0,2	0,1	0,0
Right bank (H, W)	0,0	0,1	0,2	0,3	1,0	1,1	1,2	1,3	2,0	2,1	2,2	2,3	3,0	3,1	3,2	3,3

Here we use 1 or K to define the position of the boat in any state, therefore, (1, 1) is the initial situation in which three husbands and three wives i.e. their married couples are standing on the left bank of the boat. Boat is also located on this bank. In this situation, it is possible to move to five situations in which only three are acceptable i.e. (K, 5), (K, 6), (K, 9) are in favour.

(K, 2) not acceptable chance
(K, 3) not acceptable chance
(1, 1) (K, 5)
(K, 6)
(K, 9)

Graph is

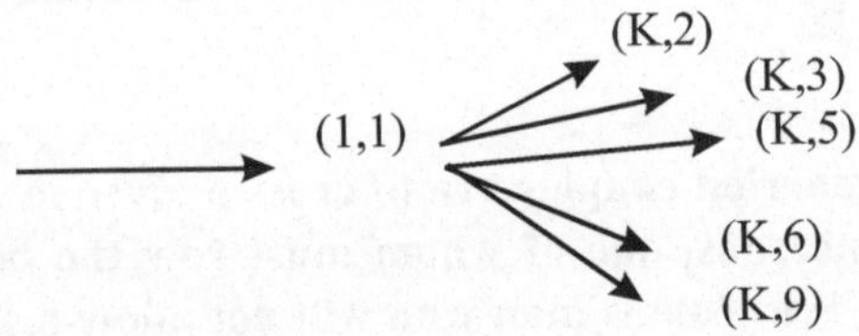

From (K, 5) we can only return to (1, 1) so this is not a very beneficial movement from (K, 6), we can move to (1, 2) which is not allowed and to (1, 5) from (K, 9) similarly (1, 5).

(K, 5)
(1, 1) (K, 6) (K, 2) Not permissible.
(K, 9) (1, 5)

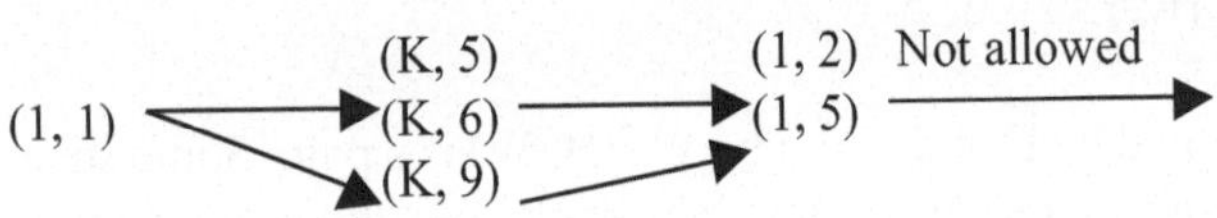

From (1, 5) the non trivial valid move is (K, 13) whereas (K, 7) and (K, 10) are not allowed. Then we adopt the case of figure given below :

(1, 1) (K,6) / (K,9) (1,5) (K, 13), (1,9) (K, 11) (1, 6) (K, 8) (1, 4) (K, 12) (1,11) / (1,8) (K, 16)

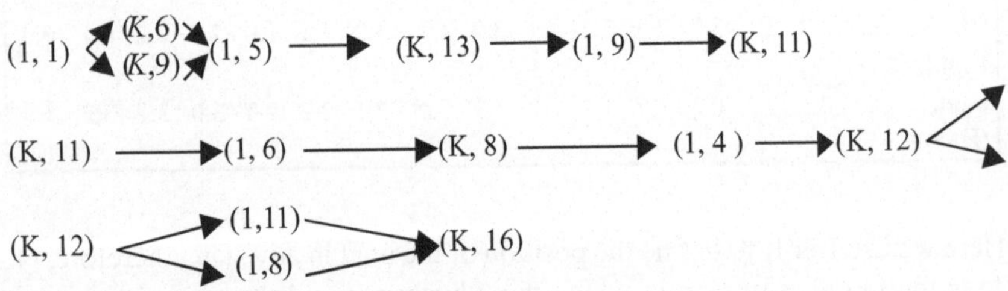

(b) What are Macros? Explain two differences between Macros and Templates. **5**

If you perform a task repeatedly in Excel, you can automate the task by using a macro. A macro is a series of commands and instructions that you group together as a single command to accomplish a task automatically. Instead of manually performing a series of time-consuming, repetitive actions, you can create and run a single macro — in effect, a custom command — that accomplishes the task for you.

Here are some typical uses for macros :

· To speed up routine editing and formatting
· To combine multiple commands; for example, inserting a table with a specific size and borders, and with a specific number of rows and columns
· To make an option in a dialog box more accessible
· To automate a complex series of tasks

Two differences between Macros and Templates :
(i) Macros can be created that can reduce many keyboard and mouse actions to a single command, mostly used to automate the routine work.
A **template** determines the basic structure for a document and contains document settings such as AutoText entries, fonts, key assignments, macros, menus, page layout, special formatting, and styles.

(ii) Macros are recorded in separate sheets in the workbooks.
Templates are created to create other workbooks of the same type.

(c) What is "Alignment"? Explain the four alignment options which can be used for document alignment. 7

Alignment is the positioning of text/matter in a cell. In general, by default in Excel the text is left aligned and the numbers are right aligned. Alignment is done in two ways which are Vertical and Horizontal alignment. Vertical alignment determines whether text is positioned at the top, bottom or center of the page.

The various horizontal alignment options are :
General - the text is left aligned and the numbers are right aligned. This is the default status.
Left - aligns the contents to the left of the cell.
Center - aligns the cell contents to the center of the cell.
Right - aligns the contents to the right of the cell.
Fill - fills the selected cells with the single character.
Justify - this option is selected with multiple lines of text as it wraps the contents from left to right.

Center Across Selection - centers the text across multiple columns.

The various vertical Alignment options are :
Top - aligns the text at the top of the cell.
Center - places the text in the center of the cell.
Bottom - aligns the text on the bottom of the cell.
Justify - wraps the text from top to bottom.

(d) What is a URL in Internet? Explain the fields of a URL through an example. 5

The **URL** is the address of a resource, or file, available on the Internet. The URL contains the protocol of the resource (e.g. http:// or ftp://), the domain name for the resource, and the hierarchical name for the file (address). For example, a page on the internet may be at the URL http://www.gullybabapublishinghouse.com/define/u/url.shtml. The beginning part, http:// provides the protocol, the next part www.gullybabapublishinghouse.com is the domain, the main domain is gullybabapublishinghouse.com, while www is a pointer to a computer or a resource. The rest, /define/u/url.shtml is the pointer to the specific file on that server.

The URL could point to other things, CGI programs, Java programs, graphic files, or other resources available on the Internet. Abbreviation of Uniform Resource Locator, the global address of documents and other resources on the World Wide Web. The first part of the address indicates what protocol to use, and the second part specifies the IP address or the domain name where the resource is located. **For example**, the two URLs below point to two different files at the domain gullybabapublishinghouse.com. The first specifies an executable file that should be fetched using the FTP protocol; the second specifies a Web page that should be fetched using the HTTP protocol:

- ftp://www.gullybabapublishinghouse.com/orderbooks.exe
- http://www.gullybabapublishinghouse.com/index.html

(e) What is a Domain Name System (DNS) ? What are the bases of classifications of DNS ? Explain with two examples each. 5

Addresses are essential for virtually everything we do on the Internet. The IP in TCP/IP is a mechanism for providing addresses for computers on the Internet. Internet addresses have two forms:
(i) person understandable which are expressed as words
(ii) machine understandable that are expressed as numbers also called IP addresses.

Domain Name System (or Service or Server), is an Internet service that translates domain names into IP addresses. Because domain names are alphabetic, they're easier to remember. The Internet however, is really based on IP addresses. Every time you use a domain name, therefore, a DNS service must translate the name into the corresponding IP address. For example, the domain name www.example.com might translate to 198.105.232.4.
The DNS system is, in fact, its own network. If one DNS server doesn't know how to translate a particular domain name, it asks another one, and so on, until the correct IP address is returned.

The following can be a typical person understandable address on the Internet:
username@host.subdomain.domain
Hosts are, in general, machines at a particular location. Resources of a host machine are normally shared and can be utilised by many users on the Internet. A user is given an account by system administrator, which allows him to use the resources of the machine.
The *username* in general, is the name of your Internet account for logging into the host machine. *Logging in* is the process of gaining access to your account on a computer, which is shared by several users.
Hosts and local networks are grouped together into *domains*, which are grouped into one or more larger domains. For an analogy a host computer is considered as an apartment building in a housing complex and your account is just an apartment in it. Domain may be an apartment complex, a town, or even a country.
Sub-domains may correspond to organizations such as NASA or CompuServe. Domains are **classified as non-geographic and geographic** below is the list of various common domain names. The domain names in India come under a larger domain ".in".

Non-Geographic domains

Code	Applicable for
.com	commercial organisations
.net	network organisations
.gov	parts of governments
.edu	organisations of higher education
.mil	non-classified military networks

.org	organisations that do not fit the commercial or educational designations

Example : www.ebay.com, www.gullybaba.com

Few Geographic Domains

Country	**Domain Name**
AUSTRALIA	.au
CHINA	.cn
GERMANY	.de
INDIA	.in
JAPAN	.jp
UNITED KINGDOM	.uk
UNITED STATES	.us

Example : www.ip**australia**.gov.**au**, www.chinaview.**cn**

Q2(a). What are dialog boxes? Explain the steps to create and run a dialog box. 5

A box that appears on a display screen to present information or request input. Typically, dialog boxes are temporary -- they disappear once you have entered the requested information.

In the Macintosh and Microsoft Windows interfaces, there is a convention that any menu option followed by ellipsis points (...) will, when selected, bring up a dialog box. Options without ellipsis points are executed directly.

Create Dialog Boxes :

1. Choose **Insert -> Macro -> Dialog** command.

This will display the Forms Toolbar automatically on the worksheet and two buttons (OK and CANCEL) in

the dialog box. The frame of the dialog box can be separately moved if you click on its border or frame and

the title can be changed.

2. Place the control in the dialog box as you placed it in the worksheet.

3. Click the right mouse button on the control while it is still selected.

4. Choose **Format -> Object** and click on control tab in the Format Object dialog box.

The additional controls which can be placed in the worksheet are :

Edit Box	This box can be used to enter text or numeric data.

Text	maximum 255 characters can be entered.
Integer	range is -32765 - 32767
Number	any valid number
Reference	valid cell reference
Multiline Edit	allows word-wrap in the control
Vertical Scrollbar	places vertical scrollbar against the control

List Box linked to Edit Control (Combination List-Edit or Combo List-Edit) - These are two different controls which work in combination to each other. You can either choose an item from the list or enter the item in the edit box.

Combination Drop-down Edit Box (Drop-down Combo List-Edit) - Similar to Combo List-Edit except that the list is drop-down list.

Run Dialog Boxes

Choose **Tools -> Run Dialog** command.

or

Click on the **Run Dialog** tool

(b) What is a protocol ? Explain and two commonly used Internet protocols. **5**

A standard way of communicating across a network. A protocol is the "language" of the network. A method by which two dissimilar systems can communicate. TCP is a protocol which runs over a network.

Refer to June04, Q1(b).

(c) What is Format Painter? Give the steps involved in applying Format Painter. **5**

This feature of Excel provides the facility to copy the format of cell(s) to the selected cells easily and quickly by clicking on the Format Painter tool button(picture given below) on the Standard Toolbar.

Applying Format Painter :

1. Select the formatted cells whose format you want to copy.

2. Press the left mouse button on the Format Painter tool button.

3. Drag the mouse pointed through the cell(s) where you want to apply the formatting.

This formatting technique can be repeated without going through the steps given above. If you double-click the Format Painter tool button, the cursor remains active until you click on the button again.

Q3(a). What is a Search Engine in Internet? List any six search engines available on Internet. **5**

Search Engine : A program that searches documents for specified keywords and returns a list of the documents where the keywords were found. Although search engine is really a general class of programs, the term is often used to specifically describe systems like AltaVista and Excite that enable users to search for documents on the World Wide Web and USENET newsgroups. Typically, a search engine works by sending out a spider to fetch as many documents as possible. Another program, called an indexer, then reads these documents and creates an index based on the words contained in each document. Each search engine uses a proprietary algorithm to create its indices such that, ideally, only meaningful results are returned for each query. Now follows the **list of famous search engines** : Google,Lycos, Excite, Hotbot, Infoseek, Alta Vista, The Scout, Infoseek.

(b) What is the remainder left after dividing?
1! + 2! + 3! + ... + 100! by 7? **5**

The given expression is 1!+2!+3!+4!+5!+6!+7!+.............+ 100! Divisor = 7

If the above expression is divided by 7.

Let the remainder is R

Let the given expression is written by P

$\therefore P =$ 1!+2!+3!+.........................+100!

Let**Quotient** is Q and we have dividend = divisor **Quoitent** + Remainder

$$P = 7Q + R$$

$$7Q = P - R$$

$$7Q = 1! + 2! + 3! + 4! + 5! + 6! + 7! + \ldots\ldots + 100! - R$$

If R =0, the Number is divisible by 7

$$7Q = 873 + 71 + \ldots\ldots + 100 - R$$

We check for values from R = 1 to 5 and other values we may find that for R = 5, then we find 7Q = O-R exists and thus R = 5 is only single value.

Thus R = 5 is the remainder.

(c) Write three differences between a work book and a work sheet. 3

Following are the three differences between a work book and a work sheet :

(i) A workbook is the MS Excel file in which you enter and store related data. A worksheet (also known as a spreadsheet) is a collection of cells on a single "sheet" where you actually keep and manipulate the data.

(ii) Each workbook can contain many worksheets. But reverse is not possible. (It's a lot like a book. One book contains an entire story. Each page of the book contains part of the story.)

(iii) Often one workbook has a single theme, such as a personal budget. Each worksheet would then have a part of the theme, such as the budget broken down by month.

(d) 'Databases can be created in MS-Excel.' True or False? Give reasons for your answer. 2

True, databases can be created in MS-Excel.

Reason : Database is the most powerful feature of MS Excel and simplified tool to store, manage and analyse data.

In MS-EXCEL, database can be created in two ways :

1. Enter the data in the form of table in the worksheet. You can enter the data as shown. This is the simplest way to create the database.

2. Use Data Form command.

Q4(a). Explain the meaning and purpose of the following: 6

(i) AutoFormat

This is a built-in table format which can be applied to the range of cells This feature includes the formatting of numbers, border alignment, font, colour, row height and column width.

To apply Autoformat to a range of cells follow the given steps :

1. Select the range of cells.
2. Select **Autoformat** option from the **Format** menu.
3. Choose the appropriate format from the list of **Table Format**.

Click on OK.

(ii) Pivot Table

A pivot table is an interactive worksheet table you use to summarise and analyse data from an existing list or table. You can update a pivot table whenever changes occur in the original source data. The original data remains intact, and the pivot table stays on the worksheet you created it on.

You can create a pivot table from source data that resides in:

1. A Microsoft Excel list or database.

2. An external database, such as a table or file created in an application or database management system external to Microsoft Excel.

3. Multiple Microsoft Excel consolidation ranges.

4. Another pivot table in the same workbook.

(iii) Custom Control

A software routine that adds some enhancement or feature to an application. Custom controls are written to provide as little as a few graphical interface improvements to as much as providing full imaging, spreadsheet and text editing extensions to the application. Depending on the development system, custom controls are either linked into the application when it is written or maintained as independent executable files that are called at runtime. DLLs, VBXs and OCXs are examples.

Example : instead of typing-in the response, you can select the appropriate option from the drop-down list. The tool buttons that are used to draw control objects are found on the

Forms Toolbar. To display this toolbar -

Choose **View -> Toolbars**.

(b) Give the steps involved in applying advanced filters in a worksheet. **4**

These filters are used to filter the data on the basis of more than one field. Using the same database, suppose you want to view only those records where the sale was more than 200 in the third quarter and more than 300 in the fourth quarter. To get the results, follow the given steps :

1. Enter the data as given below.

	H	I
3		
4	QTR3	QTR4
5	>200	>300
6		

2. Choose **Data -> Filter -> Advanced Filter** command.

3. A message dialog box is displayed that asks you to assume the top row of the data range as the header row. Click on OK.
4. A dialog box is displayed with two kinds of action :

a) Filter the list, in-place - displays only those records that match the criteria.
b) Copy to another Location - to copy the records that match the criteria to another location in the worksheet, leaving the database range as it is.
Select the first action, i.e., **Filter the list, in-place**.

5. Specify the list range as A3:E9, and the criteria range as H4:I5.
6. Click on OK.

(c) What are the uses of charts in Excel? What is a Chart Wizard? Explain two different types of charts. **5**

Charts are the graphic component of Excel. The data which is entered as tables can be viewed in the graphical form as charts which makes the figures of data effective, interesting, easy to understand, and easy to analyse and compare data.
Chart can be of two types :

Embedded Charts - These charts are included in the worksheet and can be moved, copied, and resized as any other graphical object. It's advantage is that it can be viewed alongwith the data and many charts can be inserted.

Chart Sheet - Separate Chart Sheets are inserted when a chart is created. It contains only one chart.

The **Chart Wizard** is a series of dialog boxes that guides you through the steps required to create a new embedded chart or modify settings for an existing embedded chart. It displays either five steps or two steps, depending on what is selected. If worksheet data is selected, all five steps are displayed because you're creating a new chart. If you've selected an existing chart to modify it, only two steps are displayed. When you choose the Finish button in any of the steps, the ChartWizard finishes your chart for you.
MS-Excel offers 15 different major chart types, each of which has at least one subtype, or variation. You can change the chart type to present your data most clearly and effectively. The two chart types are :

(i) Pie Chart

These are the best charts to compare the percentages of the sum the data series. It represents only one data series.

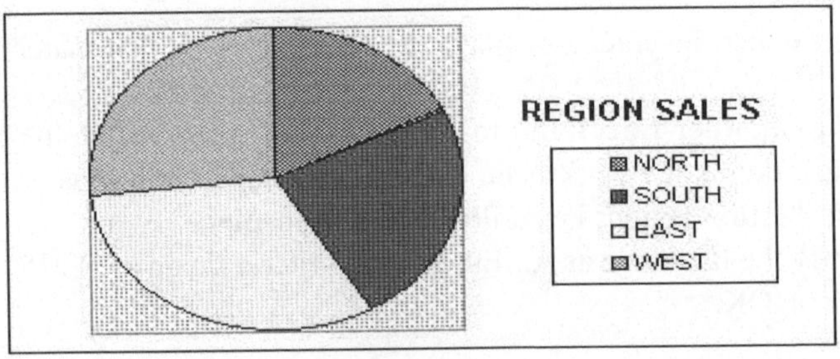

(ii) Column Chart

This consists of a series of vertical columns that allow comparison of the relative size of two or more items.

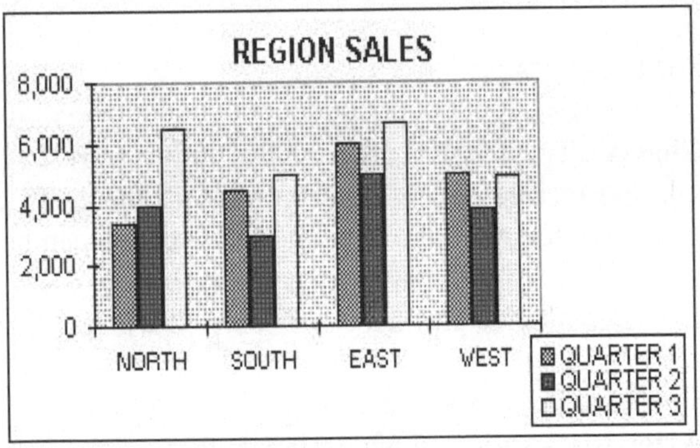

Q5(a). Explain the steps involved in displaying, editing and deleting a Scenario Manager. **6**

In Microsoft Excel, you can create and save sets of input values that produce different results as scenarios. A scenario is a group of input values called changing cells saved with a name you provide. Each set of changing cells represents a set of what-if assumptions that you can apply to a workbook model to see the effects on other parts of the model. You can define up to 32 changing cells per scenario.

Following are the steps involved in displaying a Scenario Manager :

1. Choose **Tools->Scenarios**... command.

2. In the **Scenario Manager** dialog box, select the scenario that you want to display.

3. Choose the **Show** button. The changing cell values for the selected scenario appear in the changing cells on the worksheet. The worksheet is recalculated to reflect the new values.

4. Repeat steps 2 and 3 to display other scenarios.

5. Choose the **Close** button.

Following are the steps involved in editing a Scenario Manager :

The need may arise to modify the scenarios that have been created. The changes could be in the name given to the scenario, the cell references or the values of the changing cells. To make modifications in the scenarios, follow the given steps :

1. Choose **Tools->Scenarios...** command.

2. In the **Scenario Manager** dialog box, select the scenario you want to edit.

3. Click on the **Edit** button. The **Edit Scenario** dialog box appears.

4. In the **Scenario Name** box, type the new name, if you want.

5. Edit the **Changing cell** references, if you want.

6. Edit text in the **Comment** box, if you want.

7. Click on the OK button. The **Scenario Values** dialog box appears. Make the required changes.

8. To save the changes made to your scenario, choose the **OK** button.

Following are the steps involved in deleting a Sccnario Manager :

1. Choose **Tools->Scenarios...** command.

2. In the **Scenario Manager** dialog box, select the scenario that you want to delete.

3. Choose the **Delete** button.

4. To delete additional scenarios, repeat steps 2 and 3.

5. Click on the **Close** button.

(b) What is e-mail? Explain three common points between e-mail and postal mail services. 4

Electronic Mail is the service that is available to people on a local area network or on the global Internet. It is one of the most commonly used services on the Internet, as this service is more convenient than normal postal system. E-mail does not require the person receiving the mail to be available (logged into the destination computer) at the time of receiving the mail. It is easier to send e-mail than postal mail, as you do not need to paste a stamp or search for an envelope, just create the message and send it.

Following are the common points between e-mail and postal mail services :

➢ You put on e-mail message into electronic envelope and place an electronic address on it.

➢ You do not worry, when the e-mail is read.

➢ You then hand over the envelope to someone else (the network) for delivery.

➢ You can forward e-mail to a forwarding address. The e-mail system routes it to the forwarding address.

➢ Your message may come back to you if your mail cannot be delivered. (This is called bounced mail as it "bounces" back to you).

(c) Prove that the sum of the squares of the first n integers is $\frac{(2n)(2n+1)(2n+2)}{24}$. **3**

We have to prove that sum of the squares of the first n integer n is

$$= \frac{2n\,(2n+1)\,(2n+2)}{24}$$

Mathematically which may be written as;

$$1^2+2^2+3^2+4^2+\ldots\ldots\ldots+n^2 = \frac{2n\,(2n+1)\,(2n+2)}{24}$$

i.e. $P(n) : 1^2+2^2+3^2+4^2+\ldots\ldots\ldots+n^2 = \frac{2n\,(2n+1)\,(2n+2)}{24}$ ....(1)

Let n = 1, $1^2 = \frac{2\times 1(2\times 1+1)(2\times 1+2)}{24}$

$1 = \frac{2(3)(4)}{24}$

$1 = \frac{24}{24}$

1 = 1

L.H.S. = R.H.S

$\Rightarrow P(1)$ is true.

Let us suppose that P(K) is true

putting n=k in (1) we have

$1^2+2^2+\ldots\ldots+K^2 = \frac{2K\,(2K+1)\,(2K+2)}{24}$ ....(2)

i.e. P(K) is true

Now we want to check equation (1) is also true for k+1, so, we replace K by

K+1 to last term of L.H.S. i.e. in K^2 which become $(K+1)^2$
adding $(K+1)^2$ to both side of equation (2) we have

$$1^2+2^2+3^2+\ldots\ldots\ldots\ldots+K^2+(K+1)^2 = \frac{2K(2K+1)(2K+2)}{24}+(K+1)^2$$

$$= \frac{2K(2K+1)(2K+2)+24(K+1)^2}{24}$$

$$= \frac{4K(K+1)\{K(2K+1)+6(K+1)\}}{24}$$

$$= \frac{(K+1)}{6}\left\{2K^2+K+6K+6\right\}$$

$$= \frac{(K+1)}{6}\left\{2K^2+7K+6\right\}$$

$$= \frac{(K+1)}{6}\{(2K+3)(K+2)\}$$

$$= \frac{(K+1)\times 2\times 2}{6\times 2\times 2}\{(2K+3)(K+2)\}$$

$$= \frac{(K+1)2}{24}\{(2K+3)(2K+4)\}$$

$$= \frac{2(K+1)(2K+3)(2K+4)}{24}$$

$\therefore$ P(n) is true for n = (K+1)
i.e. P(K+1) is true
$\therefore$ By principle of mathematical induction P(n) is true for all natural number n.

Hence $1^2+2^2+\ldots\ldots\ldots\ldots+n^2 = \frac{2n(2n+1)(2n+2)}{24}$ proved.

(d) Prove that the sum of two odd numbers is odd. **2**

Let n and (n+1) are two odd numbers and their sum is n+(n+1) be odd, so we may write :
$\therefore$ P(n) : n + (n+1) is odd number ....(1)
Let n = 1
P(1) : 1 + (1+1) = 3 which is an odd number
$\therefore$ P(1) is true.

Let us suppose (1) is true for n = k i.e. P(K) is true
$\therefore$ K + (K+1) = 3m (We have to remember that an odd number is always divisible by 3 and m is any integer)

Now we have to show above statement is also true for K + 1, so we change n to (K+1) in (1) it becomes :

$$(K+1)+(K+1+1) = (K+1)+(K+2)$$

$$= K+1+K+2$$

$$= 2K+3 \text{.............................}(3)$$

We see in R.H.S. of expression(3), first term 2K is divisible by 3, as we have suppose K is divisible by 3, and in second term 3 is divisible by 3 i.e. whole R.H.S. term 2K+3 is divisible by 3(since sum of two odd numbers is always divisible by (3).

Thus we can say that (K+1)+(K+1+1) is divisible by 3 i.e. P(n) is true for (K+1)

∴By principle of Mathematical Induction P(n) is true for all natural numbers n.

Finally, sum of two odd numbers is an odd number, hence proved.

CS-612 : PC SOFTWARE SKILLS
JUNE -2006

Note: Question number 1 is compulsory. Answer any three questions from the rest.

Q1(a). Johan is a Honest milkman supplying milk in two houses. One day the two ladies ask for 40 liters of milk each. One lady was carrying a fifty liters CAN and other a thirty liters CAN. Milkman has to divide the milk equally between the two ladies without using any other measurement. How he will manage exactly given fourty liters to each lady.

Full 80 Ltr.	Empty 50 Ltr. CAN	Empty 30 Ltr. CAN

	Milkman	Lady A	Lady B
Step – 1	80 L	0 L	0 L
Step – 2	30 L	50 L	0 L
Step – 3	30 L	20 L	30 L
Step – 4	60 L (30 + 30)	20 L	0 L
Step – 5	60 L	0 L	20 L
Step – 6	10 L	50 L	20 L
Step – 7	10 L	40 L	30 L
Step – 8	40 L	40 L	0 L
Step – 9	0 L	40 L	40 L

Equally Distribution

(b) What is an Address Book, and why is it required? How are new addresses added to the Address Book ?

Address Book in context of E-mail is a convenient place where contact information for retrieval by programs i.e. Microsoft Outlook Express are stored. Normally every mail reader allows address book facility to maintain a database of regularly used addresses. All addresses can be categorized in different groups of receivers like address book we maintain manually. It is used because :

1. In the address book, you get a place to store email addresses, home and work addresses, phone and fax numbers, conferencing information, instant messaging addresses and personal information such as date of anniversaries and birthdays.
2. It supports lightweight Directory Access Protocol for using Internet directory services.
3. Group of contacts can be created to make it convenient to send email to a set of people, such as relatives, friends and business associates.
4. It can be shared with other users.
5. You can import your personal address book from numerous popular email programs.
6. Send and receive business cards
7. Print all or part of your Address Book for your record in office as well as residence.

Following procedure is to be followed for giving reply to an arrived email

1. To add names directly from e-mail messages to your Address Book

You can set up Outlook Express so that when you reply to a message, the people you reply to are automatically added to your Address Book. In addition, any time you send or receive a message in Outlook Express, you can add the recipient's or sender's name to your Address Book.

To add all reply recipients to your Address Book

In Outlook Express, on the Tools menu, click Options.

On the Send tab, click Automatically put people I reply to in my Address Book.

To add an individual name to your Address Book from Outlook Express

· In a message you are viewing or replying to, right-click the person's name, and then click Add to Address Book.

· In the message list of your Inbox or other mail folder, right-click a message, and then click Add Sender to Address Book.

2. To add a contact to your Address Book by manually typing the details

On the Outlook Express toolbar, click Tools, and then click Address Book.
In the Address Book, select the folder to which you want to add a contact.
On the Address Book toolbar, click New, and then click New Contact.
On the Name tab, type at least the first and last name of the contact. This is the display name.
A display name is required for each contact. If you enter a first, middle, or last name, it will automatically appear in the Display box. You can change the display name by typing in a different name or by selecting from the drop-down list. The drop-down list will contain variations of the first, middle, and last name, as well as anything you typed in the Nickname box or the Company box on the Business tab.
On each of the other tabs, add any information you would like to include.

· Be sure to include an e-mail address for your contact. While your Address Book can be used for many purposes, its most immediate benefit is in providing e-mail addresses when you are composing mail.
· If you include a contact's street address on the Home tab or the Business tab, you can click View Map located on each of these tabs to display a printable street map showing the contact's address.

(c) What are Cell References ? Explain three ways of giving cell references, with examples of each implemented and explained through formulae.

A reference identifies a cell or a range of cells on a worksheet and tells Microsoft Excel where to look for the values or data you want to use in a formula. With references, you can use data contained in different parts of a worksheet in one formula or use the value from one cell in several formulas. You can also refer to cells on other sheets in the same workbook, to other workbooks, and to data in other programs. References to cells in other workbooks are called external references. References to data in other programs are called remote references.

Relative vs. absolute references : Depending on the task you want to perform in Excel, you can use either relative cell references, which are references to cells relative to the position of the formula, or absolute references, which are cell references that always refer to cells in a specific location. If a dollar sign precedes the letter and/or number, such as $A$1, the column and/or row reference is absolute. Relative references automatically adjust when you copy them, and absolute references don't.

Relative references : When you create a formula, references to cells or ranges are usually based on their position relative to the cell that contains the formula. In the following example, cell B6 contains the formula =A5; Microsoft Excel finds the value one cell above and one cell to the left of B6. This is known as a relative reference.

	A	B
5	100	
6	200	=A5
7		

When you copy a formula that uses relative references, Excel automatically adjusts the references in the pasted formula to refer to different cells relative to the position of the formula. In the following example, the formula in cell B6, =A5, which is one cell above and to the left of B6, has been copied to cell B7. Excel has adjusted the formula in cell B7 to =A6, which refers to the cell that is one cell above and to the left of cell B7.

	A	B
5	100	
6	200	=A5
7		=A6

Absolute references : If you don't want to adjust references when you copy a formula to a different cell, use an absolute reference. For example, if your formula multiplies cell A5 with cell C1 (=A5*C1) and you copy the formula to another cell, Excel will adjust both references. You can create an absolute reference to cell C1 by placing a dollar sign ($) before the parts of the reference that do not change. To create an absolute reference to cell C1, for example, add dollar signs to the formula as follows: =A5*$C$1

Labels and names : You can use the labels of columns and rows on a worksheet to refer to the cells within those columns and rows. Examples of labels are "Price," "Quantity," and "Total." Or you can create descriptive names to represent cells, ranges of cells, formulas, or constant values.

About labels and names in formulas : Worksheets often have labels at the top of each column and to the left of each row that describe the data within the worksheet. You can use these labels within formulas when you want to refer to the related data. You can also create descriptive names that are not labels on the worksheet to represent cells, ranges of cells, formulas, or constants. Note By default, Microsoft Excel does not recognize labels in formulas. To use labels in formulas, click Options on the Tools menu, and then click the Calculation tab. Under Workbook options, select the Accept labels in formulas check box.

Use labels to represent cells : When you create a formula that refers to data in a worksheet, you can use the column and row labels in the worksheet to refer to the data. For example, the following example contains columns labeled Product 1, Product 2, and Product 3. To calculate the total value for the Product 1 column, use the formula =SUM(Product 1).

	A	B	C	D
1	Division A	Product 1	Product 2	Product 3
2	East	30.00	70.00	110.00
3	West	40.00	80.00	120.00
4	Total	=SUM(Product 1)		

Or if you need to refer to the Product 3 amount for the East division (that is, the value 110.00), you can use the formula =Product 3 East. The space in the formula between "Product 3" and "East" is the intersection operator. This operator designates that Microsoft Excel should find and return the value in the cell at the intersection of the row labeled East and the column labeled Product 3.

3. D references : If you want to analyze data in the same cell or range of cells on multiple worksheets within the workbook, use a 3-D reference. A 3-D reference includes the cell or range reference, preceded by a range of worksheet names. Excel uses any worksheets stored between the starting and ending names of the reference. For example, =SUM(Sheet2:Sheet13!B5) adds all the values contained in cell B5 on all the worksheets between and including Sheet 2 and Sheet 13.

Refer to the same cell or range on multiple sheets by using a 3-D reference

The workbook must contain more than one worksheet. For more guidelines for using 3-D references, click ».

Click the cell where you want to enter the function.

Type = (an equal sign), enter the name of the function, and then type an opening parenthesis.

Click the tab for the first worksheet to be referenced.

Hold down SHIFT and click the tab for the last worksheet to be referenced.

Select the cell or range of cells to be referenced.

Complete the formula.

(d) Differentiate between splitting of windows and freezing of window

panes.

There are several differences between the two.

1. You can reposition the split crossbar as you do windows (position mouse over a bar, right-click and hold, move mouse, unclick). You cannot move the frozen sections without unfreezing/freezing all over again.

2. Freeze actually immobilizes everything above and to the left of the cursor. You can use the arrow keys, page-up, and so on to go up or left as far as you want (watch the Name Box), but you won't see the frozen section move.

3. Split allows you to move the two to four sections almost separately. Click inside one section. Move left/right. Only the two sections that are on top of each other will move, not the other two. Similarly, moving up or down will move only the two side-by-side sections, not the other two.

(e) State and prove Jung's theorem.

Ans. Refer to Page No. 172, 173, Q6(b).

(f) How can names be given to a range of cells ? What are the rules for defining range names ? List two valid and two invalid range names.

Named Ranges are a powerful tool in Excel that allows you to assign a meaningful name to a single cell or a range of cells. For example, you can assign the name "BookRate" to cell C1 and then use the name "TaxRate" anytime you would normally use the cell C1, such as =A5*BookRate.

Adding Named Ranges

To create a new Named Range from Excel, use the following procedure: Select the cell or range of cell that you want to assign a name to. Go to the Insert menu, select the Name menu item, and type your name in the text box.

Rules for defining range names

A range name can contain letters, numbers, and underscores, but not spaces or special punctuation characters. Moreover, it cannot be the same as a normal cell reference.

Example of valid and unvalid, "AA10" is not a valid range name because "AA10" is the name of a normal cell reference (row 10, column "AA"). Also Book Rate is unvalid due to space present between Book and Rate.

RateBook, and TaxRate are the valid range names.

2(a). What is a Domain Name System (DNS) ? Explain the terms user

name, host, domain and sub-domain in the context of an Internet Address.
Refer to Dec,2005. Q1(e).

(b) Differentiate between a Worksheet and a Workbook. Give three ways to restrict access to your workbook.
Refer to Chapter-5, Q6 and Q7.

3(a). What is the utility of viewing a worksheet in multiple windows ? Explain four ways of arranging the windows on the screen.
Following are the utilities of viewing a worksheet in multiple windows:
(i) You may need to view two parts of a worksheet simultaneously.
(ii) A worksheet can have many views or separate windows as you want, each being independent of each other (in terms of scrolling, not data!)

Now Refer to Chapter-7, Q4, Page No.-50.

(b) Explain two ways to share information with people having common interest, on the Internet.
Following are the two ways to share information with people having common interest on the Internet :
(i) Mailing Lists : E-mail provides a mechanism for groups of people who have common interests to establish and maintain contact. Such interest groups are referred to as mailing lists (lists for short), after all they are mailing list of the members' e-mail addresses. We can subscribe to any of such lists. We will receive copies of all the mail sent to the list. We can also send mail to all the subscribers of the list.
We can become a list subscribers, by contacting the list's administrator. There exist two types of list administrators: human or computer program called listserv. Our request to subscribe may sometimes be refused. Do not get disappointed, there will be plentiful more lists that will accepts your subscription.

(ii) Usenet and Newsgroups : There are many ways to meet people and share information-using Internet. One such way is through Usenet *newsgroups*. These are special groups set up by people who want to share common interests ranging from current topics to cultural heritage. There are currently thousands of Usenet newsgroups. The Usenet can be considered as another global network of computers and people, which is interwined with the Internet.
Usenet is like a living thing: New newsgroups get added, the groups which have too much traffic get broken up into smaller, specialised groups, and the groups even can dissolve themselves. The newsgroups are really meant for interaction of people who share your interests. You can post your own questions

as well as your answers to the questions of others, on the Usenet. Usenet has its own set of rules and manners, governing behaviour; most of them are based on common courtesy. Unfortunately, not everybody follow them.

Q4(a). How can data in a database be filtered ? Explain Auto filters and Advanced filters.

Refer to Chapter-10, Q4, Page No.-73.

(b) What is a template ? Also explain why it is called a Special Workbook.

Refer to Chapter-11, Q4, Page No.-82.

(c) State Goldbach's conjecture. Why is it called a conjecture, and not a theorem ?

Ans. Goldbach's conjecture : All the numbers of the form $2^{2n}+1$ are prime. The above statement is called conjecture, not a theorem be cause it be comes 125 at n=5, which is not prime

Q5(a). Explain the following terms, with examples :

(i) Mailing Lists and Mail Reflectors

Mailing Lists : Refer Q3(b) in this paper.

Mail Reflectors : E-mail address that acts as an alias, redistributing all mail received to another address or to a mailing list. Individuals use mail reflectors to hide their true identities or to forward messages following a change of e-mail address.

The same method can be used to address a particular group of people – for example, Gully Astrology Point might create mail reflectors for all staff (staff@astrologyeverywhere.com), for new clients (new@astrologyeverywhere.com), former clients (former@astrologyeverywhere.com), and so on.

(ii) Telnet

Refer to Chapter-12, Q1(iii), Page No.-86.

(iii) Autotemplates

Refer to June,2001. Q6(b), Page No.-209.

(b) Show that for all positive integers $n, 2^{2n-1}+1$ **is divisible by 3.**

Ans. P (n): $2^{2n-1}+1$ is divisible by 3

Let n=1,

P (1): L.H.S=$2^{2\times 1}+1=2+1=3$ which is divisible by 3 Hence it is R.H.S

$\therefore$ P (1) is true

$\therefore$ We can say P (n) is true for n = k, i.e. P (k) is true &

P (k): $2^{2k-1}+1$ is divisible by 3

$\therefore 2^{2k-1}+1 = 3m$

$\therefore 2^{2k}.2^{-1} = 3m-1$

$\therefore 2^{2k}=(3m-1)2$

changing n to k+1 in $2^{2n-1}+1$ it becomes

$$2^{2(k+1)-1}+1 = 2^{2k} . 2^{2-1} +1 = 2^{2k}. 2+1$$

$=\{(3m-1)2\}2+1$

$=12m-4+1$

$=12m-3$

$=3(4m-1)$

(which is a factor of 3)

i.e. $2^{2(k+1)-1}+1$ is divisible by 3

: P(k+1) is true

: By principle of mathematical induction P(n) is true for $\forall$ n. Proved

CS-612 : PC SOFTWARE SKILLS
DEC -2006

Note: Question number 1 is compulsory. Answer any three questions from the rest.

Q1(a). A father has two sons. Four years ago, the father was three times as old as his eldest son and four years hence, the eldest son will be twice as old as the younger son. If the younger son is now 8 years old, find the father's present age. **[7]**

Let age of father = x years
Let age of eldest son = y years
Let the age of younger son = z years

Four year ago

Age of Father = x - 4
Age of Elder Son = y - 4
Age of Younger Son = z - 4

Condition

$(x - 4) = 3(y - 4)$
$x - 4 = 3y - 12$
$x - 3y = -8$ ....(i)

Four years Hence

Age of Father = x + 4 years
Age of Elder Son = y + 4 years
Age of Younger Son = z + 4 years

Condition

$(y + 4) = 2(3+ 4)$
$y + 4 = 2z + 8$
$y - 2z = +4$ ....(ii)

Give z = 8 years put in (ii)

$y - 2 \times 8 = +4$
$y = +4 + 16 = 20$

$\boxed{y = 20}$ years put in (i)

$x - 3 \times 20 = -8$
$x - 60 = -8$
$x = -8 + 60$
$x = 52$ years

therefore, present age of father = 52 years

(b) Summarize the working of any two of the following: [6]

(i) E-mail

* E-mail passes from one computer, known as a mail server, to another, as it travels over the Internet. This can be compared to a letter that makes stops at different postal stations along its way, before reaching the recipient.
* Once it arrives at the destination mail server, it is stored in an electronic mailbox until the recipient retrieves it.
* This whole process will take only seconds, allowing you to quickly communicate with people around the world at any time of the day or night.

(ii) Telnet

A TELNET connection is a Transmission Control Protocol (TCP) connection used to transmit data with interspersed TELNET control information.

1. When a TELNET connection is first established, each end is assumed to originate and terminate at a "Network Virtual Terminal", or NVT. An NVT is an imaginary device which provides a standard, network-wide, intermediate representation of a canonical terminal. This eliminates the need for "server" and "user" Hosts* to keep information about the characteristics of each other's terminals and terminal handling conventions. All Hosts, both user and server, map their local device characteristics and conventions so as to appear to be dealing with an NVT over the network, and each can assume a similar mapping by the other party. The NVT is intended to strike a balance between being overly restricted (not providing Hosts a rich enough vocabulary for mapping into their local character sets), and being overly inclusive (penalizing users with modest terminals).

***NOTE :** The "user" Host is the Host to which the physical terminal is normally attached, and the "server" host is the Host which is normally providing some service. As an alternate point of view, applicable even in terminal-to-terminal or process-to-process communications, the "user" Host is the Host which initiated the communication.

(iii) Search Engine

A search engine operates, in the order : (a) Web crawling, (b) Indexing, (c) Searching.

Web search engines work by storing information about a large number of web pages, which they retrieve from the WWW itself. These pages are retrieved by a Web crawler (sometimes also known as a spider) — an automated Web browser which follows every link it sees. Exclusions can be made by the use of robots.txt. The contents of each page are then analyzed to determine how it should be indexed (for example, words are extracted from the titles, headings, or special fields called meta tags). Data about web pages are stored in an index database for use in later queries. Some search engines, such as Google, store all or part of the source page (referred to as a cache) as well as information about the web pages, whereas others, such as AltaVista, store every word of every page they find. This cached page always holds the actual search text since it is the one that was actually indexed, so it can be very useful when the content of the current page has been updated and the search terms are no longer in it. This problem might be considered to be a mild form of linkrot, and When a user comes to the search engine and makes a query, typically by giving key words, the engine looks up the index and provides a listing of best-matching web pages according to its criteria, usually with a short summary containing the document's title and sometimes parts of the text. Most search engines support the use of the boolean terms AND, OR and NOT to further specify the search query. An advanced feature is proximity search, which allows users to define the distance between keywords.

(c) Explain the features of the following with example: [6]

(i) Goal Seek

Refer to Chapter-11, Q2(ii). Page No.-81

(ii) Solver

Refer to Chapter-11, Q2(i). Page No.-80

(d) Suppose m & n are integers, such that $n^2 + 1 = 2m$. Prove that m is the sum of squares of two integers. [4]

We have

$$n^2 + 1 = 2^m$$

$$\therefore m = \frac{n^2+1}{2} = \frac{n^2}{2} + \frac{1}{2} = \left(\frac{n}{\sqrt{2}}\right)^2 + \left(\frac{1}{\sqrt{2}}\right)^2$$

$$P(n): \left(\frac{n}{\sqrt{2}}\right)^2 + \left(\frac{1}{\sqrt{2}}\right)^2$$

let n = 1, $P(n) = \left(\frac{1}{\sqrt{2}}\right)^2 + \left(\frac{1}{\sqrt{2}}\right)^2 + \left(\frac{1}{\sqrt{2}}\right)^2$ which is sum of squares of two integers

Let us Suppose P(k) is true

$\therefore P(k): \left(\frac{k}{\sqrt{2}}\right)^2 + \left(\frac{1}{\sqrt{2}}\right)^2$ which is sum of squares of two integers.

(Let) $\therefore \left(\frac{k}{\sqrt{2}}\right)^2 + \left(\frac{1}{\sqrt{2}}\right)^2 = (x)^2 + y^2$ where x and y are integers.---(i)

changing n to k + 1 in $P(n): \left(\frac{k}{\sqrt{2}}\right)^2 + \left(\frac{1}{\sqrt{2}}\right)^2$ it becomes

$$\left(\frac{k+1}{\sqrt{2}}\right)^2 + \left(\frac{1}{\sqrt{2}}\right)^2 = \left(\frac{k}{\sqrt{2}}\right)^2 + \left(\frac{1}{\sqrt{2}}\right)^2 + \left(2\frac{k}{\sqrt{2}}\right) + \left(\frac{1}{\sqrt{2}}\right)^2$$

$x^2 + y^2 + \left(\sqrt{2}k\right) + \left(\frac{1}{\sqrt{2}}\right)^2$ from (i)

which is sum of squares:-

$\therefore$ P(k+1) is true

i.e., P(n) is true for n = k + 1

$\therefore$ P(n) is true for every n

$\therefore m = \left(\frac{n}{\sqrt{2}}\right)^2 + \left(\frac{1}{\sqrt{2}}\right)^2$ is true

hence proved.

(e) What is domain name ? Name any four top domain names. [3]

A name that is entered into a computer (e.g. as part of a Web site or other URL, or an e-mail address). These names are technically hostnames.

E.g. www.gullybaba.com is a domain name.

Every domain name ends in a top-level domain (TLD) name, which is always either one of a small list of generic names (three or more characters), or a two characters territory code. Top Domain Names first implemented in 1985 were : com

.edu

.gov

.net

.org

.mil

(f) Explain, with example, how charts in Excel are used in analysis. [4]

Refer to Chapter-9, Q3. Page No.-67

2(a). What do you understand by the term Internet Protocol ? Explain HTTP protocol and what it is used for. **[5]**

Refer to Dec,2005, Q2(b). Page No.-107

Hypertext Transfer Protocol (HTTP) is a method used to transfer or convey information on the World Wide Web. Its original purpose was to provide a way to publish and retrieve HTML pages.

HTTP is a request/response protocol between clients and servers. The originating client, such as a web browser, spider, or other end-user tool, is referred to as the user agent. The destination server, which stores or creates resources such as HTML files and images, is called the origin server. In between the user agent and origin server may be several intermediaries, such as proxies, gateways, and tunnels.

(b) If three persons (equally able) can jointly finish/complete three jobs in three days, then 100 persons (of the same ability) can jointly do 100 such jobs in how many days? **[5]**

I man = x

II man = y

III man = z

$\because$ all three are of same capacity = p (let)

$\therefore x = y = z = p$

$\therefore x + y + z = p + p + p = 3p$

$\because$ (x + y + y) does 3 jobs in = 3 days

$\therefore$ 3p does 3 jobs in = 3 days

$\therefore$ 3p does 1 job in = 3×3 days = 9 days

$\therefore$ p does 1 job in = 9×3 = 27 days

100 men = 100 p

jobs = 100

$\because$ p men does 1 job in = 27 days

$\therefore$ 100 men does 1 jobs in = $\frac{27}{100} \times 100$ days

= 27 days

i.e., we conclude that,

100 persons of same ability jointly do

100 such jobs in 27 days.

3(a). Explain the following functions giving examples for each:

(i) LEN ( )

Refer to Chapter-8, Q2(f).

(ii) FLOOR ( )

Floor function returns a number rounded down based on a multiple of significance.

The syntax is: Floor(number, significance)

number is the number that you wish to round down.

significance is the multiple of significance that you wish to round a number to.

Note: If the sign of the number and the significance parameters are different, the Floor function will return the #NUM! error.

(iii) CEILING ( )

Refer to Chapter-8, Q2(j).

(b) Comment on the statement "Every graph is not an Euler's graph". Using a diagram, illustrate different parameters which decide that a graph can have an Eulerian walk or not. [4]

A graph that has neither self loops (i.e., an edge having the same vertex as both its end vertices is termed as self graph) non parallel edges (i.e. all edge having same pair of end vertices are called parallel graph).

Where in other words, a figure which has walk which is a finits alternating sequences of vertices and edges $v_0, e_1, v_1, e_2, v_2, ---v_{k-1}, e_k, v_k$ beginning and ending with vertices such that v_{i-1} and v_i are the end vertices of the edge e_i, $1 \le i \le k$, and all the edges are distinct). The walk may be open or close for graph.

On the other hand, an euler graph is a graph which contains closed walk only. Here closed walk we mean graph which begins and ends at the same vertex.

For supporting our answer are may take some diagrams.

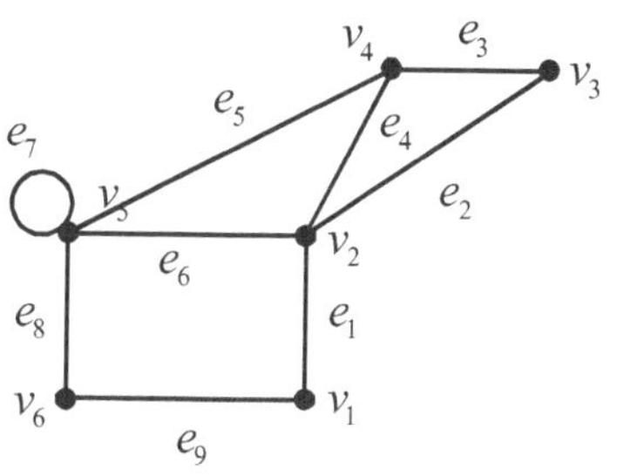

Figure : I

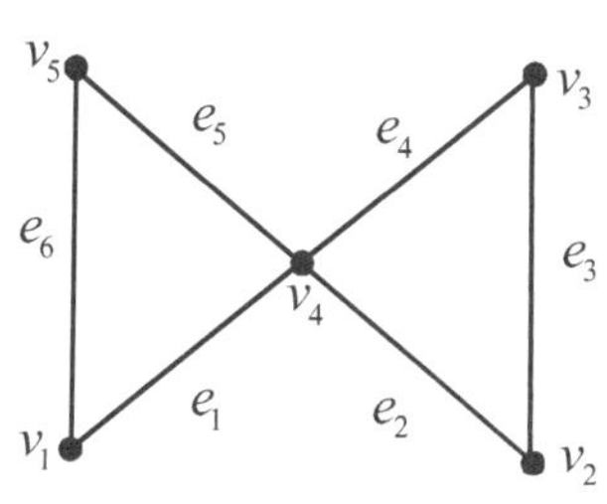

Figure : II

In figure I

Sequence $v_2, e_2, v_3, e_3, v_4, e_5, v_5, e_7, v_5, e_6, v_2$ is a closed walk there fore it is an Euler graph.

and the sequence $v_1, e_1, v_2, e_4, v_4, e_3, v_3, e_2, v_2, e_6, v_5$ is an open walk. Thus above figure may noted as simple graph also.

In figure II we see that there close walk with sequence $v_1, e_1, v_4, e_2, v_2, e_3, v_3, e_4, v_4, e_5, v_5, e_6, v_1$. Therefore, it is only Every graph.

Thus we conclude that "Euler graph is not an Euler graph. Hence Proved.

Q4(a). What do you understand by the term Custom Controls ? List the sequence of steps involved in creating custom controls. **[5]**

Refer to Chapter-7, Q5. Page No.-51.

(b) How do we use FTP ? Discuss any three FTP commands. **[5]**

Refer to June,2005. Q3(a). Page No. 129.

5. Write short notes on any four of the following: **[10]**

(a) Autofit

Refer to Chapter-6, Q1(ii). Page No.-96.

(b) E-commerce

Refer to Chapter-12, Q1(i). Page No.-85.

(c) Auto templates

Refer to June,2001. Q6(b). Page No. 209.

(d) DNS

Refer to Dec,2002. Q4(ii). Page No. 186.

(e) Pivot tables

Refer to Dec,2002. Q5(b). Page No. 188.

CS-612 : PC SOFTWARE SKILLS
June, 2007

Note : *(i)* Question number 1 is **compulsory**.
(ii) Attempt any **three** questions from the rest.

1. (a) Given 13 cricket balls, one of them heavier than the rest, how can you determine it, in not more than 3 weighings, using decision tree?
Refer to Chapter-1, Q.No.-8, Page No.-9

(b) Explain the concept of filtering a database in MS-Excel using Autofilters and using Advanced filters.
Refer to Chapter-10, Q.No.-4, Page No.-75

(c) What is the difference between 'Internet' and 'Network'? What is the role of TCP/IP in Internet? Also, list the hardware components used in the Internet.

A network is an interconnection of a group of computers. Networks may be classified by what is called the network layer at which they operate according to basic reference models considered as standards in the industry such as the four-layer Internet Protocol Suite model. While the seven-layer Open Systems Interconnection (OSI) reference model is better known in academia, the majority of networks use the Internet Protocol Suite (IP) as their network model.

Types of networks:

Personal Area Network (PAN), LAN, MAN, WAN, and Internetwork and types of it are Intranet, Extranet, and Internet.

Internet is a specific internetwork, consisting of a worldwide interconnection of governmental, academic, public, and private networks based upon the Advanced Research Projects Agency Network (ARPANET) developed by ARPA of the U.S. Department of Defense – also home to the World Wide Web (WWW) and referred to as the 'Internet' with a capital 'I' to distinguish it from other generic internetworks.

Participants in the Internet, or their service providers, use IP Addresses obtained from address registries that control assignments. Service providers and large enterprises also exchange information on the reachability of their address ranges through the BGP Border Gateway Protocol.

This implies that Internet is the subset of Network but Network is not the subset of Internet. Internet provides various services like E-mail, World Wide Web, Remote access, Collaboration, File sharing, Streaming media, and Voice telephony (VoIP) which can not be available on other types of networks.

Role of TCP/IP in Internet : A key communication protocol used in the Internet is called, the Internet Protocol. The Internet uses a set of rules called TCP/IP, which governs the sending and receiving of data on the Internet. TCP stands for Transmission Control Protocol whereas IP stands for Internet Protocol. They are collectively known as TCP/IP. The TCP helps in sending large block of information (text data) by dividing the data into data packets. It also adds special information i.e. the packet position in the document, error correction code etc. The IP puts destination address information on such packets. IP software allows a computer to send and receive data. IP does not handle all the problems that can arise. A computer using the Internet also needs TCP software to provide reliable, error free communication whereas Routers help to transfer information from source computer to destination computer. On Internet it is not necessary that all packets follow the same path in transfer. Routers balance the load on various paths that exist on the network. To make better utilization of Internet we use certain tools like Telnet, Gopher etc. Telnet is a tool, utilized for logging on remote computers on the internet. Its specification is part of the TCP/IP documentation.

Hardware components : (i) Modem, (ii) Computer, and (iii) Internet connection.

(d) What is Chart Wizard in MS-Excel? Write the step-by-step method to create charts using Chart Wizard. What are the components of Chart Wizard?

Refer to June-2002, Q.No.-3(b)(ii), Page No.-195
& Refer to Chapter-9, Q.No.-2, Page No.-66

(e) What is a template? Explain with an example.

Refer to Chapter-11, Q.No.-4, Page No.-82

2. (a) Prove that for any prime p = 5, $p^2 + 2$ is composite.

Refer to Chapter-2, Q.No.-8, Page No.-21

(b) What is a Function Wizard in Excel? What are its uses?

Refer to Chapter-8, Q.No.-2, Page No.-54

(c) What is the use of GOAL SEEK? Explain with an example.

Goal seek : Often you know the result you want a formula to return but not the input values the formula needs to reach that result. To solve such a formula, you can use goal seek feature. With this, MS-Excel varies the value in a cell you specify until a formula dependent on that cell returns the result you want.

Goal Seek saves you from performing time-consuming trial-and-error analysis. To seek a specific solution to a formula:-

1. Enter the data in the sheet.

2. Choose **Tools→Goal Seek...** command. The **Goal Seek** dialog box is displayed.

3. In the Set cell box, enter the reference or the name of the cell containing the formula for which you want to find a specific solution.

4. In the **To value** box, enter the value you want as the result.

5. In the By changing cell box, enter the reference of the cell containing the value to be changed in solving for the result that you want.

6. Choose the **OK** button.

For example, if the answer is 56, and the first number is 8, what is the second number? Is it 8 multiplied by 7, or 8 multiplied by 6? You can use Goal Seek to find out.

Create the following Excel 2007 spreadsheet

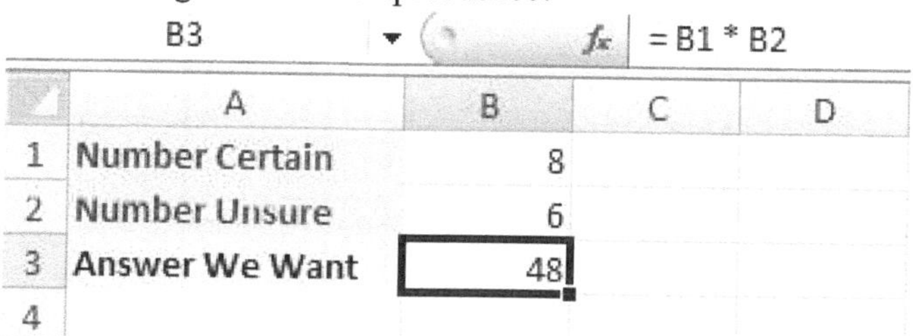

In the spreadsheet above, we know that we want to multiply the number in B1 by the number in B2. The number in cell B2 is the one we're not too sure of. The answer is going in cell B3. Our answer is wrong at the moment, because we has a Goal of 56. To use Goal Seek to get the answer, do as the following:

From the Excel menu bar, click on Data

Locate the Data Tools panel and the What if Analysis item. From the What if Analysis menu, select Goal Seek

The following dialogue box appears:

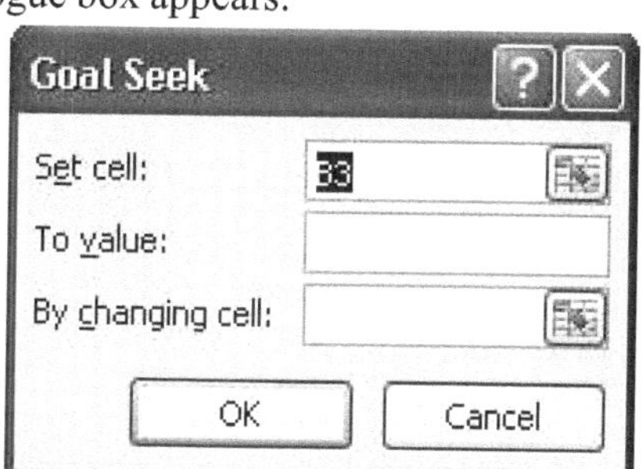

The first thing Excel is looking for is "Set cell". This is not very well named. It

means "Which cell contains the Formula that you want Excel to use". For us, this is cell B3. We have the following formula in B3:

= B1 * B2

So enter B3 into the "Set cell" box, if it's not already in there.

The "To value" box means "What answer are you looking for"? For us, this is 56. So just type 56 into the "To value" box

The "By Changing Cell" is the part you're not sure of. Excel will be changing this part. For us, it was cell B2. We're weren't sure which number, when multiplied by 8, gave the answer 56. So type B2 into the box.

Your Goal Seek dialogue box should look like as below:

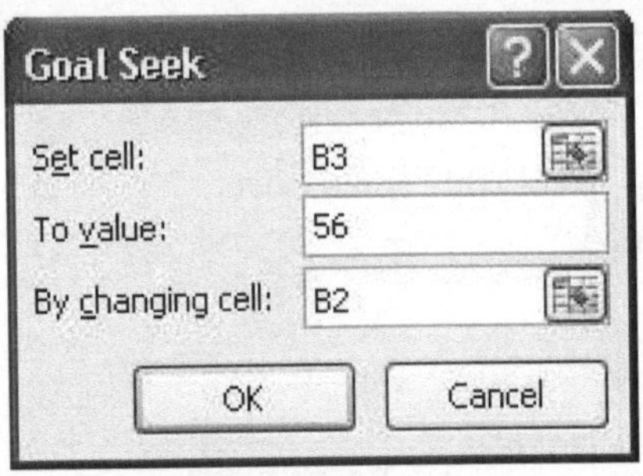

Click OK and Excel will tell you if it has found a solution:

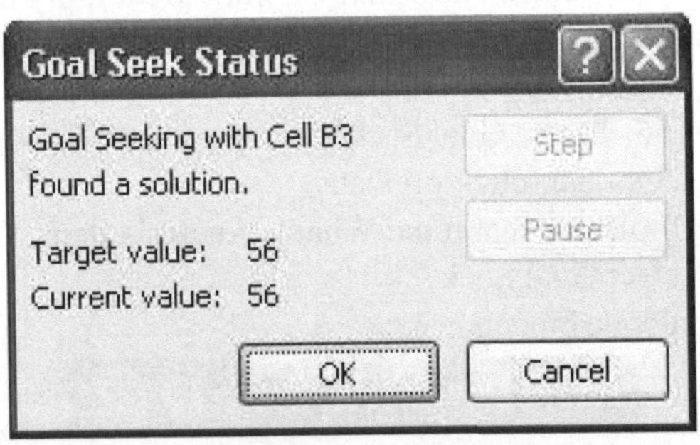

Click OK again, because Excel has found the answer. Spreadsheet will look like this one:

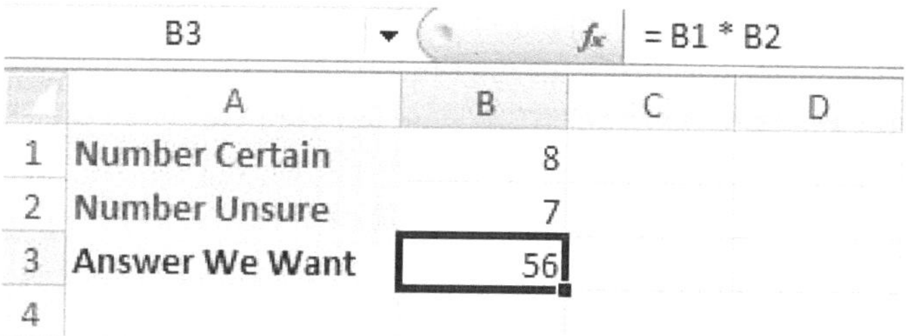

Excel has changed cell B2 and replace the 6 with a 7 which is the correct answer.

3. (a) Prove that for every integer n > 2, $(n!)^2 > n^n$.

Refer to Chapter-3, Q.No.-4, Page No.-26

(b) What is meant by URL? What are its components?

Refer to Dec-2005, Q.No.-1(d), Page No.-104

4. (a) Compare the different types of Internet connectivity mechanisms.

Refer to Chapter-12, Q.No.-7, Page No.-95

(b) Explain how the access of workbook in Excel can be restricted from other users.

Refer to Dec-2004, Q.No.-6(b), Page No.-144

5. (a) Write short notes on any *two* of the following:

(i) HTTP

Hypertext Transfer Protocol (HTTP) is a communications protocol used to transfer or convey information on intranets and the World Wide Web. Its original purpose was to provide a way to publish and retrieve hypertext pages. HTTP is a request/response protocol between a client and a server. The client making an HTTP request—such as a web browser, spider, or other end-user tool—is referred to as the user agent. The responding server—which stores or creates resources such as HTML files and images—is called the origin server.

Typically, an HTTP client initiates a request by establishing a Transmission Control Protocol (TCP) connection to a particular port on a host (port 80 by default; see List of TCP and UDP port numbers). An HTTP server listening on that port waits for the client to send a request message.

Upon receiving the request, the server sends back a status line, such as "HTTP/ 1.1 200 OK", and a message of its own, the body of which is perhaps the requested file, an error message, or some other information.

(ii) Telnet

Refer to Chapter-12, Q.No.-1(iii), Page No.-85

(iii) FTP

Refer to Chapter-12, Q.No.-1(iv), Page No.-85

(iv) Domain Name System

Refer to Dec-2005, Q.No.-1(e), Page No.-104

(b) Explain the following functions giving example for each:

(i) EXACT( )

EXACT (text1, text2) : Compares two text strings and returns TRUE if they are exactly the same, otherwise FALSE. It is case-sensitive but ignores formatting differences.

Text1 - is the first text string.

Text2 - is the second text string.

Example

= EXACT("poor", "pour")

(ii) IF( )

IF(logical_test, value_if_true, value_if_false) : Returns one value if logical_test evaluates to TRUE and another value if it evaluates to FALSE. Upto seven IF functions can be nested.

Logical_test - is any value or expression that can be evaluated to TRUE or FALSE.

Value_if_true - is the value that is returned if logical_test is TRUE.

Value_if_false - is the value that is returned if logical_test is FALSE.

Example IF (35>19, 35,0)

(iii) MOD( )

MOD(number, divisor) : Returns the remainder after number is divided by divisor. The result has the same sign as divisor.

Number- is the number for which one wants to find the remainder.

Divisor- is the number by which one wants to divide number.

Example

= MOD(15, 2)

= MOD(15,–2)

CS-612 : PC SOFTWARE SKILLS
December, 2007

Note : *(i)* Question number 1 is **compulsory**.
(ii) Attempt any **three** questions from the rest.

1. (a) Prove that the product of four consecutive natural numbers cannot be the square of an integer.
Refer to Dec-2003, Q.No.-1(a), Page No.-163

(b) With the help of an example, explain how to enter a formula, do some calculations and also mention how to edit the formula in MS-EXCEL.
Refer to Chapter-8, Q.No.-1, Page No.-53

(c) Summarize the basic features of any search engine. Also, list the basic options that would be available on them.
Refer to June-2005, Q.No.-1(b), Page No.-118

(d) What is the significance of Domain Name System? List any three geographic and non-geographic domain names.
Refer to Dec-2005, Q.No.-1(e), Page No.-104

2. (a) With respect to MS-EXCEL, what are internal and external databases? List any two external databases. Also, explain any one way to create a database in EXCEL.
Refer to Chapter-10, Q.No.-5, Page No.-76

(b) With the help of an example, explain the application of a decision tree. Also draw the decision tree for the example problem.
In decision analysis, a "decision tree" — and a closely related model form, an influence diagram — is used as a visual and analytical decision support tool, where the expected values (or expected utility) of competing alternatives are calculated.
Now Refer : Chapter-1, Q.No.-6, Page No.-6

3. (a) Write the basic functionally of the following in MS-EXCEL :
(i) Format Painter
Refer to Chapter-6, Q.No.-1(iii), Page No.-46

(ii) Function

Refer to Chapter-8, Q.No.-2, Page No.-54

(iii) Chart Wizard

Refer to June-2002, Q.No.-3(b)(ii), Page No.-195

(b) Write the process of sending an attachment (either a text file or image) through an email.

Refer to June-2003, Q.No.-1(d), Page No.-175

4. (a) What is the remainder left after dividing 1! + 2! + 3! + ... + 100! by 7 ?

Refer to Dec-2005, Q.No.-3(b), Page No.-108

(b) List any five important features of any GUI browser.

Refer to June-2003, Q.No.-3(a), Page No.-178

5. Write short notes on any four of the following :

(a) Decanting Problems

Refer to Chapter-1, Q.No.-3, Page No.-3

(b) Minimum spanning circles

Refer to Chapter-3, Q.No.-13, Page No.-30

(c) FTP

Refer to Chapter-12, Q.No.-1(iv), Page No.-85

(d) Gopher

Refer to Chapter-12, Q.No.-9, Page No.-97

(e) Doughnut and Radar charts

Refer to Chapter-9, Page No.-70

CS – 612 : PC Software Skills
June, 2008

Note : (i) Question number 1 is **compulsory**.
(ii) Answer any **three** questions from the rest.

Q1. (a) Define "decanting problems". Discuss a methodology to solve a decanting problem. Suppose you have three jugs with capacities 8, 5, 3 litres but none are calibrated. Jug A is filled with 8 litres of milk. Suggest a methodology to divide this 8 litres of milk into two equal parts.

Ans. First Refer : Refer to GPH Book Q.No.-3, Page No.-3

Now, to solve this problem : we can take following steps.

Let us suppose that 8 litres vessel Ps X, 5 litre vessel is Y and 3 litres vessel is Z.

	X	Y	Z
STEP 1	8	0	0
STEP 2	0	5	3
STEP 3	3	5	0
STEP 4	3	2	3
STEP 5	6	2	0
STEP 6	6	0	2
STEP 7	1	5	2
STEP 8	1	4	3
STEP 9	4	4	0

(b) Find the smallest prime P such that
Q = 2 × 3 × 5 ... × P + 1 is a composite number?
What are the next two such composite Q's? **What are the prime factors of Q?**

Ans. Q = 2×3×5×7×11×13×.........× P +1

Consider the number Q formed by multiplying each of the primes up to and including and adding 1 to the result.

Euclid now moves in to the kill. Here, he asserts, is a number that is larger than P, and yet one is not divisible by any of the primes up to P-for division by any of these numbers leave a remainder of 1. Q is a Prime ! But it may be asked : "Granted that Q is not divisible by 2, 3, 5, ...yet couldn't be divisible by same prime different from all of these ? After all, Q is a number vastly bigger than P!" Q may indeed have divisors, Euclid would concede: but they must be different from 2, 3, 5, ..., P.

The Method yield the following primes for P set at 3, 5, 7.

$2 \times 3 + 1 = 6 + 1 = 7$

$2 \times 3 \times 5 + 1 = 30 + 1 = 31$

It skips 5, 11, 13, 17, 19 etc.

(c) What is "Format Painter" of MS Excel? How is it applied?

Refer to GPH Book Dec-2005, Q.No.-2(c), Page No.107

(d) Explain the functioning of following commands w.r.t. Netscape Navigator?

(i) reload frame (ii) load images (iii) refresh

(iv) open file in editor (v) mail document

Ans. Netscape Navigator is a www graphical browser. It is available for downloading free of cost at the site with the URL http://home.netscape.com

Functioning of the following commands w.r.t Netscape Navigator :-

(i) Reload Frame : The active frame in the current document is reloaded from where it has been loaded initially. This is necessary when the "transfer is interrupted".

(ii) Load Images: Usually, the images will be embedded in the E-mail messages. These icons which represent images have to be expanded. This can be done with this menu option.

(iii) Refresh : This will clean the RAM. So, the browser window will look blank.

(iv) Open file in Editor : We can open a local document in the Netscape Editor.

(v) Mail Document : Mail the current document to the address specified in TO box.

Q2. (a) Determine all positive integers for which $2^n + 1$ is divisible by 3.

Ans. The given expression is $2^n + 1$. We wish to determine all positive integers for which $2^n + 1$ is divisible by 3.

i.e. $n \geq 1, 2, 3, \ldots\ldots n$

Now for

$n = 1$	$2^n + 1 = 3$
$n = 2$	$2^n + 1 = 15$
$n = 3$	$2^n + 1 = 9$
$n = 4$	$2^n + 1 = 17$
$n = 5$	$2^n + 1 = 33$
$n = 6$	$2^n + 1 = 65$
$n = 7$	$2^n + 1 = 129$

It is observed that whenever n is a odd positive integer i.e. 1, 3, 5, 7,.....2^n +

1 is divisible by 3. And for odd n, we can rewrite the given expression as

$2^n - (-1)^n$

This expression for the form $a^n - b^n$ is always factorable. Therefore, for all positive odd n integers, the expression $2^n + 1$ is always divisible by 3.

(b) Explain five categories of functions provided by Excel. Give one example of each category.

Refer to GPH Book June-2004, Q.No.-3(a), Page No.152 or Chapter-8, Q.No.-2

Q3. (a) What do you mean by the term IP address, in a computer network? Briefly describe the utility of IP addressing?

Refer to GPH Book Dec-2003, Q.No.-5(a), Page No.171 or Chapter-12, Q.No.-5

(b) Explain the utility of following Internet tools :

(i) Finger

(ii) Internet Relay Chat

(iii) Multiuser simulation environment

(iv) Multicast Backbone

(v) VAT

Refer to GPH Book Chapter-12, Q.No.-8, Page No.97

Q4. (a) Briefly describe the following terms related to Internet :

(i) HTTP2

Refer GPH Book to June-2007, Q.No.-5(a)

(ii) Telnet

Refer to GPH Book Chapter-12, Q.No.-1(iii), Page No.85

(iii) FTP

Refer to GPH Book Chapter-12, Q.No.-1(iv), Page No.85

(iv) DNS

Refer to GPH Book Dec-2005, Q.No.-1(e), Page No.104

(b) Explain the working of following Excel functions, giving example of each:

(i) EXACT( )

(ii) IF( )

(iii) MOD( )

Refer to GPH Book June-2007, Q.No.-5(b), Page No.232

Q5. (a) Write the steps to hide/unhide, split and freeze window panes.

Ans. Hiding / Unhiding windows

You can temporarily hide the same of the windows to clear the workplace.

(1) Choose Window – Hide to hide the active window

(2) Choose Window – Unhide to unhide the hidden window.

Split & Freeze window Panes : Refer to GPH Book June-2005 Q.No.-5(a)

(b) You are given three integers X_1, X_2, X_3. Prove that the average of two of these must be an integer.

Ans. We are given X1, X2 & X3, Now if want that the average of all or atleast two of these must be integer, than we take all the number must be an even number. If all the numbers are in the form of even number than the average result is always be an integer. Now, we take $X_1 = 2$, $X_2 = 4$ $X_3 = 6$. So,

$$f(x)_1 = \frac{2+4+6}{3} = 4 \text{ integer}$$

$$f(x)_2 = \frac{2+4+6+8+10}{5} = \frac{30}{5} = 6$$

So, if we take the input as even number than the result of average of these number must be an integer.

CS – 612: PC SOFTWARE SKILLS
December, 2008

Note : (i) Question number 1 is **compulsory.**
(ii) Answer any **three** questions from the rest.

Q1. (a) A boatsman must ferry across a river with a wolf, a sheep and a bundle of fodder. His boat is too small to carry more than himself and one of the passengers at a time. He cannot leave the wolf alone with sheep or the sheep alone with the fodder. Show how he can cross without any detriment to either sheep or fodder.
Refer to GPH Book, Q1(a), Page No.146

(b) What is Internet? How does it work?
Refer to GPH Book, Q1(b), Page No.146

(c) What is a Search Engine? What are the different types of search engines?
Ans. First Refer to GPH Book, Q3(a), Page No.108
Types of Search Engine : For the most part, Internet search tools fall into two main types. First the online directory is typified by "Yahoo" and "Lycos." A second type, the search engine, is represented by other web sites such as "Hotbot" and "Alta Vista." The difference between these two is the strategy they use to compile their site listings. However, a third type of the search utilities are hybrids of these two approaches and combine the two into a comprehensive package. The idea behind the hybrid search engine is to offer "the best of both worlds."
Directory-Based Search Services
For directory-based search services, the primary frame of reference is the subject matter. The site listings are compiled and reviewed manually. For example, Yahoo, the best known Internet Directory, dedicates staff to review and categorize site suggestions and then adds them to a specific directory on Yahoo.
The Search Engine
In contrast, the unmanned Search Engine completely automates the process of indexing the sites and totally removes the human component. A software robot called a spider or crawler gathers sites from across the web as it scans pages and connects to associated links. One particular advantage is that the spider will automatically return to the same site periodically to check for new content or new pages.
Examples of unmanned search engines include :

Google
http://google.com
The mother of all search engines that puts the world of the Internet at your fingertips.
Alta Vista
http://altavista.digital.com/
Alta Vista is a huge, fast web index provided as a service to the Internet community by Digital Equipment Corporation.

(d) Define Macros of Excel. Explain the different options available to run a Macro.

Ans. If you perform a task repeatedly in Excel, you can automate the task by using a macro. A macro is a series of commands and instructions that you group together as a single command to accomplish a task automatically. Instead of manually performing a series of time-consuming, repetitive actions, you can create and run a single macro — in effect, a custom command — that accomplishes the task for you.

Here are some typical uses for macros :

· To speed up routine editing and formatting

· To combine multiple commands; for example, inserting a table with a specific size and borders, and with a specific number of rows and columns

· To make an option in a dialog box more accessible

· To automate a complex series of tasks

Running the Macro means to repeat the action recorded as a macro. To run the Macro, steps are :

1. **Tools → Macro...**command is selected.

2. In the Macro Name/Reference box, the macro name is typed or selected.

3. The **Run** button is clicked on.

Or

Tools → Months is chosen.

Or

Ctrl + Shift + M key combination (that has been defined as the option before recording the macro) is pressed.

(e) Define a function in Excel. Explain any three of the Excel functions with the help of examples.

Refer to GPH Book, Q.No.-3(a), Page No.152

Q2. (a) What is a chart in Excel? How many types of charts are available

in Excel? Give examples of any two charts.

Refer to GPH Book, Q.No.-1, Page No.66, and Q.No.-3, Page No.67

(b) What is a protocol? Explain any two commonly used Internet protocols.

Ans. A standard way of communicating across a network. A protocol is the "language" of the network. A method by which two dissimilar systems can communicate. TCP is a protocol which runs over a network.

Now Refer to GPH Book, Q.No.-1(b), Page No.146

Q3. (a) What is a Decision Tree? Solve the following problem using Decision Tree:

"You have been given 12 (twelve) coins, one of which is different from the rest in weight, how will you pick it in three weighings? Also draw the decision tree for the given problem.

Ans. A decision tree (or tree diagram) is a decision support tool that uses a graph or model of decisions and their possible consequences, including chance event outcomes, resource costs, and utility. A decision tree is used to identify the strategy most likely to reach a goal. Another use of trees is as a descriptive means for calculating conditional probabilities.

Now Refer to GPH Book, Q.No.-8, Page No.9

(b) What is a URL? Explain the parts of URL.

Refer to GPH Book, Q.No.-3(b), Page No.131

Q4. (a) What is a Pivot Table? What is the use of pivot table? How do you create it?

Refer to GPH Book, Q.No.-1(e), Page No.121

(b) Prove that

$$S_n = \left(\frac{1}{2}n(n+1)^2\right)$$

for sum of first n cubes by method of induction.

Refer to GPH Book, Q.No.-2, Page No.33

Q5. Write short notes on any *five* of the following :

(a) FTP

Refer to GPH Book, Q.No.-1(iv), Page No.85

(b) E-mail

Refer to GPH Book, Q.No.-1(v), Page No.85

(c) CEILING( )

Refer to GPH Book, Q.No.-2(j), Page No.57

(d) Template

Refer to GPH Book, Q.No.-4, Page No.82

(e) NCSA Mosaic

Ans. The University of Illinois' National Center for Supercomputing Applications (NCSA) contributes significantly to the worldwide cyberinfrastructure for science and engineering, operating some of the world's most powerful supercomputers and developing the software needed to efficiently use these systems.

Mosaic or NCSA Mosaic is the web browser credited with popularizing the World Wide Web. It was also a client for earlier protocols such as FTP, Usenet, and Gopher. Its clean, easily understood user interface, reliability, Windows port and simple installation all contributed to making it the application that opened up the Web to the general public. Mosaic was also the first browser to display images inline with text instead of displaying images in a separate window.

(f) Netscape Navigator

Refer to GPH Book, Q.No.-1(d), June 2008

(g) FLOOR( )

Ans. In Excel, the Floor function returns a number rounded down based on a multiple of significance.

The syntax for the Floor function is :

Floor(number, significance)

number is the number that you wish to round down.

significance is the multiple of significance that you wish to round a number to.

CS – 612: PC SOFTWARE SKILLS
June, 2009

Note: Question Number **1** is **compulsory**. Attempt **any three** questions from the rest.

Q1. (a) Why MS-Excel is used? Explain its various features that make it easier to user.

Refer to Chapter-5, Q. No.-1 and Q.No.-2, Page-41

(b) What are Decision Trees? What kind of problems can be best solved using decision trees. Assuming one such problem, show its proof.

Ans. Refer to Q.No.2(b), Page No.-233

The conclusion is that decision tree helped us turn a complex data representation into a much easier structure.

Now Refer to Page-6, Q.No.-6

(c) Explain various components of the Internet. Also, explain the working of an Internet.

Refer to Page-90, Q.No.-5. Now Refer to Page No.-97, Q. No.-8

(d) Write the steps to create a chart in MS-Excel. Also, explain the different types of charts that can be created in Excel.

Refer to Page-66, Q.No.-2 and Q.No.-3

(e) Explain the four methods used for connecting to the Internet.

Refer to Page-95, Chapter-12, Q.No.-7

Q2. Write short notes on the following:

(a) Gopher

Refer to Page-203, Q. No.-1(c) (i)

(b) Goal Seek

Refer to Page-168, Q.No.-(ii)

(c) URL

Refer to Page-104, Q.No.-(d)

(d) Decanting Problems

Refer to Page-3, Chapter-1, Q.No.-3

(e) HLOOKUP( ) and VLOOKUP( )

Refer to Page-61, last a part and part b.

Q3. (a) Prove that if two integers *'a'* and *'b'* are each of the form 4k+1, their product is also of the same form.

Refer to Chapter-2, Q.No.-6, Page No.-21

(b) What is meant by Cell References? Explain the three ways in which cells can be referred, with an example of each.

Refer to Page-42, Q.No.-5

Q4. (a) What are Macros? Explain their utility in MS-Excel. Write steps for recording and running a macro.

Refer to Page-240, Q.No.-d

(b) What are the advantages of an Email service? Explain the use and importance of following Email components.

(i) BCc

Ans. BCC is an abbreviation used in email, which means simply Blind Carbon Copy. A normal email address can have three classes of email recipients: the To recipients, the CC recipients, and the BCC recipients.

The To recipients are thought of as the primary recipients of the email, the CC recipients are those who are receiving carbon copies of the email, and the BCC recipients are those who are receiving carbon copies of the email, but whose addresses no other recipients can see.

(ii) Cc

Refer to December-2004, Q.No.-5(a), Page-140-141

Q5. (a) What are bookmarks used for in a browser? Write steps to create and view a bookmark.

Ans. Bookmark : A list of pages a user likes to frequently visit. Netscape® Navigator and Explorer® have a "bookmark" menu item which allows users to add favorite sites via the Bookmark option. A term equivalent to the conventional bookmark used by readers to indicate position in a text book where they left it while reading it last time.

(b) What are firewalls? Explain their purpose for any network.

Ans. A firewall is a system which prevents unauthorized use and access to your computer. A firewall can be either hardware or software. Hardware firewalls provide a strong degree of protection from most forms of attack coming from the outside world and can be purchased as a stand-alone product or in broadband routers. Unfortunately, when battling viruses, worms and Trojans, a hardware firewall may be less effective than a software firewall, as it could possibly ignore embedded worms in out going e-mails and see this as regular network traffic. For individual home users, the most popular firewall choice is a software firewall. A good software firewall will protect your computer from outside attempts to control or gain access your computer, and usually provides additional protection against the most common Trojan programs or e-mail worms. The downside to software firewalls is that they will only protect the computer they are installed on, not a network.

It is important to remember that on its own a firewall is not going to rid you of your computer virus problems, but when used in conjunction with regular operating system updates and a good anti-virus scanning software, it will add some extra security and protection for your computer or network

(c) Differentiate between FTP and TELNET. Also, write steps to transfer a file to and from FTP Server.

Refer to Page-86, 3rd , 4th Point

To transfer files using FTP, take the following steps:

(i) Start an FTP session.

(ii) Click on the file or directory you want to transfer. If you do not see the file or directory you want to transfer, you can use the working directory field above each of the file systems to change to the directory that contains the files or directories you want to transfer, or to change to the directory that you want to transfer files or directories into, by typing the fully qualified path.

(iii) Click the arrow button in between the local file system and the remote file system to transfer the file or directory.

CS – 612: PC SOFTWARE SKILLS
December, 2009

Note: Question Number **1** is **compulsory**. Attempt **any three** questions from the rest.

Q1. (a) Explain the following functions in MS-Excel:

(i) Formatting a column

Ans. Using Menu Commands

To Set the columns Width

1. Select any cell(s) in the column(s) to change its width.

2. Choose **Column** option from the **Format** menu.

3. From the cascading menu, chose **Width**.. option.

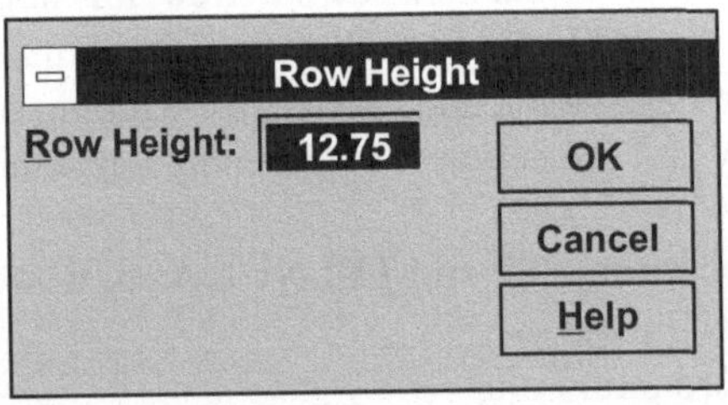

The other options available for formatting columns are:

AUTOFIT SELECTION- It adjusts the width of the column according to the widest entry in that column.

To Set the Row Height

1. Select the cell(s) of the row(s)

2. Chose Format->Row-> Height.

3. Give the height of the row as shown below.

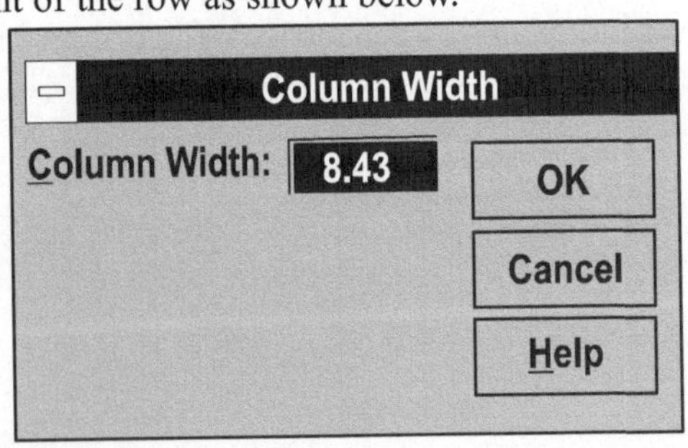

(ii) Creating a data series

Refer to June-2005, Q.No.-1(a), Page-117

(iii) Inserting or deleting rows and columns

Ans. Insert & delete columns & rows: Select column(s) or row(s) using the headings (A, B, C or 1, 2, 3...).

Right-click, choose Insert or Delete to insert/delete columns/rows.

(iv) Format painter

Refer to June-2003, Q.No.-2(c)(ii), Page-177

(b) Describe the working and need of the DNS in resolving the Internet Addresses.

Refer to Chapter-12, Q.No.-5, Page-90

(c) What is an Internet? Explain its components and at least four uses.

Refer to Chapter-12, Q.No.-5, Page-90

(d) Explain the use of Pivot table. Write the steps for creating pivot table from source data resides in workbook.

Refer to Chapter-10, Q.No.-3 (i), Page-74

(e) Explain the best way of solving Decanting problems and provide a solution for the following problems:

You are provided a 12 *l*. Vessel filled with water and two vessels of 9 *l* and 5 *l* capacity. How can you divide 12 *l* water into two equal portions?

Refer to Chapter-1, Q.No.-4, Page-5

Q2. (a) Prove that the product of four consecutive natural numbers cannot be the square of an integer.

Refer to Dec-2003, Q.No.-1(a), Page-163

(b) Explain the following terms briefly:

(i) News groups

Ans. Refer Page No.-94, (ii)

(ii) Mail Reflectors

Ans. A program that sends out files or EMAILS in response to a command embedded in an email. For example, a mail reflector may administer a DATABASE of software manuals and might respond to an email containing the command 'manual' followed by the name of the manual by sending the designated manual as an attachment.

(iii) FTP

Refer to Chapter-12, Q.No.-1(iv), Page-86

(iv) Address Book

Refer to Chapter-12, Q.No.-1(viii), Page-88

Q3. (a) Explain at least two tools and two services of the Internet.

Refer to Chapter-12, Q.No.-5, Page-90

(b) Explain the purpose of following options used for data sorting and filtering in MS-Excel:

(i) Sort by and (ii) Then by

Ans. By which column would you like to sort your data? Excel lets you support by up to three different fields, in the order you specify. For example, in your budget spreadsheet, you might sort by Department, and then, for each department, by Category, and then by Date. This would show you, for each department, a list of expenditures for each category, sorted by date.

(iii) All

Ans. Show all of the records in this column. You generally use this if you've already filtered the information and you now want to un-filter a particular column.

(iv) Blanks

Ans. This a one of the option in sort order. Blanks always come at the end.

Q4. (a) What are search engines? Explain in detail any two search engines.

Refer to Dec-2008, Q.No.-1(c), Page-239

(b) Define a scenario. Write steps for creating and editing a scenario.

Refer to Dec-2004, Q.No.-4(b), Page-139

Q5. Write functions in MS-Excel to achieve the following tasks:

(a) Generate a random number greater than or equal to 0 but less than 2500.

Ans. To generate the random number, use the RAND(), to generate the random number, but don't want the number to change every time the cell is calculated, you can enter = RAND() in the formula bar and press, F9 to change the formula to a random number.

= RAND ()*2500

(b) Assign grade 'A' if percentage is greater or equal to 75, 'B' if percentage is less than 75 but greater than or equal to 60 and 'C' otherwise.

Ans. Calculate the percentage of the grade and Assign the grade according to condition.

If (percentage >=75, A, B, If (percentage >= 60, C, false))

(c) Return the initials from strings contained in first name, second name and combine with last name.

Eg. Ram Kumar Sharma to R.K. Sharma

Ans. Old-text—is the text you want to Replace

New-text—is the text you want to Replace old text with.

Ex:- = substitute ("Ram Kumar Sharma", "R.K. Sharma")

(d) Compare two strings, if they are same return one string else concatenate the two strings and return.

Ans. Joint several text items into one text item. The "&" operator can be used instead of CONCATENATE to joint text items.

Text1, text2...- are 1 to 30 text items to be joined into a single text item. The text items, can be text strings, numbers, or single-cell references.

Example: = CONCATENATE ("Soft", "ware")

EXACT (text1, text2)

Compares two text strings and returns TRUE if they are exactly the same, otherwise FALSE. It is case-sensitive but ignores formatting differences.

Text1- is the first text string.

Text2- is the second text string.

Example: =EXACT ("Poor", pour")

(e) Assuming a list of 10 projects with their cost. Calculate the total money spent on projects.

Ans. 1. Select cell any cell.

2. Type " = sum(" in the cell.

3. Use the mouse point to drag select cells containg cost of all to projects.

4. Type the closing round bracket ") " to complete the function.

5. Press the ENTER key on the keyboard.

CS-612: PC SOFTWARE SKILLS
June, 2010

Note : *Question Number 1 is* **compulsory**. *Attempt* **any three** *questions from the rest.*

Q1. (a) Explain the use of custom controls on the worksheet. Also, write the steps to create custom controls.

Refer to Page No.-51, Q.No.-5

(b) Prove that there is at least one prime number between $x^2$and $(x + 1)^2$ for all integers x satisfying $1 \le x \le 20$.

Refer to Page No.-18, Q.No.-1

(c) What is meant by domains in DNS? How are they used for network addressing?

Refer to Page No.-104, Q.No.-1(e) & Page No.-90, Q.No.-5

(d) What is a template in MS-Excel? How is it different from Auto templates? Explain the use of Autotemplates.

Refer to Page No.-82, Q.No.-4 & Page No.-209, Q.No.-6(b)

(e) Why Search Engines are used in web? Explain the features of any two Search Engines.

Ans. Refer to Page No.-156, Q.No.-4(c) & Page No.-169, Q.No.-3(a).

Three essential features of a web search engine (crawling, indexing, and searching). Because of the limited resources available on the platform on which it ran, its indexing and hence searching were limited to the titles and headings found in the web pages the crawler encountered. Usually all features are supported by modern day search engines.

(f) Explain the concept of minimum spanning circles using an example.

Refer to Page No.-172, Q.No.-6(b)

Q2. (a) How does the Internet work? Explain the role and function of all hardware devices used between client and server machine.

Ans. Refer to Page No.-90, Q.No.-5

A hardware device that acts on behalf of other devices for purposes such as data storage and security. A **proxy server** can locally cache frequently accessed documents in order to reduce the level of Internet traffic to a remote server. A proxy server also may support a proxy firewall, thereby serving as both a logical and physical barrier.

Modem Or called **Mod**ulator **Dem**odulator. It is a sort of communication device that converts binary electrical signals into acoustic signals for transmission over telephone lines and converts these acoustic signals back into binary at the receiving end. Conversion to acoustic form is known as modulation; conversion back to binary form is known as demodulation .

(b) At what time after 4 PM is the minutes hand of a clock exactly aligned with the hour hand?

Refer to Page No.-10, Q.No.-11

Q3. (a) What are the similarities and differences between the FTP and TELNET? Also, write the steps to download a file from the FTP server.

Refer to Page No.-245, Q.No.-5(c)

(b) Write a step by step procedure to get the values of the given formula.

$m = \frac{x^3 + y^2 + z}{y}$ **where, the values of x, y and z are given. The values of m must be saved in new column.**

Refer to www.gullybaba.com download section.

Q4. (a) What is a difference between E-mail and online chatting? Explain the different components of an E-mail.

Ans. An email is a text document which is sent to your Internet Service Provider server when you press the 'send' button. There it sits for a little while, from a few microseconds to an hour or so, whenever the mail server batch process outgoing email. This document is transmitted as a single file, including attachments, to another server, the recipients Internet Service Provider incoming mail server, by way of servers which forward all mail to the closest address available. The message then resides on the incoming server until downloaded by the recipient.

Online chatting is a conversation between two or more people at computer keyboards, which is made up of data packets sent for every line, return key press, or other interrupt, and without delay, to each computer that is logged into the chat session. So, each packet that a computer sends out might be cloned into several hundred packets, to allow all the logged on users, even the 'lurkers', to receive a person's words.

Now Refer to Page No.-140, Q.No.-5(a).

(b) Explain the use of Autofilters and Advanced filters in MS-EXCEL with the help of an example.

Refer to Page No.-75, Q.No.-4

Q5. Write a short note on the following:

a) HTTP

Refer to Page No.-231, Q.No.-5(a)(i)

b) Pivot Table

Refer to Page No.-165, Q.No.-(iv)

c) GOAL SEEK

Refer to Page No.-168, Q.No.-2(b)(ii)

d) Decision Trees

Refer to Page No.-233, Q.No.-2(b)

CS-612: PC SOFTWARE SKILLS
December, 2010

Note : *Question Number 1 is* ***compulsory****. Attempt* ***any three*** *questions from the rest.*

Q1. (a) Prove that for any prime $P \geq 5, P^2 + 2$ is composite.
Refer to Page No.-190, Q.No.-1(a)

(b) What are the different Internet connectivity mechanisms? Compare and contrast between them.
Refer to Page No.-95, Q.No.-7

(c) What is the purpose of macros in Excel? How can macros are recorded and run? Explain using an example.
Refer to Page No.-83, Q.No.-5,
Recording a Macro:
1. Click on Tools, Macro, Record New Macro. Activate the Macro Recorder
2. Here you can give your macro a name and you can enter a shortcut for your macro (both optional). You can store your macro in three workbooks. If you choose to store your macro in Personal Macro Workbook, the macro will be available to all your workbooks (Excel Files). This is because Excel stores your macro in a hidden workbook that opens automatically when Excel starts. If you choose to store your macro in New Workbook, the macro will only be available in an automatically new opened workbook. If you choose to store your macro in This Workbook, the macro will only be available in the current workbook.
3. Finally, Click on Stop Recording.

Note: if you accidentally close the Stop Recording box, go to View, Toolbars, Stop Recording to turn it back on while recording a macro.
Now Refer to Page No.-240, Q.No.-1(d)

(d) A user want to send a 10MB document file as an Email attachment to her friend named "RAM". User wants that a copy of this mail must be send to "MALA", but without informing and knowledge of "RAM". Write a step by step procedure to perform the above task of the user.
Steps to email an attachment to RAM, Refer to Page No.-175, Q.No.-(d).
Steps to send same mail to MALA with informing and knowledge of RAM : Write email id of MALA in BCC textbox. BCC is an abbreviation used in email, which means simply Blind Carbon Copy. A normal email address can have three classes of email recipients: the To recipients, the CC recipients, and the BCC recipients.

The To recipients are thought of as the primary recipients of the email, the CC recipients are those who are receiving carbon copies of the email, and the BCC recipients are those who are receiving carbon copies of the email, but whose addresses no other recipients can see.

(e) Assume X and Y are integers, such that $(X^2 + 1) = 2Y$. NOW, Prove that Y is the sum of squares of two integers.

Refer to Page No.-221, Q.No.-(d)

(f) What is meant by protocol? Explain the importance of HTTP in Internet and its use.

Refer to Page No.-107, Q.No.-2(b) & Page No.-223, Q.No.-2(a)

Q2. (a) How do we use FTP? Also, write any three FTP commands.

Refer to Page No.-129, Q.No.-3(a)

(b) What is firewall in networking? Explain, how does it protect network from hackers and viruses?

Refer to Page No.-245, Q.No.-5(b)

Q3. (a) Write the difference between absolute, relative and mixed cell references using an example for each.

Refer to Page No.-213, Q.No.-1(c)

(b) Write the parameters of the following MS Excel functions. Also, give an example for each.

(i) CEILING.

Refer to Page No.-57, Q.No.-(j)

(ii) FLOOR.

Refer to Page No.-224, Q.No.-3(a)(ii)

Q4. (a) What is the reminder left after dividing 1!+2!+3!_ _ _ _ _ _ _ _ _ +100! by 7?

Refer to Page No.-205, Q.No.-2(b)

(b) What is an importance of Pivot table in Excel? Explain the different operations that can be performed on Pivot tables.

Refer to Page No.-121, Q.No.-1(e)

Q5. Write short notes on the following:

(i) TELENT.

Refer to Page No.-86, Q.No.-1(iii)

(ii) ISP.

Refer to Page No.-87, Q.No.-1(vii)

(iii) Decanting Problems.

Refer to Page No.-3, Q.No.-3

(iv) Scenario.

Refer to Page No.-139, Q.No.-4(b)